ON
BEING
A POET

ON
BEING
A POET

JUDSON
JEROME

Cincinnati, Ohio

Library of Congress Cataloging in Publication Data

Jerome, Judson.
   On being a poet.
 Includes index.
1. Poetry-Authorship. 2. Poetics. I. Title.
PN1059.A9J47 1984   809.1   84-15286
ISBN 0-89879-148-0

ACKNOWLEDGMENTS

Much of this material appeared in different form in my columns in *Writer's Digest* and *Cedar Rock*. Most of my own poems are included in *Thirty Years of Poetry: 1949-1979*, Cedar Rock Press, where Myrtle's poems also appear.

"Disillusionment of Ten O'Clock" and "The Poems of Our Climate" from *The Collected Poems of Wallace Stevens;* © 1956 by Alfred A. Knopf, Inc.

"Lower the Standard" from *The Bourgeois Poet* by Karl Shapiro, © 1964 by Random House, Inc.

Excerpt from "The Lesson of the Moth" from *The Lives and Times of Archy and Mehitabel* by Don Marquis. © 1927, 1930, 1933 by Doubleday & Company, Inc. Reprinted by permission of the publisher.

"Love Poem" from *The Selected Poems of John Frederick Nims,* © 1982 by the University of Chicago Press.

"Two Tramps in Mud Time" and "The White-Tailed Hornet" from *The Poetry of Robert Frost* edited by Edward Connery Lathem. © 1936 by Robert Frost. © 1964 by Lesley Frost Ballantine. © 1969 by Holt, Rinehart and Winston. Reprinted by permission of Holt, Rinehart and Winston, Publishers.

"Thoughts on Looking into a Thicket" from *As If* by John Ciardi, © by Rutgers, the State University, 1955. Reprinted by permission of the poet.

"The Neural Lyre: Poetic Meter, the Brain, and Time" by Frederick Turner and Ernst Poppel is reprinted from *Poetry,* August 1983, © 1983 by the Modern Poetry Association.

"Fenced-in Fields" by X. J. Kennedy from *Claims for Poetry,* Donald Hall, editor, © 1982 by the University of Michigan Press. Reprinted by permission of the poet.

Excerpts from "Leaving the Motel" from *After Experience* by W. D. Snodgrass, © 1960 by W. D. Snodgrass. Reprinted by permission of Harper & Row, Publishers, Inc.

Excerpts from "Daddy and Lady Lazarus" from *Ariel* by Sylvia Plath, © 1963 by Harper & Row, Publishers, Inc.

"Santa Claus" from *The Collected Poems of Howard Nemerov.* The University of Chicago Press, © 1977. Reprinted by permission of the author.

For Marty, Sandy, Michelle, Beth, Polly, Topher, Kirstin, Britta and Charisma

CONTENTS

INTRODUCTION: THE POETIC CALLING

This book is about experiencing poetry. I've written two books about the craft of poetry and its technical elements (*The Poet and the Poem* and *The Poet's Handbook,* both published by Writer's Digest Books), but this one focuses on more subjective aspects. Why do we write poetry at all? For whom are we writing it? What do our words convey to others—about ourselves and about other things? What effect does our poetry have, or do we want it to have, on the world at large? In addition, Appendix I deals with practical details regarding getting poetry to print.

But here I'm going to tell you the beginning of the story of how I became seriously involved with the art. I think you may identify with it if you think poetry is, should be, or is becoming central to your life. The story will also give us a chance to examine together a poem—T.S. Eliot's "The Love Song of J. Alfred Prufrock"—that I believe touches an important nerve in every twentieth-century poet. "Proof-rock" might be a way of saying "touchstone," a piece of hard black stone such as jasper or basalt used to test the quality of gold or silver. "Dreams are the touchstones of our characters," said Henry Thoreau. Rub your dreams on this poem and see what you learn about yourself.

But also try to see it as a I first did. Imagine a drab classroom of the University of Oklahoma in the spring of 1944. As a freshman in that classroom, just having turned seventeen in February, I was the first member of my lower-middle-class southwestern family to go to college, so I had accelerated my graduation from high school in Houston, Texas, in order to get as much college credit as possible before being drafted into World War II. I was immature in every way, weighing a hundred pounds, five feet tall, looking like an eleven-year-old. I felt unsophisticated, inferior, and yet cockily defensive as I tried to relate to the older and bigger freshmen around me.

This was our first English class of the second semester. I had already had English composition and was now being introduced to literature. The professor, Charles C. Walcutt, sat on the desk with his long legs pulled up, his knees under his chin. We watched him flip one cigarette butt after another across the room. Each butt sailed in an arc over the slanted glass windbreak at the window and dropped through the open slit. With a lazy sigh of condescension he warned us that we probably wouldn't understand "Prufrock," but nonetheless he read it—in a dry, low-keyed way that seemed to me the height of urbanity.

It was very moving to me as I heard the college girls come and go, talking of student government. I hungered after the sophistication of professors such as Mr. Walcutt. I even took up smoking cigarettes and got sick on them. He and other intellectuals had a kind of knowing sneer about what seemed to me wondrous and mysterious things. I probably practiced that sneer.

I went through a lot of unconscious modeling of such men. I was almost giddy with admiration for a wizened old philosophy professor, the Platonist Gustav Muller. I walked up and down the sidewalk outside his house at night, watching him move about his lighted, book-lined study puffing his pipe. I hoped that just by chance he might come out for a stroll, and I might casually fall in step alongside him as he walked to the corner drugstore, and I could ask him, in a sophisticated way, the meaning of life. No doubt I adopted Eliot as a model as well—or at least the fictional Eliot known as J. Alfred Prufrock. Eliot himself must have done some posturing, projecting himself as a central sensibility into old men in this and other poems.

I never much liked the later poems of Eliot—and haven't read through the *Four Quartets* to this day—but I cut my poetic teeth on "The Love Song of J. Alfred Prufrock." From that poem I learned such formal possibilities as the interplay of irregular but insistent rhyme; varying line length; loose but never quite flabby meter; the mixture of humor and seriousness; the use of images from everyday life, science, social behavior—indeed from all areas of life that had not seemed "poetic" to earlier poets; the tone of cynical, almost haughty sadness; the stance of the alienated, self-deprecating narrator; and above all the music, the rich, scintillating orchestration of sounds, rhythms, cadence, conversational and rhetorical tones. . . . Well, if those qualities don't characterize some of my youthful poems, it's not for lack of trying.

Furthermore, the experience of grappling with "Prufrock" made me feel that poetry was my calling. The word "calling" (or, in its Latinate form, "vocation") implies that God, or the Muse, or some cosmic force has called you to a kind of dedication that will order and give direction to your life. Though, of course, I could not have recognized it then, the major ambition of my life was to write a poem as good as that one. As good? Well, one that would mean as much to other people as that poem meant to me, a poem that could express exquisitely, artfully, and permanently the feelings and thoughts we all share. I wanted to create something readers could identify with, as I identified with the psychological anguish and wit of Prufrock, a poem that as insightfully as Eliot's defined a central theme of our times. (The odes of Keats have probably brought a similar sense of identification to more readers than have any other poems.)

To experience such a calling is a little like falling in love, to have a vision of the unattainable. I'm sure it has happened to you: Some poem seemed to crystallize your values and goals. You, too, may have fallen in love with poetry and the idea of being a poet. Perhaps that's why you're reading this book right now. In some ways falling in love is a kind of mental disorder, a sickness. Expectations are always so much greater than reality—or, at least, so very different from reality. The very expectations can be destructive, spoiling appreciation of everything that doesn't measure up to them. But normally after the fever, the experience that follows is actually deeper and more satisfying than anything imagined in the midst of rapture. You are no longer "in love"; you simply love. Or, if you have experienced this calling, you no longer worry about being a poet; you simply write poetry. I hope this book leaves you loving poetry still, though no longer in love with a vision. Rather, it should be like the love one has for a seasoned mate, valued as much for faults as for virtues, loved for being real—not for being a projection of one's fantasies.

Yet the vision, however unattainable, remains important in many ways. I still love "Prufrock"—which by now is a seasoned mate of my mind. I reread it with fond amusement such as one feels when looking at old photos. It reminds me, above all, of how much I had to grow.

I will intersperse these chapters with poems of my own that seem at least somewhat relevant to the prose discussion. In the one that follows I deal with what I long considered a burden of my life—that immaturity I have told you about. Eliot seems to have adopted the posture of an old man early in life. For me that was impossible.

THE YOUTHFUL LOOK

Chronic apologizer! Damn!
My moment of assertion is absurd.
Always I am slipping from silence like
a punctured, squawking bird.

Ingratiatingly self-effacing,
I see in the mirror no face, in the face no eyes,
and as I put myself down here
I disappear in lies.

Never to speak without smiling, no
protest intact, no searing of anger clean
or gesture sure. I walk in short
trousers; my knees can be seen.

I know my faults. I say it here.
No Hamlet, no, nor even Prufrock, I.
Accepting no yesterdays, I will say
"I'm sorry," and grin when I die.

The Dignity of Man, indeed:
I have no stature as I have no age,
and, if a man, consign all my
dignity to the page.

Here is a challenge for you which I'd like to explain. If I had suggested to the editors of Writer's Digest Books that they publish a collection of my poetry or of poetry by myself and others, they wouldn't seriously consider it. Their books are mainly for people who want to learn how to write—and so this is a book for such people. But if I'm correct in what I most deeply believe about our mutual art, you'll learn more from the poetry I quote in this book (by myself and others) about how to write poetry than you will from the prose. I think you'll remember the poetry longer. And some of these poems—or other poems they lead you to—will be for you what Eliot's poem was for me, the catalysts that make you aware of your calling and, at the same time, imbue you with some very specific techniques and goals that will enable you to undertake the practice of our art in a committed way.

Let me know if I'm wrong. For that matter, I wouldn't mind your letting me know if I'm right.

Judson Jerome
Downhill Farm, 1984

PART I:
INSIDE
THE
POET

My guess is there's something you want to get *out*. Of course I don't know a thing about you personally. But I know we share at least a common humanity and an interest in poetry, so I have some guesses. Moreover, I have engaged in a lot of intimate discussion and correspondence with poets at all stages of development from childhood to old age, from raw amateurism to consummate professionalism, asking what makes people like us get involved—sometimes painfully, troublingly involved—in so thankless an art.

And the most common denominator I have found is the overwhelming urge we feel to express something. That "something" may be along the lines of opinions or beliefs. It may be emotions that might overwhelm if not outpoured. Or it may be experience we want to make available to others. The urge that human beings have to express themselves is one of the glories of our species. Our belief that what we have suffered, learned, and enjoyed is somehow significant fuels our grandest achievements and our most profound probing. But in its raw and natural form, the urge to express doesn't make very good poetry. Given that we all have plenty that we want to get out of our systems (and, we hope, into the world's literature), the first question is how that energy relates to art.

But Part I may not be the place for you to start. This book need not be read sequentially. Part I talks about some of the internal dynamics that lead to poetry; Part II relates that to readers and listeners—those we want to reach; Part III considers the effect this interaction of poet and audience has on the poem itself; and Part IV pertains to the way our poetry fares in today's social and aesthetic climate. If your primary interest is in getting your work into print, you might want to start with the Appendix. Begin with the aspect that seems most relevant.

But remember that whenever I say "you," I probably mean "me." I started one of my books (*Poetry: Premeditated Art*) with this sentence: "I have written in the first person—for I had no other person available." I can't write "objectively" about poetry or making poems. I can only write about what I perceive to be the way my experience has been interlaced with poetry. There is a lot more unabashed autobiography in this book than in *The Poet and the Poem* and *The Poet's Handbook* because as I have grown older and learned more it has seemed more honest to call my spades spades. And since bias was unavoidable, I thought it only fair to give you the experiential basis from which my own arose. So "Inside the Poet" is, in truth, a kind of subtitle for the book. What it means is "inside Jud." And you'll find a number of characters and recurring themes threaded through the abstract discussion and quoted poems, a tapestry that tells a story that inescapably qualifies all I say.

CHAPTER I:
SCRATCHING
WHERE
IT
ITCHES

What Is Poetry?

You aren't alone. Practically everyone from time to time feels a desire or even a need to write poetry and wonders what that means and what it requires. Most just plunge right in, either fitting their words to the forms of verse assimilated in childhood or, more commonly these days, simply breaking lines where they feel like it, improvising freely. Others, like you, seek a deeper understanding of what poetry is all about. I assume that's what you're seeking, or you wouldn't even have read this paragraph.

Some, and this may also apply to you, are looking beyond the moment's need for self-expression. They are thinking of writing poetry for publication, thinking of poetry as an art form, asking themselves whether they could or should regard themselves as poets. These are some of the questions to which this book is addressed.

Assuming you find such questions relevant, I would guess that you have an itch you need to scratch—and for some reason you think poetry is the way to scratch it. Why poetry? First of all, what *is* poetry? You'll find as many definitions as there are writers on the subject, but for the time being, let me suggest a very simple answer: Poetry is writing that uses line breaks. That is, instead of continuing the margin,

> you break the stream
>   of words
>   and place
> them   where
>   you please.

Notice that this simple definition applies to form, not to content. You can use poetic form to say anything you wish, even, as I just did, to make a point in the midst of expository prose. You can use it for story or song or instructions for the use of a power mower. It's the form that makes it poetry—and the quality of writing in that form can be good, bad, or indifferent.

That simple distinction between two forms of writing may not satisfy you. Some people reserve the word *poetry* for writing that they especially like, that which they find especially imaginative or moving or exalted. They may use the term *verse* for writing in roughly the same form which they do not especially like, or which they regard as merely humorous or trivial. We might never agree about whether a given piece of writing meets those subjective criteria, but we can recognize in a moment, by a glance at the page, whether the writing uses the line break as a device. If it uses the line, let's call it poetry, at least for now. That allows for the possibility of such a thing as *bad* poetry, and in my experience that's a category that is often useful.

Why have human beings—in all cultures and throughout history—so often chosen to write using line breaks? Well, advertisers caught on long ago to the fact that poetic form provides a way of being emphatic, of catching the eye, of suggesting more than one is actually saying. Most magazine ad copy is, in effect, commercial poetry, using not only line breaks but many other devices associated with poetry, such as consonance, rhythm, metaphor, even rhyme to zap the reader's attention. Many people throughout history have used the techniques of poetry to make writing effective, pungent, memorable, moving—and, as those advertisers know, the techniques work.

But that utilitarian explanation may not apply to your personal reasons for turning to poetry rather than some other means of expression, such as prose, to say what's on your mind. You may not be thinking of how the writing affects readers at all. Rather, your reason for writing poetry has something to do with the special nature of what you want to express. You want to write it down, more for yourself than for others, and for some strange reason prose just doesn't feel right. You have an urge, which you may not quite understand yourself, to use broken lines.

Usually, those who have that urge have been moved by strong emotions, such as love, hate, sorrow, or appreciation of beauty. A lawyer who came to one of my workshops explained his motives this way: "I have these fleeting moods, and I want to get them down." Notice that he didn't even mention communication. His need was to record, not necessarily to convey something to others.

The Voice from Beyond

One term commonly used about the urge to write poetry is *inspiration*. In workshop after workshop I have heard people discuss the mysterious urges that moved them to write poetry. At one of these, a navy veteran who had become a college student, wanted to know whether he was a poet. Before he put too much energy into writing (he had begun recently and had been encouraged by his professor), he wanted some assurance that he *could* be inspired. His question reflects a curious but common attitude toward poetry. If you take a talent test for music, you might expect objective measures, such as something which could indicate your ability to distinguish and reproduce tones and rhythms. But most people seem to think that the skills for writing poetry will come naturally if you have the basic qualification: inspiration.

A widely published poet-professor at the same workshop reported that one group of his poems simply came over him: "I began hearing these voices," he said, "more and more clearly." A portly poetess said God spoke to her every morning. Her poems came unbidden to her mind, and she wrote them down the way they came. (One might be amazed to see how inclined God was to use clichés and vague abstractions and to express Him- or Herself in dog-trot and ineptly rhymed lines.)

"I am sure God does speak to you," I said. "And to me, too. In fact, I'm sure you wouldn't deny that God speaks to each of us."

"Oh, no," she said, horrified to think she might have seemed to be making an immodest claim for some special status.

I told her (and the group) that, insofar as I could understand the matter, some faculty of our consciousness is, indeed, in touch with the wellspring, tuned to whatever purpose creation has and responsive to universals beyond our comprehension. Similarily, we are wordlessly in touch with one another—perhaps with the dead and unborn as well as with the living. These messages are coming in at all times, piling up like unread mail for most of us.

There is nothing very remarkable or special about inspiration. The word implies we have been "breathed into," that an influence from outside is affecting our thoughts and actions. It would be immodest to deny that such influences play upon us, to claim that we are independent of that eternal, mysterious stream. The phenomenon is as common as consciousness itself.

Looked at another way, we bob along on an eternal flow of private thought, feeling, and language, picking out only a minute portion to express or even become aware of. We don't know the source. It may be the popping of synapses or racial memory or intergalactic communica-

tion or the tireless whisper (like the night song of crickets) of God providing us with personal and instantaneous guidance. Call it inspiration
if you will.

   The problem is not to be inspired or to know whether one is inspired. Rather, the problem is what to do with the inspiration when it
comes. We can't process it all. I suspect that civilized humanity has
suppressed those faculties we call ESP simply to avoid overload, for
they are much more active in children, in the brain-damaged, and in
primitive societies such as the bushmen than they are in "normal"
Western adults.

   On the other hand, too much awareness can be blinding. While
those who cannot see with their eyes develop their other faculties to
heightened sensitivity, those who *can* see probably could not bear such
intense stimuli of hearing, touch, taste, and odor as the blind experience daily. And those accustomed to using "reason," or left-brain faculties, do so by tuning out contradictory or confusing impulses from
other lobes of awareness. The arts, including poetry, require a great
deal of right-brain activity (a matter discussed more fully in Chapter
11). As Shakespeare pointed out, "The lunatic, the lover and the poet /
Are of imagination all compact." Unfortunately, poets sometimes
sound like blithering idiots because they don't know what to do with
all the stimuli they are receiving.

   You can't help being inspired, nor can you become inspired by will-
power. Trying to be inspired is like trying to have an orgasm. If inspiration isn't apparent to you, the main thing you have to do is relax, stop
trying, and let it happen.

Active and Passive

   We are likely to be confused because the image of accomplishment
we cultivate in our civilization is that of conscious effort. One takes
command, one manages, manipulates, controls. But poetic receptivity—which Keats called "negative capability"—requires passivity, surrender, acceptance. I came to understand this better from working
with clay than from writing poetry and tried to express the paradox
this way:

CLAY

Give it *self*. Tear off a chunk and pound.
Hand heat and pressure make it round. It? Round?

It. Round. For every squeeze an opposite
impression comes from you and makes it it.

So shape is negative, but fat and real,
and regular if turned upon a wheel.

Turned? Rather, though your foot impels below,
it seems to *turn*. You hold—and it would *go*.

You educate it merely, thin it down,
as verbally it spins into a noun:

a pot, a thing in space, with out and in
you gave it. You. Your hands and discipline.

The clay is damp and finely granular,
less pliable than you, and yet you are

except for *some*thing, like this clay, this pot,
a self imposed on nothing, shaped from not,

defined, a hunk of motion with a name,
for every pot you make, not quite the same.

When modeling a statue, for instance, you don't "make" a nose. You
keep pushing, pulling, working the clay in apparently random ways,
until a nose emerges. The conscious control, often so swift it seems intuitive, is to *stop* meddling when a curve or dent or mass seems right. It
is the ability to stay the hand, to recognize the worth of what has
emerged, to know what one wants to keep.

And usually one has in mind no clear image of what the finished
work will look like: Even sketches, even subjects of portraiture, provide only the roughest guidance. One has to put aside preconceptions
and be responsive to the medium itself and to the features already
formed rather than to seek to reproduce some design from a blueprint.

This is true in all the arts, indeed in most right-brain activities, including friendship and love. One cannot "make" love, but by conscious will you may achieve the passivity and receptivity that enable
love to occur. When writing poetry, you can open your awareness to
that eternal stream. But you should expect the full and indiscriminate
abundance of consciousness to be more formless and full of garbage
than *Finnegans Wake*. That stream is not poetry, of course. As the computer folk say, "garbage in, garbage out." Simply putting down whatever comes to mind is, first of all, impossible: There is too much. Sec-
ondly, it is artless.

Art is selection, and that *is* an active function. You have to choose
from the innumerable images and words that flood through the mind
those worth saving, those that go together, those that have some co-

herency, direction and significance, however subtle their relationship. The role of selection will be discussed more fully in the next and later chapters. But at this point many of those millions who write poetry lose interest. They are gratified and fascinated by the inspiration pouring in, and they are sometimes eager to try to get some of it down on paper. But they are less enthusiastic about the work required to turn all that dictation from beyond into a work of art. Their itch is, like that of the lawyer I mentioned, more to record than to communicate.

They may not understand their own itch. It's more satisfactory to scratch your own back than to have someone do it for you because *you* know where it itches. But what need are you trying to satisfy when you write poetry? It's not always easy to tell.

The Old Stamp Collector

As an adolescent I collected stamps, and after a few years I began to wonder why. I had noticed that some students joined our high school stamp club to meet new people, socialize, to make dates. Some seemed to have been pushed into philately by parents who thought stamps would teach them geography. Some had dreams of buried gold—thinking they might find rare stamps worth millions in their uncles' attics.

Those with such peripheral interests soon dropped out. The Stamp Club of Stephen F. Austin High School in Houston in the early 1940s wasn't really the center of much social or sexual action. Not much geography (or any other academic subject) was being learned there. No one in the history of the club even had gotten rich by finding a rare stamp. And a lot of allowances were being spent in response to comic-book ads which lured neophytes with introductory offers of packets of stamps.

Those of us who stuck with stamp collecting had social and educational needs, just like the others, but we satisfied those some other way. We ignored the ads. We realized that we were about as likely to find a walnut-sized diamond in the gravel of the driveway as a valuable stamp in Uncle's attic. In retrospect I think the only explanation for my continuing interest was that I liked stamps.

The little boogers just turned me on. I loved especially the dim old canceled ones, each thin tissue that I knew had borne a message from somewhere to somewhere else many years ago. I liked those better than the gaudy, exotic ones from French colonies in Africa—the kind most common in those packets from the dealers. I even stopped looking up my stamps in the catalog to find their mythical "market value." I liked stamps for themselves, not their monetary value.

Then, about my sixteenth year, I met someone who *really* liked stamps. An elderly gentleman learned from an acquaintance that I was interested, so he invited me to see his collection. One evening I located his elegant apartment, was invited in—and there his collection lay in the lamplight. Or *part* of it was on display. The whole collection consisted of many albums, most under lock and key in glass cases. It clearly represented considerable investment of time and money over the previous half century. It was surely accruing value. The old man spoke sadly of the time when his heirs would auction it off for thousands of dollars, as none of them were interested in continuing to build it. But it was obvious that he had not lavished his love on stamps for financial speculation.

And though he enjoyed sharing his hobby with me and would no doubt have relished getting together with other connoisseurs, he was not using philately to satisfy some social urge. He must have learned a great deal of geography and history, not to mention the chemistry of paper and glue and the secrets of printing processes, but he was not collecting stamps to satisfy some scholarly or technical interest. He just loved stamps. Each one in his tweezers under the magnifying glass was a cherished object.

He was generous, too. He gave me a couple of dozen stamps which were by far more rare and valuable than any others in my collection. Had he found in me the spark of a true collector, he might have put me—a virtual stranger—in his will. But his greatest gift to me was one he did not intend to give and might have regretted had he known about it. By his kindly example he showed me that I was not really a stamp collector and would never be one.

I could not imagine myself a half century later with a collection comparable to his—even if I were assiduous and lucky. And though I admired him for having achieved what he had, I knew I did not want to emulate him. He intended to inspire me. What he did was liberate my energy from stamps and allow it to move on to other things. Those stamps he gave me were among the last added to my little collection.

His example was important in another respect as well. He made me burn to discover what it was in this world I could care about in the way he cared about stamps. I am reminded of a poem by Don Marquis' creation, archy the cockroach. He is talking about a moth who had no desire greater than to fry himself on a light bulb or flame. Archy (who used only lowercase letters because he wasn't heavy enough to push down the shift key on the typewriter) concludes:

> i do not agree with him
> myself i would rather have

> half the happiness and twice
> the longevity
>
> but at the same time i wish
> there was something i wanted
> as badly as he wanted to fry himself

We all need something to dedicate ourselves to—at the most extreme something to live for, even to die for. The old man had found a focus on his life, and poetry came to replace stamp collecting in mine.

Pitfalls of Poetry

For many of the millions, young and old, who dabble in poetry the way adolescents of Houston used to dabble in philately, I would like to serve as that kindly old man. One of the benefits this book may provide is to liberate your energy from *writing* poetry altogether. I hope it will, at the same time, make *reading* it a more profound and satisfying experience.

Why should I, or anyone, want to discourage people from writing poetry? For one thing, if you get past the point of writing it down and begin to think about getting it published, you should know you're swimming in a sea full of sharks. I would like to help such poets save their allowances. The poetry sucker ads don't appear in comic books, but in many other respects they resemble those that attempt to reach into piggy banks to sell packets of cheap, gaudy stamps to unwary kids. In the Appendix, "Publishing Poetry," I will discuss some of the vanity rackets you should beware of, especially fake contests and anthologies.

The ante is higher when it comes to poetry, and you get less in exchange. The contests, agents, publishers, teachers, and conferences that hang around the fringes of the world of poetry indicate there must be a rather large market to exploit. Serious poets, like serious stamp collectors, are not likely to be distracted by such ads, but there are too few serious ones to make the ads worthwhile anyway. Those ads pay off because there are so many who are confused in sorting out their interests, those who are not scratching where they really itch.

Particularly sad are those whose interest in poetry is actually a misguided social urge. I can give you a composite case history of the sort of person I mean. Let us imagine a highly intelligent, sensitive young man who feels unappreciated. His family members have little respect for him—perhaps classifying him as "intellectual" or otherwise odd, as one who doesn't fit their narrow stereotype of manliness.

In school he may have been called an "underachiever," that is, someone whose work does not measure up to his potential as indicated by test scores. He may have few friends—again because he doesn't fit the narrow local stereotypes. Essentially he is lonely, and though he is regarded as a kind of failure by family, acquaintances, teachers, and bosses, he senses (probably rightly) that he is superior in ways unrecognized by those who deal with him daily.

He remembers one exception: Mrs. Bloom, who was his third-grade teacher. (You'll meet her again in Chapter 15.) She herself was not much appreciated by the pupils or other teachers. But she paid attention to our hero, drew him aside and told him he had a light under his bushel, that he was "special," or "talented." Moreover, Mrs. Bloom used to rhapsodize over poetry, which was one of the reasons her pupils didn't respect her.

Now, in his late twenties, buried in a routine job, socially (and especially sexually) isolated, fearing that he will sink into the sea of anonymity and conformity around him, he remembers Mrs. Bloom and poetry and begins writing down his feelings in short, obscure bursts of language he calls poems. And he starts noticing "Poetry Wanted" ads in writers' magazines.

Willa Cather wrote a moving story, "Paul's Case," about such a boy. Paul did not turn to poetry, however. He turned to larceny. With money stolen from his employer he took a train to New York and lived in a luxury hotel for a few weeks—really scratching where it itched. When he was found out, he committed suicide.

Poetry is comparatively harmless, but perhaps less satisfying for such a young man's needs. If what you are looking for is social recognition, intimacy, ease of the pangs of loneliness, poetry is like bad breath. It drives people further away. If you can get anyone to read it (which isn't easy, outside a poetry club), you find that they don't understand you any better. Maybe they misunderstand you more. At best it is a lonely activity—not only writing it, but all the requirements of learning to write it: studying, reading poetry of the past, analyzing techniques, and staying aware of contemporary literary currents.

Not even published poetry has much of an audience, and this young man's work is not likely to be published unless it be at his own expense or in the newsletter of his poetry club (or perhaps church). There must be at least ten times as many people in this country writing poetry as reading it. Imagine all those poets running around trying to get someone to sit still and pay attention!

Even that vague goal of "recognition" is an illusion. I doubt that our young man could name ten living American poets. Can you? Now try sports stars, rock stars, movie stars, novelists—and I'll bet you have better luck. There is no wealth to be gained. Poets don't support themselves by writing poetry: That is literally impossible (as I discuss further in the Appendix). Writing poetry in search of such rewards is a guaranteed way of digging your rut deeper. It only makes the itch more intense.

Some of us go right on writing poetry, as that old man collected stamps, because the activity is satisfying in itself. We love poetry for its own sake. We're not saints—or I'm not. Sometimes I wish for more attention or recognition or appreciation. Sometimes I wish people understood me better. Sometimes I'm lonely. Sometimes I experience sexual hunger. Sometimes I hanker a little after fame or fortune. But I usually don't confuse those itches with poetry. I don't think poetry will rescue me, as Prince Charming rescued Cinderella, from all the anguish and deprivation in my life. When I'm involved with poetry— reading it, studying it, writing it, writing about it—I can pretty well clear my head of other matters and scratch that itch.

Otherwise I don't know how I could do it at all. If, while writing a poem, I were also trying to do something else besides write that particular poem as well as I could, I would be hopelessly confused. And because I genuinely like poetry—good poetry, that is—I don't find it difficult to maintain my focus. You might be surprised to know how many people who write poetry don't enjoy reading it. No wonder they can't concentrate on writing it well! I enjoy sex, but I don't do it for fame and fortune, and so I have no difficulty keeping my mind on the activity at hand.

Poets who are publishing hardly ever join poetry clubs. They are no more likely to do so than that old man would have to hang around our high school meetings. Poetry is not a means to get into society. Rather, it is for most poets a way to get out of society into delicious solitude. To tell you the truth, I generally feel guilty about the time I devote to poetry because I enjoy it so much and it isolates me from others and interferes with my chores.

Strangely, this satisfaction has little to do with anyone reading what I have written, though I like my work to be read. I enjoy the adulation I reap at poetry readings, but I don't think I write poetry for that reason. In fact, readings are as frustrating as they are pleasing, for people always get something different out of the poems than I thought I put into them.

There are a number of dangers in defining oneself as a poet or in choosing poetry to scratch an unspecified itch. The first is that of being overly impressed by one's own fertility. I know of an elderly Canadian poet who is very proud of having over five thousand of her poems published in good magazines. She writes very well, but I think she would have done better for herself and the world if she had spent more energy on five hundred, or even fifty—giving those few a better chance of enduring in our literature. I suspect that because she thinks of herself as a poet she feels she has to be turning out something new all the time.

There is the danger of attributing some kind of supernatural quality to ordinary inspiration. If one begins to notice the subconscious stream—which is normal, and present in each of us—it seems like a mystic experience. Perhaps it is, for all I know, but it is not nearly so remarkable as it first appears. If you've ever been "straight" among people who are stoned, you know how amusing, pathetic, and finally tiresome a heightened responsiveness to that stream can be. People abnormally aware of the most commonplace garbage running through their minds suddenly start making pretentious announcements, winding through endless verbose sentences, giggling at each bubble as it pops in the stew of consciousness.

Without benefit of drugs, many beginning poets seem carried away by the miracle of shards and half-digested lumps of phrasing that happen to drift past their inner eyelids. Since they don't know where all that stuff is coming from, they figure it must be divine, therefore precious, therefore worthy of recording. My advice is, when you get what seems a startling notion, relax: There's plenty more where that came from. And it won't seem nearly so startling if you wait and become accustomed to the flow. Only then will you be able to distinguish the significant from the insignificant.

There is the danger of attaching too much importance to yourself as the chosen oracle of divine intelligence. I suspect that when it comes to ability, intelligence, talent, we are all alike (yet individual), as the bumps on an orange. The fact that we have thoughts and feelings and that our minds ride a stream of language is no more (or less) remarkable than that we can digest our food or conceive children. Surely we are not all equally effective as poets, but the difference is not that God makes some material available to some and denies it to others. You will write better when you stop thinking you are so special, that your talent is some kind of halo or mark of Cain which sets you apart from ordinary mortals. Then you will start concentrating on writing well, working harder—and that is, finally, what makes the difference between good poets and poor ones.

Another danger in this style of self-definition is that of becoming tempted to take the easy way. The sheer abundance of inspiration gives one almost too much to choose from, and in that situation it is altogether too easy to avoid the difficult or dangerous or embarrassing, to exercise one's virtuosity in arpeggios of triviality.

It is an indulgence to wallow in mere fancy. A whirl of dry leaves might remind you of a fairy dance, sending your imagination reeling into realms in which those tatters of dead oak have a fairy queen and king holding court in some palace of the sewer. Don't get the idea that if you write something down in broken lines it is any less silly than it would be in prose or ordinary conversation.

A good poem always contains an element of risk. One poet-professor at a workshop gave us a very polished poem tripped off on the occasion of a friend's calling him on the phone to ask about the names of God. The poem, in an amusing, erudite, almost smug fashion, ran through gods of various cultures and the etymology of our word "god." But the poem remained at arm's length. I said (dramatizing by falling to the floor on my knees) that I wanted the poem to cry out in desperation: "I don't *know* the name of God!" A matron poetess, whose perceptions were often straight to the point, said, "He wants you to bleed a little." That was exactly what I wanted.

Poetry that stays with us always reaches into the areas of doubt and dismay of a poet's most serious concerns. Even good light verse does this. It works the themes about which a poet feels deeply ambivalent, about which he or she doesn't know the answers. A poem of certainty or solid belief is almost bound to sound like propaganda—a sermon or a lecture. But the tide of inspiration is so rich that it is easy to escape significant encounters and spend one's passion on the brilliant, empty bubbles of random association or conventional ideas that fail to challenge either the poet or the reader.

Congestion is also a danger. Indeed, the navy veteran should have worried about too much rather than too little inspiration. His professor had taught him about the complexities, the double meanings, the multilayered truth, of much good poetry, giving the impression that the very texture of poetry was ingenuity, a fabric of language so packed and imaginative that a few lines could occupy a college class for an hour of explication. Having been a professor for twenty years, I know well the temptation—the need to fill those hours, to remain on top, to stun the students again and again with one's cleverness and arcane knowledge. And it is true enough that poets generally have packed much more into their lines than an army of explicators will ever dig out.

But that's not the point. Good lines resonate with all those meanings because they probe to the core, not because the poet has deliberately obfuscated simple meaning and piled random association on association to keep undergraduates occupied. Our problem in the welter of inspiration is to simplify, simplify, to hear and draw out a clear strain, and if we have succeeded, yet have fished up a strand of authenticity, the complexities will cling, for all our effort.

Most dangerous of all, however, is the question the veteran raised about whether or not he was a poet. It is dangerous no matter how it is answered. I consider myself a poet at the time I'm writing a poem. The next hour I may be a mechanic or father or dishwasher. I told the veteran, "You can't help being a poet, just as you can't help being inspired. Almost all people write poetry at least occasionally in their lives, and at such times they are poets."

But of course my answer merely evaded the true intent of his question. Most of us recognize that you *become* a carpenter or accountant or doctor by study, effort, and slow acquisition of skill. But many think that one "is" a poet as a dog is a dog, without studying or analyzing dogness. I get many letters telling me about this. My correspondents often say that I'm wasting my time picking poems apart and insisting that people think about them. They assure me that *they* are poets, and they know poets don't analyze: They just warble like Shelley's skylark "in unpremeditated art."

For them poetry is not an activity; one can be a poet, they believe, without writing a line. Each has staked out a position by proclaiming, "I am a poet!" I guess they mean year in, year out, day and night. It must be a very insecure position to hold. I would be subject to creeping doubts that maybe, down deep in my psyche, I'm *not* a poet. Maybe folks will find me out! I think I'd get tired of maintaining the pose. I had fun with that idea in this poem:

HELIUM: AN INERT GAS

My ego, like a pink balloon,
  bobs on a string behind
or floats above me where I sit—
  self-affacing, kind.

Sometimes I hug it to my chest
  getting in and out of cars
or ask my friends to hold it for me,
  especially in bars.

My boss says keep it out of sight
  in the kneehole of my desk.
In traffic, how it dances, jerks
  in nervous arabesque!

I should not bring it to the table,
   but when I come, it comes,
though kids giggle and point at it
   and pummel it with crumbs.

Sometimes I dream it drifts away
   above the curling sea,
though it is safely under the sheet
   between my wife and me.

My doctors, friends, and family
   all wonder what's inside.
I think they'd like to pop it, watch
   it flabbily subside.

Poeting

You are a poet when you are poeting, writing poetry, then and only then, and even at that moment you don't know with any certainty that it's so. The thought itself would be a distraction, as if in the midst of a difficult concerto a violinist were to reflect, "Wow! I'm really doing an excellent job!" She'd miss a note for sure. There's a kind of meditative state required for any creative art, including that most basic one of orgasm, which demands that the mind be on a plane of awareness that transcends such petty concerns as vanity. (I discuss that trance in Chapter V.)

You can't help wondering from time to time whether your work will make it to the anthologies, whether it will be explicated by busy professors and numb undergraduates in some space-age Intro to Lit, whether your clicking keyboard is somehow engraving your words on a slab of Olympus. But these thoughts are simply more of the junk rolling down the stream of fancy, comparable to the dreams of the scullery maid that Prince Charming someday will come along. If you could ask God whether you are a poet, a voice would thunder from the heavens: "None of your business! Get to work!" But I once expressed my doubt that God would be much concerned.

THE UNCHOSEN

I guess I have a deficiency. God never
said boo to me when as a boy I stood
straining in church with muscular endeavor
for the sweet squirt of salvation. I never could
see why He spoke to this or that old lady,

sending her, hallelujah, down the aisle.
Was I alone in the congregation vile?
Or was their claim of spirit something shady?
And now when I read poets who simply Know,
drinking their imagery from God's own cup,

whose poems "just come," and then, like Topsy, grow,
whereas I always have to make them up,
with never a tremor saying *Break this line*
or *Save this phrase, regardless of its beat*,
hear no obscurities which seem Divine,

and, knowing not God's measure, still count feet,
I yearn that reason give me some relief
(besides those lapses when my mind, not soul,
is not so much inspired as out of control).
Non-linear God, help Thou my unbelief!

Yet it is also true that I have to label myself in some basic way; I do, after all, call myself a poet, even though I might not write poems more than a few times per year. That old man was a stamp collector. He no doubt had some job to support his habit (as poets require some income to support theirs). He had many other functions in life as a man, citizen, husband, father, friend. But stamp collecting was probably the activity for which he had the deepest respect and deepest love. That way of defining a role, you see, does not depend upon the recognition of others. There is no way he can be exposed as a fraud. In his darkest, most troubled nights he needn't wrestle with self-doubt: Maybe I'm *not* a stamp collector! He knew how he liked to spend his leisure. He knew where he itched.

CHAPTER II:
ARTLESSNESS
AND
ART

Artlessness is the apparently uncontrollable urge we have to express ourselves, indeed, to express our most intimate selves. For some reason we think, even as very young children, that poetry is the appropriate medium for saying the things we feel most strongly—and often most secretly.

If you have decided that poetry is the best way to scratch where you itch, you will quickly find yourself in a conflict between artlessness and art, for art is the process of rearranging, distorting, and disguising those artless outpourings to make them, if not necessarily shapely and beautiful, at least suitable for public consumption. Part of you wants to spill out the raw thought and emotion of your most intimate consciousness, and another part wants to shape what spills, in order to give it an aesthetically pleasing form and perhaps to make the raw material unrecognizable.

You may not recognize that the conflict is there, and even if you become aware of it, you may not understand it or be able to resolve it. I've been writing poetry for nearly a half century, seeing my work published for more than forty years, and writing about poetry in *Writer's Digest* and many other magazines and in books for a quarter of a century. Still I don't understand it fully and don't always know what to do about that conflict in my own work.

But why bother? Why do we want to say these things at all? It is probably a healthy impulse for the psyche, like the body, to discharge at moments of overload—not only to void itself of waste but to erupt in involuntary laughter, tears, sighs, and smiles. These are all symptoms of overload: Your consciousness suddenly has more than it can deal with in equanimity, and a physical response surges to the surface. Another way of responding to that need to discharge is, for many of us, to put words on paper—usually in the broken lines of poetic form.

We know that those who bottle up their feelings, who never find any way to express them, suffer terrible psychological repercussions—sometimes including violent outbursts. Even as children, long before we are conscious of the danger, we sense that we will be better off if we get things "off our chests." Some of you may be offended by the suggestion that poetry arises from the discharge of excess, but remember that many of the feelings we need to express are tender and beautiful. It can be as perilous to repress feelings of affection and pleasure as it is to repress those of anger and grief.

One of my early poems, written when I was about eight (the only copy now in the Judson Jerome Collection of the Boston University Library), is a sentimental expression of love for my mother. I may have had difficulty in telling her how much I loved her, but putting it in a poem somehow made it seem more acceptable to utter feelings our culture inhibits little boys from uttering. In one respect the poem probably represented a kind of spontaneous overflow of genuine feeling. But it's also interesting that the poem is metrical, rhymed, and uses words such as "weep," which I am sure I never used in daily conversation. The art—that is, the pains I took to decorate this expression of simple affection—enhances and strengthens the impact of the original impulse, however awkwardly. In that simple example you can see that art does not necessarily compromise the honesty of artless outpourings.

But sometimes it does. We may be ashamed of what we want to say and distort it to make it seem more acceptable. Or imagine someone who has fallen in love, and certainly isn't ashamed of it, yet is too shy or embarrassed to express the feeling in any intelligible way. Such a person may resort to a poem that means a great deal to the author and very little to anyone else. Often we can't define, even to ourselves, what we are feeling. Sometimes the words echoing in our heads seem to demand expression whether we understand them or not. And sometimes the mere act of expressing those words helps us clarify our feelings.

I once talked with a young poet, Charisma Flecksteiner, about her first published poem (which appeared in September 1980 in the first issue of *Tiger and Lambs,* a magazine of poetry by children which has since folded). Charisma was nine when she wrote this:

THE EDGE

The wings of a bird
are like the edge
of the sun, and the edge

of the sun is like
the edge of love.

Three years later I asked her why she wrote it. "I was just sitting and thinking," she said, "about the way words flow together, and the difference the little changes made—all the details." The feeling she wanted to express apparently had little to do with birds, the sun, or love. It was a feeling about language, and the images and the apparent subject of the poem appear to have been rather arbitrary. That is, she felt like playing with words and in the process came up with some words that made sense.

But mere playing with words, even finding a way to make them make sense, is still artless. The finished poem, however, also has elements of artistic form. What moved her to break the lines so that each had two beats? (Surely she didn't realize that she was using a combination of iambs and anapests.) Why do we put things in patterns at all? Did she like the enrichment of the word "edge" that resulted from putting it twice at the ends of lines? What is so attractive about repetition—of ideas, of sounds, of phrases? Why do we invent figures of speech, in this case a string of similes? What sense of drama caused her to arrive at a climax with the word "love"? Each of these questions points to the use of artistic techniques, but so far as Charisma knew, she was merely expressing herself. Maybe art is one of the feelings we have to express. Maybe we have an artless need to be artful.

That example radiates childish innocence, but much that we need to express is distasteful or even forbidden. In Chapter VIII I discuss some of the therapeutic functions poetry can serve, often requiring that we elude the censors outside and inside our minds. But I should warn you at the outset of this discussion that learning how to write poetry is likely to be a much more disturbing and challenging matter than picking up a few writing techniques. In order to make art out of your artless impulses, you will have to explore those impulses and their sources in greater depth and with more candor than most people ever do.

Well, you don't *have* to. You don't have to read this book or any other about what it means to be a poet. You can simply pour out the strains of your unpremeditated art in any way you please, without deep self-examination. But poetry will ultimately be more satisfying to you, and your writing will be more likely to endure, if you force yourself to dig a little around the roots of your psyche.

The Serpent in the Garden

The great Irish poet W.B. Yeats wrote, "Love has pitched his mansion in / The place of excrement," an acknowledgment that from the moment of birth our tenderest and most uncontrollable bodily functions are associated with one another—and condemned. That association and conflict are fundamental in much of our best poetry. They throw our psyches into turmoil and generate feelings that human beings generally need desperately to express. But we face powerful inhibitions to such expression.

From our earliest consciousness we suffer contradictory feelings about our genital area—the source of so much of our natural satisfaction and filth. Imagine the fresh mind of the infant. He has just experienced sensual pleasure and relief. At that moment a creature ten times his size, one from who he has received love and sustenance, begins hauling him around physically, changing diapers over his howling protests. A message is planted deep, though, of course, wordlessly. That message means: Something about my natural self elicits fearsome reactions from those I depend on and love.

At the same time, the baby is learning that goodness consists of learning to manage natural impulses, to tidy them up, hide them, live as though they didn't happen, flush them away, to cover artlessness with art. We gain love and approval from strong, powerful, omnicompetent giants by developing such restraint. Our most rooted dependencies on others—mother, father, mate—are stained by this association before our minds can develop any defense.

The dynamics of civilization begin with manhandling infants to change diapers. We couldn't survive as healthy beings or coexist unless we learned to restrain and control our functions of elimination and sexuality, and we customarily do this by developing an attitude of shame and disgust toward those functions. (Interestingly, one anthropologist has suggested that the earliest tool developed by our species may have been the predecessor of toilet paper. Disease would have killed us off without it; and, as the only mammal habitually to walk erect, so our waste does not fall free, we are unique in requiring that tool.) In all cultures love is glorified and celebrated, but there is no culture that does not repress, or attempt to repress, many forms of sexual behavior.

We come to fear and abhor what we also enjoy and cannot avoid. To work, to make civilization possible, the fear and revulsion must be firmly rooted in the subconscious, must operate swiftly, intuitively, irrationally. We must learn to flinch at the functions of our own body as a forest animal fears fire.

If controls are necessary, as surely they are, can't we have control without terror? Can't we restrain ourselves without hating ourselves? A mature, rational person can perhaps arrive at a nonjudgmental understanding and rise above those primitive responses, but that isn't possible for the infant, and that early conditioning is almost impossible to eradicate fully.

I can give you an example from personal experience. Much of the emotional energy of our lives goes to working out our relationships with those giants that hover over us in infancy. In my case it was a painful struggle in regard to my father because it happened that he was a miserable man who made his family miserable as well:

ALCOHOLIC

My father (didn't everybody's?) drank—
the Dread Disease, plague of his generation—
and we were patient, swallowed down his spite,
and understood him as he thrashed and sank,
and all forgave (oh, life means brief duration!)
and all refrained from saying wrong or right.
We knew, in dry, bright Oklahoma City,
the only cure for drink was love and pity.
We knew the flesh was frail, with delicate breath,
and so indulged each other into death.

But when he dared me—cursing me, demanding—
and shuffling scrawnily down halls of my mind,
sagging his jaw, speaking with tongue gone blind,
should I have answered him with understanding?
He cannot help the things he does, we said.
(He grinned and snitched a ten and drove off, weaving.)
His heart, we said, is spotless—but his head
disturbed. (Late I would hear him, racketing, heaving.)

Years after he was gone I think I saw
how we insulted him, drove him along:
His spirit we called nerves, said nerves were raw,
denied his holy sanction to be wrong.
The sonofabitch (God bless him) drank and died
because we understood away his pride.

Much later I began to understand and value the fearful limits he imposed on my childhood and was able to get past the regret and anguish to appreciate how even his sickness helped form me and contribute to my art. Mountain Fork is a stream where we fished in the Kiamichi Mountains of Okalahoma—or, rather, he fished and I paddled:

ON MOUNTAIN FORK
discipline:
> the whispering *S* of line
above the canoe, the weightless fly thrown through
a gap in the branches, spitting to rest
on the still pool where the bass lay,
> wrist true
in the toss and flick of the skipping lure.

love:
> silence and singing reel, the whip
of rod, chill smell of fish in the morning air,
green river easing heavily under, drip
of dew in brown light.
> At the stern I learned
to steer us—wavering paddle like a fin.

art:
> tyrannous glances, passionate strategy,
the hush of nature, humanity slipping in,
arc of the line, ineffectual gift
of a hand-tied bug, then snag in the gill, the snap
and steady pull.
> His life was squalid, his
temper mean, his affection like a trap.
I paddled on aching knees and took the hook.
My father shaped the heart beneath my skin
with love's precision:
> the gift of grief, the art
of casting clean, the zeal, the discipline.

Though the poem says nothing of the changing of diapers or repression of sexuality, it reflects the pain of acceptance and finally appreciation of a father's arbitrary power. I learned from the exquisite art of his fly fishing, which rose so cleanly from the ugliness and misery of his life, ways in which I, too, could turn suffering into creative force and beauty. And though I resented much that happened in our lives, I also loved him, and the poem, written long after his death, is not a complaint but a tribute.

So, I think, must any artist eventually recognize the wellspring of his artless urges. What happens to our minds when we begin to think of ourselves as bad by nature, as those infantile encounters on the changing table are likely to make us do? For instance, we learn to believe that to want is bad. But we can't help wanting. Therefore, to get what we want, we have to pretend that we don't want it. We have to sneak up on satisfaction. Learn manners. Learn art. Don't reach for the candy before it's offered. Don't become sexually aroused. The best way to win love is to pretend that we don't desire. To gain acceptance requires a mask.

If others—especially those we are closest to and love most—knew what we were really like, what we really wanted, they would reject us. That's just as true of many "good" feelings as of "bad" ones. As I've suggested, lovers also fear at times that others will learn the secrets of their inner natures. In some contexts people feel a need to hide the noblest of impulses, even charitable ones. Fear of such rejection is the serpent lying at the bottom of the mind. The human being is the animal that covers its private parts (though in different cultures what is considered "private" may vary). Art's imitation of nature is our desperate attempt to regain Eden, to create by our own ingenuity that paradise of naturalness from which we are excluded by our knowledge.

Perhaps in view of this we can understand why so many are moved—one might say driven—to write poetry. As we grow, we forget the original pain and confusion, forget what it was all about. We are left with a horrifying sense of uniqueness: I alone am evil. Others (especially the giants who tend me) apparently do not experience longing and need. I must learn, the maturing person tells himself, how can I overcome, or seem to overcome, my fearful desires. It feels like a partial suicide, as I have to kill off aspects of my essential self. Meanwhile I must find some way of expressing the complex internal drama that is tearing me apart.

It is, finally, beneficial to learn not to need—especially to learn not to inflict one's needs on others. One of my poems deals with this theme—and the ambivalence in which it leaves one. I began with an allusion to a saying from the days of the Great Depression, "God must love the poor; He made so many of them":

LOVING MY ENEMIES

I must love my enemies: I have made
so many of them. Whether I, drowning, flailed
rescuers, or, terrier-nervous, yapped,
defending God knows what from God knows whom,
or thought I was the jester, licensed to wound,
I drove you all away. I wanted room

to grow my crooked stem, so sprouted thorns,
or, as self-consuming candle, blindly burned
in guttering isolation, or vacuum-drained—
as a black hole does the sky—all warmth and light.
Emperor of sunny nursery play,
I took all as due, nor wondered how or why.

Pursuit of justice was a good excuse
to wear the jackboots of some public cause
and stab a friend for a stranger's brief applause.
It simplified affection's murky snarl
to make such clean incisions. I have hurled
babies and bathwater out for a better world.

But mostly I won your enmity with love
too fast too soon, my overwhelming wave
of self too bountiful, too gladly given.
To save yourselves from my self you were driven
if not to anger, to politic escape.
I said I love you: You foresaw a rape.

You must have loved me, enemies, to have left,
dreading the waste and smother of my gift,
sensing my naked need to be received.
Hard love withholds indulgence: You withheld.
Such closeness would have scalded both of us.
You could avoid what could not be repelled.

Safer, of course, to love thus at a distance—
a dream of faces gone, but nearly kissed—
blending across the years without resistance,
yin lost in yang, and none knows when or how.
But there is safety even in my bower,
for I love you still—but do not need you now.

The Artifacts of Loneliness

I don't mean to imply that our wellspring of artless impulse is without joy and caring and gratification, but even our positive expressions are likely to be hedged and guarded because of our sense of isolation and our recognition of the necessity of restraint. A gnawing ache at the pit of the stomach arises from our vague, unspecific sense of unworthiness. And loneliness. Sometimes it seems that no one in the world—especially those closest to us—feels what we feel, feels what we dare not name. Intimacy is frightening. We go to bed with a lover fearing that our secrets will be involuntarily revealed in sleep. And our deepest desire is the same as our deepest fear: to be understood, to be deeply known.

What do we do about it? A lot of us write, as I said in "The Youthful Look" (quoted at the end of the Introduction). Others paint or make music or cook food or decorate homes or collect firearms or do something else that they may or may not call expressing themselves. The activities are all distantly related to their motives. A sweet old lady shows her painstaking needlework. Who would dream it was a response to her toilet training? A florid executive shows us the Porsche in his garage which he polishes and takes apart and puts back together and takes out only on dry summer weekends. Who could associate it with his battle with his sexuality? A cellist brings an audience to tears with his rendering of Ernest Bloch's rhapsody, *Schelomo*. Who would suspect that he meant it as a loving tribute to his Jewish parents? Who would dream that Jack Sprat's wife spent a lifetime justifying herself in compensation for an infantile sense of unworthiness?

ALL THE SORE LOSERS

"You win," he said, and shrugged. She nodded,
in dark recesses chalking one more score.
  (A stave gave way in her corset, but
she thought she would not need it any more.)

That night she took a torch, descending
by dripping stairs her endless, echoing halls.
  The flame was smoky, oily, but
gleamed on the trophies ranked along the walls.

Eight shapes of sweating brass were lovers
frozen in postures of athletic play,
  graceful, with swollen muscles, but
corroding here beyond the reach of day.

Here were the scalps of ladies who
befriended her, and then revealed their faults.
She bore their smiling manners, but
their stinking pelts now hung here in these vaults.

A golden likeness of her daughter
evoked the time she found *that* trollop wrong.
She had her son in silver, but
did he give up—or merely go along?

With her husband she had taken pains
to get him, not at once, but piece by piece.
Thus no one saw him suffer, but
grow daily leaner as she grew obese.

Now picking over his bone structure
she knew where he was fallible, joint by joint,
so durable and pearly, but
he steadily surrendered, point by point,

and now, she reckoned, had lost track
of all his losses and the total due.
She cackled, counting. Time would prove
that she and she alone was right. She knew.

Some write fiction. And we must understand and agree that, of course, the stories are about imaginary people in imaginary places. A story lures us with its guise of entertainment. Sit back, it says. I'll amuse you, divert you, astound you, maybe frighten you or make you sad, but relax: You needn't concern yourself with the person behind all this.

Drama is an even more impersonal form, the mode that most thoroughly suppresses the personality of the author. It is there, of course, and a perceptive reader senses beyond the story the engagement of its creator. But if the author of fiction or drama knows his craft well, he almost never stands forward to say in his own voice, "Look at me, listen to me." His values and the passion of his concerns are communicated indirectly through the invented story.

The same is generally true of many kinds of poetry: narrative, satirical, philosophical, didactic, or dramatic. But the most common type of poetry today is the lyric. When most of us think of "a poem," we have in mind a relatively short personal lyric, the form in which the poet at least pretends to speak out directly on themes that deeply move him. The poem usually takes up no more than a single page—rarely as long as two hundred words, often a few dozen or less.

It doesn't promise a reader much entertainment. We don't expect a good laugh or a gripping tale or a rich tapestry of life—though many good poems provide these rewards. Some poems are somewhat like musical compositions. They communicate pleasure in sheer sound, rhythm, rhyme, harmony, repetition, floating cadences, which can be appreciated more or less separately from meaning. But musical delight is not often the reason poems are written or why they are read. The most common type of poem gives us little but the feelings or perceptions or thoughts of the poet. It is like a brief, often quite passionate personal letter or essay. Often it's a cry from the heart.

Jailhouse Blues

I am reminded of a joke about a group in a restaurant opening Chinese fortune cookies and reading each message aloud: *Beware of strangers; You bring joy with your smiles,* and so on. Then one of the party opened a cookie and read: *HELP! I AM A PRISONER IN A CHINESE COOKIE FACTORY!* That is the message of many a lyric poem: *Help! I am a prisoner!*

To some extent many of us feel as though we were cut off from the rest of the world by gray walls in our minds. We are desperate to escape, but those walls are also our protection. Could we survive in the daylight? Would people stone us if we were free to walk outside? Notice that the anonymous message in the cookie gave no directions to bring help. Similarly, the poet who writes one of these cries from the heart probably doesn't really expect anyone to do anything about his complaint.

In fact, he might be embarrassed if he thought anyone really understood. Often he disguises his misery with wit, symbolism, fiction, figurative language, unconventional grammar, strange arrangement of words on the page, or other devices. He is crying out, "I want to be understood." But he fears that if he is, he will be rejected, detested, and though he cannot stop himself from sending out his appeal, he dreads its reception. *If others—especially those I am closest to and love most—knew what I am really like, what I really wanted, they would reject me. Yet I am so lonely in my dungeon.*

I don't know any solution for that classic dilemma of poets. It won't do (we are right in suspecting) to express ourselves too clearly, too blatantly. Art would dissolve into feeling, and raw, naked life is indeed offensive to many, even to ourselves. Our dignity and nobility may depend upon our capacity for inventing ingenious disguises. Or we might make light of our problem, as I tried to do in this poem:

HELP! I AM A PRISONER IN A
CHINESE COOKIE FACTORY!

I sell. All sell something, but all say
selling one's soul or hole or art is crime.
What kind of woman do you think I am? I am.
What you pay me to say, I say. In rhyme? I rhyme.

A hack of a magic mirror, I give you back
your image as you dream you should appear.
You name it, Bud: I answer like an echo
and simulate submission, front or rear.

My heart is that fabled singer, Orifice,
who goes to Hell to save Your Idiocy.
My mind, a calculator, leaps to the touch
of buttons. Selfless, I sell—of self am free.

Yet my venality is all in vain:
I have not rooted out my deepest I—
for when the cookie crumbles, still there comes
(distant, anonymous) this comic cry.

I hope no one knows what I meant by that.

The Art of Lying

How much does communication have to do with our urge to write,
after all? Simplemindedly, we might regard language as intended to
convey meaning and pointless when not used for that purpose, but my
experience tells me otherwise. For instance, on a long boring drive I notice that words dance continually in my head, arranging themselves in
patterns of sound and meaning, even though I don't speak them.

Sometimes I speak to the empty car, unconsciously prompted by
the pleasure, or perhaps simply the need, of expression. I could hardly
claim even to be talking to myself, for I'm not listening. I'm not thinking things out. The verbal spring in the recesses of my brain (like that in
yours) seeps or flows or gushes perpetually whether I'm asleep or
awake, alert or somnolent. Unconsciously productive as my heart, it
pulses on, whether anyone is listening or not, like an abandoned radio.
Communication is only occasionally the use to which I put that constant stream.

So it is not surprising that much poetry is obscure. It may never
have been intended to be understood. One might suppose that if a poem appears in print it had meaning for *somebody*, but that's not true, ei-

ther—at least in any ordinary sense of "meaning." Maybe the poet paid someone (with money or other favors) to print it. Maybe some editor thought, "The more obscure, the artier." Maybe someone found its very unintelligibility fascinating—as one stares at the hypnotic changes of light and shape in a burning hearth. Or maybe somebody thought that—whether *he* understood it or not—it might contain some buried message, like a scrap of code intercepted from a foreign power, and so should be passed along in hope that someone down the line can decode it.

Code, indeed, is often involved—like the code of symbols in our dreams. Much of what we need desperately to express is forbidden by polite society, and if we are to say it at all, we must consciously or unconsciously find ways to disguise it. We internalize many of society's prohibitions—and dare not say what we must deeply feel even to ourselves. It is dangerous to express such feelings—and dangerous to repress them. It is perhaps most dangerous of all if those closest to us (our parents, mates, children, closest friends) were to be aware of them.

The codes we use to evade these censors may be so involuted as to become gibberish—or so clever that they slip past understanding in a pinafore of innocence, even the poet remaining unaware of the meaning. And having gotten it out—whatever the taboo thought or feeling may have been—we feel better, whether anyone understood us or not (and perhaps especially if nobody did!).

Still other codes are cries we utter when we are not consciously aware that we need help or are crying out. The poem may be an awkward jumble of broken lines that seems to be about a sunset or a squirrel on a lawn. The poet leaves it lying around the house, or reads it aloud to a family more interested in the interrupted television show, or sends it out to magazines already adrift in such heartbreaking messages, or pays to have it printed in a booklet to be sent to heedless friends and famous strangers. What he may not realize is that his pitiful poem has nothing whatsoever to do with sunsets or squirrels.

The real message is, "I languish for lack of attention! I need to be seen as a significant person. I need love." Unfortunately, the poet may feel no better for having so indirectly expressed these needs, for having sent out these coded cries. The disregard of the world for his inept poem may only confirm the poet's sense of worthlessness and helplessness.

The Lie of Arting

So far I have been discussing the artlessness of poetry, the crude but essential need of all human beings to express some of the complexities, conflicts, and perceptions that boil in every consciousness. But if that were all it is, no one would read it for sure, except possibly psychologists. Who needs to suffer through the artless contents of other people's minds?

And, sure enough, most of the poetry in the world is little better than unprocessed raw material. You can find a lot of such poetry published in literary journals. Most of it, however, forms a subterranean tide of pages of broken lines that make it no further than the wastebasket or attic trunk or perhaps a personal love letter. On the other hand, you and I know that a few poems constitute some of the most magnificent cultural monuments of any civilization. These occur when artless self-expression is squeezed into a corset of art.

If you want to be recognized by others as a poet, you make demands on your work that you never need apply to self-expression. It is no longer a matter of whether you feel better having gotten it off your chest (even if only into your bottom drawer). Now you have to ask what effect it will have on others. *What will readers make of this? Does it make sense? Do I want it to? Will they be moved, amused, disturbed, or merely bored? Suppose they laugh at what I mean seriously—or take seriously what I meant as a joke. Will I care? How will I get the reaction I want? How can I at least hold a reader's interest?* These questions take you a long way from mere honesty or sincerity, even from the urgency of your need for expression. You are no longer merely verbalizing thoughts and feelings. You are performing, manipulating, calculating. Art is artificial. What is merely natural, this implies, is not enough.

A PIDDLING HARVEST

I was an intellectual
on chilling winter days
and would not say things plainly if
I could find other ways,

but April seemed so innocent
my sap began to rise;
the sun was kind, and I began
to throw off my disguise.

I was quite nude by summer, baked
and sweated, fang and claw,
and other natural instincts were
exposed till they were raw.

Oh, raw and red as apples glowed
all acres of my skin,
till skin could hardly stand it, so
in fall I raked all in

and somewhat blushed that harvest proved
I scarcely filled the cart.
Now twilight comes so early that
I best return to art.

The sense of natural badness that is inescapably implanted in the infant has the remarkable and sometimes glorious effect of motivating human achievement for good or ill. We are dissatisfied with nature, as we are with ourselves, and we therefore devote our energy and imagination and ingenuity to transforming whatever we find in a natural state. Granted, sometimes we overdo it. The biblical injunction to take dominion over the earth has produced some frightening pollution and distressing eyesores, not to mention devastating wars and waste of resources. One of the things the human race surely has to learn as it matures and grows in density is how to leave more of nature alone, how to value the given world. But writing poetry requires relatively harmless distortion of nature, and when the art is exercised well, the results are certainly nobler and more beneficial to humanity than the raw material of artless impulses.

Don't be fooled by the pose of professionals who claim to be indifferent to such concerns, who say their work is a spontaneous outpouring of their inner selves. That's all part of the act—and the best acting is always a convincing simulation of spontaneity. When I wrote that poem at eight, I meant what I said, and I was giving the poem to my mother in a genuine gesture of affection, but I was also probably calculating (correctly) that Mother would like it. Would anyone else? It probably never occurred to me to wonder, but, surely, there was some element in my writing of "showing off." All that meter and rhyme and fancy vocabulary didn't come merely out of love.

There was also some unconscious element of yearning for immortality. Little did I imagine that when I reread it forty-odd years later I would pack it off to Boston (in lieu of the trash can), but I must even then have wanted to make my perishable feelings imperishable, to give my life significance beyond the moment. And when you start thinking like that, you tidy things up a bit. You suck in your gut for the corset. You try harder to find precise language, memorable phrases, recognizable rhythms, effective combinations of sounds, images with impact. You are not asking, *Is this how I really feel?* but *Is this fresh—or clichéd? Is it dramatic? How is it paced? Is it intelligible? Is it vital? Does it resonate with significance?* When you ask the expert, *Is this a poem?* you are really asking yourself, *Is it art?*

Full Circle

It only adds to the confusion to realize that the greatest poetry (indeed, the greatest art) is the most honest, the most expressive—in a curious way, the most artless—after all. However tight the corset, self seeps through. (Indeed, sometimes it seems the tighter the corset, the more it seeps.) But this is one of those effects, like being loved, or being popular, or being trusted, that you can't get by trying, and the more you try, the less you achieve it.

Among great authors Shakespeare and Homer are perhaps the greatest—and the most anonymous! We know very little about either biographically, and what little is known is often in dispute. Yet one who has read their work deeply and at length has the sense of knowing the authors intimately. The plays and poems of Shakespeare, for instance, tell us about the range of his feelings and his capacity to understand human personality, human drama, the machinations of history, the secrets of the heart, and the magic of words in rendering the full panorama of life. When we have that much grasp of what a man knows and feels, we take him into our lives as a close friend, whether or not we know a single fact about the actual person who walked the streets of London.

Yet all that rich and ample self-expression leaked, as it were, through the restraints of artifice—of meter, rhyme, of fiction, fancy, and fact, most of it in the most impersonal form of all: drama. Express himself? He was doing hack work, refurbishing old plots, rewriting history to satisfy contemporary political pressures, dancing to the conflicting tunes of mass taste, patrons' preferences, and literary convention. *What will the Queen say, or the Archbishop, or those Puritan preachers? What do the company managers want? What can (and will) the actors do? What are my competitors doing? How long till opening? What costumes are available in the wardrobe? What's the news from home—and from my accountants? my lawyers? How can I work with the grippe? I'll be at this all night— and don't want to run out of ink or coal for the fire.* Such distractions might divert a man from expressing what was really on his mind—yet, by means of whatever art his circumstances required, he managed to convey a sense of himself through the fabric of artifice.

The artless need of self-expression and the artful control that makes such expression effective and memorable are like counterweights of a gyroscope. You need both—but artlessness will take care of itself. In any case, you can't learn much about it. You can't take lessons in letting it all hang out. Some few—especially those with emotional problems—may need encouragement to do so, but those of us inclined to write poetry generally do not require any such prodding. Rather, we probably should learn more about how to bottle it for public consumption. We need to channel our force of self-expression into forms that others might be interested in reading or hearing.

And, luckily, *that* is something we can learn. The techniques of art, the craft, are, of course, useless without the throbbing pressure of self behind them: an empty corset hanging on a nail. But, well, would those who were not issued selves please raise their hands?

YOU HAVE TO TOOT YOUR OWN HORN

(to be sung to the tune of "Yankee Doodle")

The flesh is weak: You need a bra
  to amplify your sweater—
and though I like the smell of you,
  I do like Lifebuoy better.

Truth is never enough: The act
  of love requires some acting.
One's friends are liars; enemies are
  sufficiently exacting.

Flatter as ye would be flattered;
  kiss as ye would be kissed.
I'd rather never go to bed
  than with a realist.

I find you as you say you are
  complete in all essentials,
but be for me the apogee—
  and never mind credentials

Don't hide your talent: Goods are good
  only when you sell them.
How can your customers know what
  they've bought, unless you tell them?

It pays to advertise. Think big.
  Eat grass, but call it clover.
Consider Jesus, Son of God.
  He nearly put it over.

CHAPTER III:
PERILS
OF
PUBLICATION

The impulse to write poetry is likely to be quickly followed by anxieties about publication. The poem may have begun as pure expression and may, in fact, never be seen or heard by another person, but as soon as it is written down, we are likely to wonder whether it should or could be made public, even if the public we have in mind is only one other person.

Some poets I have known no sooner set pen to paper (or, more likely, fingers to keyboard) than they began imaginatively rehearsing for the talk shows. There are many good reasons for trying to get your work published, and the Appendix is an extensive discussion of how to go about it, but here I want to remind you that concerns about publication are a distraction from the writing process itself. And it may surprise you to consider that such concerns are totally irrelevant to many people who find much fulfillment and satisfaction in writing poetry. Let posterity worry about what, if anything, to do with all those manuscripts piling up in the bottom drawer. You might concentrate on learning to be happy though unpublished.

Lest you hear that advice as condescending, let me describe one of the poetry workshops I offered some years ago at Downhill Farm. Fire crackled on the hearth of our log cabin in the Pennsylvania Alleghenies. The room was full of poets—seventeen of them—from places as far away as Florida, Ohio, New England. One young black woman was a telephone operator from Kansas City. A computer programmer who lived in Hawaii happened to be on the mainland at the time of the workshop and was able to attend. The youngest—a high school student from New Jersey—had published a handful of poems in his school literary magazine, and though we didn't take statistics on the oldest, there were a number of grey heads besides my own in the room.

Quite a few of them had won prizes and were widely published. In some cases this had gone to their heads—and they might have written better poetry if they had had less success in getting into print. Unfortunately, with so many subsidized literary magazines in the United States today, most of them with very little readership (see Chapter XVII), it is altogether too easy to find one that will accept your poems. I wanted those poets to understand some of the perils of publication.

Others had never had a poem accepted for publication. Some weren't sure they ever wanted to publish. For them one of my objectives was to help them feel comfortable with the idea of not doing so. There is much to be gained from writing and reading poetry apart from publication. And even if your hope is for eventual publication, active involvement in the process, which is as different from writing poetry as selling cakes is from baking them, can be postponed indefinitely, perhaps for your whole life.

In the opening session I tried to set the tone for the weekend. For the next two days we would be going over work by each poet in detail—reacting, suggesting, commenting, criticizing. They were all strangers to one another, and to me, except through correspondence, but I had read poetry by each, and there was not one present whose talent I didn't respect. Indeed, I was awed by the assemblage of such variety and so much precious ability. But I wanted to prepare the participants to be useful critics of one another. One of the great rewards of poetry can be, precisely, a gathering such as this. Sharing your poetry in any way, even by merely reading it aloud, is a kind of publication. Each of those poets had come from great distances to find an audience willing to listen, to read, and to react in return for his or her own response to the work of peers. It was important that they engage in that process as sensitively as possible.

I started our session by asking for an invocation, something like what ancient authors called an Invocation of the Muse. I asked for a few moments of silence in which we could get used to being together, absorb one another's presence, and summon from our depths the best we had to offer to the group. Whether one believes inspiration comes from above or outside or one's own subconscious, I am sure we all know that delicate seedlings of poetry can be easily drowned in a flood of ego. We had to put aside the shrill clamoring of self for recognition, attention, authority, and let some purer spirit emerge.

The Quest for Immortality

Searching for words about what we should keep in mind as we examined one another's work, I talked about the various uses of poetry in our lives. I think all poets need such perspective. The values you bring to bear as you judge your own words or those of others depend on the intentions underlying the poem. Each needs to ask himself, *Whom am I writing this for?*

There might be more possible answers than you realize at first. The audiences of poetry are many, and they have very different requirements. Few poets try to speak to only one of these audiences, and many of us who call ourselves poets would like to reach them all. But sometimes the criteria of success for one audience contradict those for another. I'm sure most of us would like to sweep the board and write poetry that is great for the ages, for our own time, for the intellectuals and the masses, for those we love and for ourselves. But some of those audiences matter to us more than others, and this affects the way we write and what we say. Moreover, if we worry too much about publication, about reaching any audience at all other than ourselves, that preoccupation may diminish the effectiveness of what we write.

Explaining this, I said I guessed that most of us present in the log cabin would be willing to skip all the other audiences if we could speak to "the ages." We don't want much: just a place in the library alongside Shakespeare. Fame in our own times, fortune, popularity, being heard and understood, and even self-satisfaction seem lesser goals.

I told them I believe the major distinction between human beings and other forms of life is our awareness of our own mortality. As I said in Chapter II, we are never satisfied with nature as we find it in ourselves or in the world around us. One source of that dissatisfaction is our knowledge that our time is limited. Much of our achievement, our restlessness, our anxiety, the labors of parental love, and the monuments of brick or intellect we use our life to build are hedges against the oblivion of death.

We are therefore likely to hope that whether or not we are personally remembered as individuals, we will be able to make some enduring difference in the world, to leave our environment transformed. One of the ways we try to do that is by writing poetry, our effort to contribute to and alter human culture. It's a presumptuous and grandiose goal. But we're saved from our vaingloriousness (if at all) only by the simple fact that, by definition, we'll never know whether we succeeded. We can write as well as possible, according to our lights, but ultimately we can't make ourselves immortal as poets by our own efforts. There's nothing we can do about it. The ages will decide what poetry is for them.

I think of my own poems as messages in bottles pitched into the sea of time, a little like the pathetic cry of the prisoner in the Chinese cookie factory mentioned in Chapter II (though I hope my messages aren't that pathetic). Maybe some of the bottles will wash ashore on some distant beach and be found by someone who just happens to be able to read them and appreciate them. Or one might think of them as children who grew up and moved away and don't write home. Some such attitude may help us dissociate our feelings from our poetry's ultimate fate.

NEW YORK
This is not a poem about
      New York, as the title implies,
or even a poem, as does
      the shape of the thing on the page,
or even a personal statement
      (all my I's are lies),
but a kind of document
      (to be found in a bottle) of an age

of dinosaurs, as if dinosaurs
      had some ferny Madison Avenue
(sluice of the swamp, of heavy
      splashing, reptile groans),
and some distant mammal caught
      in the natural network knew
eventually some creatures
      would dig up skyscrapers like bones

and put huge calcium structures
      somewhere in a cosmic museum
with Latin labels (ah, Rome!)
      affixed to nature's mistakes,
and young users of reptile-
      flesh coal all went to see them
(though professors would prove that most
      of these exhibits were fakes),

and this mammal (I) finished
      his bottle and stuffed in a song
saying
      it helps not to know
      that you know not to what
            you belong.

That poem takes the posture of speaking to the ages, but, obviously, it was meant for a contemporary audience and would have little value unless published at the time it was relevant. Already it seems dated—a political statement of a bygone era.

It was quite another matter when Emily Dickinson filed her poems away, most of them unread by any other person than herself, only to be found after her death. I once suggested that poets get ahead the way Emily Dickinson did: Try your trunk. That's a big gamble, isn't it? And Emily very nearly lost. She had sent out a few poems when she was alive, let a few people (some of them influential) know she was writing poems, and a few had recognized her highly original, if unconventional, genius. Thus before she died she had made it possible for the ages to discover her—but just barely. Her temperament was that of a recluse, and she must have intuitively known that the limelight would destroy her creative capacity.

But when her family and well-wishers began bringing out her poetry after her death, they edited it freely to make it conform to conventional notions of proper diction, punctuation, and form. It wasn't until our own century that the little packets of handwritten poems were reexamined and published in a form that reaffirmed her original intentions. Not many of us who care intensely about the exact form in which our work is presented would be willing to take so great a chance that our relatives or editors would do it right.

One function of publication is to guarantee that your work is preserved and available—and in the form in which you want it to appear. I have helped a number of people, especially elderly people, arrange to have their work self-published for this reason. (I explain how to go about it in the Appendix.) They wanted to be sure that at least a few copies of an authoritative text were left to posterity. That is not vanity. They weren't convinced that posterity would surely be interested. But, just in case, they wanted to make sure posterity would have a chance to look at and consider their work.

I suggested above that we might compare the love and hope we have for our unread poems to that which we have for our children. That love and hope, too, is often tragically unfulfilled. My friend Sandy (she uses no last name) defined the problem in a poem that might serve as an envoi for many a collection of poetry left never to see the light of day:

A DEATH IN THE FAMILY

Emily, my words
                  will not lie

patient, breathless in an airless
trunk, saving their stirrings
for only the most intimate of caresses.
No, I would welcome
no such restraints as sweet
repose.
      Rather, here,
here are my offerings, take them
while flesh still clings to the bone.
Too late, too late,
           the moment
                  has passed.
Fresh air has turned my stale words
to dust. A kind breeze holds its breath,
whispers what we have both known all along—
some things were meant to be born
                and die at home.

Many great writers have self-published some or all of their work. Rest assured that there is nothing to be ashamed of if you want to preserve your poetry in this fashion.

Or at Least a Nobel Prize

At the workshop most of the poets were more actively concerned with an audience other than posterity—the intellectuals and poetic professionals of our own time. That is, they might not hope to impress their neighbors or mothers or the masses of common readers, but they hoped to score with the editors of respected journals and publishing houses, the critics and reviewers, the academic teachers of literature, the folks at the National Endowment for the Arts, or those in the foundations, or those handing out the literary prizes, and the hundred or so poets who are "recognized" at any given time in the United States.

I pointed out that there are advantages in aiming for this elite audience. One is that this is almost the only route to becoming recognized as a literary poet—the kind found in the library alongside Shakespeare—while you are alive. Another is that you can actually learn—from writing classes, books, workshops, and active study—much that is relevant. You can read the literary journals and analyze the trends—can do what in the business world is called "market research." You can make valuable friends—and success in this area is much more dependent upon politics and connections than is generally admitted. (Most of the judges, critics, and opinionmakers would have you believe that all judgments are made on the basis of pure quality, but no one can tell you what that quality is.)

Notice that I used the word "score with" rather than "reach" to describe the impact you try to have on that elite. When we think of editors or critics or established poets or foundation executives reading our work, we aren't likely to think of them being moved. We don't think of their lives being changed or of making contact with them as people. They sniff our poems like merchants, for their own positions and reputations depend on their ability to predict what will impress others. Many decisions to publish the work of a given poet are made at cocktail parties, where recommendations are exchanged without anyone actually reading the work in question.

Sorry to sound cynical, but I know this world of the powers of poetry well, and though I don't blame anyone for trying to enter it and play the game, it is better not to confuse the values of the current literary world with those that ultimately determine literary value. To succeed in this area you have to be tuned to current trends. If you go to the library and look at the files of a trendy magazine such as *The New Yorker*, you will find that the poetry of the thirties or forties differs distinctly from that of each of the following decades. In studying literary history we learn stylistic distinctions for relatively huge hunks of time: the Renaissance, the Enlightenment, the Romantic Era. Within each, of course, are finer distinctions based on differences among individual poets and in the changing climate of opinion. For a poet trying to participate in the apparent high culture of his own time, an era may be a decade or less. It is important to know what is modern *this* year.

Obviously, the judgment of the professionals of any given time may or may not coincide with the judgment of the ages (and even that "judgment of the ages" is relative). In the mid-seventeenth century, when Donne and Milton were writing, the professionals were betting all their chips on Abraham Cowley, the T. S. Eliot of his day. Cowley is now regarded primarily as a historical curiosity. Since Eliot's death his reputation, which so dominated the literary world for nearly half a century, has similarly diminished. He is currently most widely known as the author of *Cats*.

It is important to keep such relativity in mind because most of the guidance you will get at poetry workshops, including mine, or from teachers of writing at universities is more likely to help you become a Cowley than a Donne or Milton. Such teaching is necessarily, though unconsciously, directed at helping you impress the elite and the professionals currently in vogue. It may have nothing whatsoever to do with achieving immortality as a poet, or reaching any significant readership in the general public, or saying well what you most wish to say. My personal invocation is, *Muse, I beg thee, help me tame my arrogance. Help me remember the essential triviality of tuning one's soul to the fashion, of scoring on the Dow Jones Average of literary reputation!* I have spent too much of my life (none too successfully) doing that.

The Common Touch

Though the audience of great poets such as Donne and Milton is vast over time, it is likely to be narrow in their own lifetimes. Robert Lowell, who briefly succeeded T. S. Eliot as the darling of intellectuals in twentieth-century America, was more widely known than read. His books were issued in editions of five thousand copies or less—a drop of ink in the sea of publication. Even those few hundred editors, prize givers, and recognized poets read little current poetry, except to keep up, stay on top, and remain alert to new trends. The general public is another audience entirely—people who have never read Edgar Guest, Kalhil Gibran, and Rod McKuen, much less Lowell or W. D. Snodgrass or Sylvia Plath.

One of my readers sent me a poem by a popular poet, Alice E. Chase. Each month Ms. Chase has a poem in *True Story*. She probably gets substantial pay for her work—a phenomenon almost unknown among literary poets. Apparently millions of readers like poetry of that sort, good people who just don't happen to share the snobbish values of the Establishment. I don't happen to like that kind of poetry very much myself, but I must admit that it has some qualities that would benefit more intellectual poetry. It is usually clear, readable, unpretentious, and emotionally relevant to the lives of its readers.

And those may be the people you want to write for. My Muse reminds me that I am envious in a dark corner of my soul, for I, too, yearn for a wide readership, would like my poetry to become a staple on the shopping list of the masses—not for the material reward, but simply to know that my words are echoing in the minds of millions. The Bengali poet Rabindranath Tagore, walking along a dusty road one evening, heard an ox-cart driver singing one of his poems as a song. Surely the peasant had never heard of Tagore by name, but the poet's lyrics had become a part of the peasant's cultural makeup. "That is the greatest reward a poet can have," Tagore later said: "to achieve anonymity in one's own lifetime." Though I have no idea how to help you become such a popular poet except to advise you to study and imitate the work that has succeeded, I recognize the value of that goal. I wish there were a way of getting genuinely good poetry—like much of the folk poetry of the past—to the masses. Those who come nearest doing so today are the authors of lyrics of popular songs, especially rock and country and western.

As Friend to Friend

Some write for a much smaller, but still an essentially nonliterary, public, such as their local communities, their colleagues, fellow hobbyists, or coreligionists. Their work may appear in local papers. My father, who was an oilman in the thirties and forties, published dialect verse in the Oklahoma City dailies on such subjects as gushers and roughnecking—verse much appreciated by the community of oilmen and -women. One of my correspondents calls himself "The Farm Poet." His weekly poems are syndicated in a number of rural papers where he has a following—much larger than the readership of any poetry I ever wrote—of people who might otherwise never read poetry at all. He and his readers have nothing to do with the world of literary professionals.

Others write for church publications or club newsletters. I had a warm and friendly letter once from the editor of a magazine called *Backpacker*. He told me he had a deep love for Longfellow, Browning, Keats, even Ezra Pound. He wanted me to tell my readers that he was actively seeking poetry with rhyme and meter about—of all things—backpacking! However specialized the content and audience, the poetry he selects will no doubt be good work. What has that to do with the ages, with the judgment of literary professionals, or with the masses? The Muse reminds me that a piece of soul is sacred, no matter where one finds it.

Still others write for family and friends—a genre in which the annual printed "Christmas poem" is perhaps the most familiar variety. Some of the world's greatest poetry, including many classical Japanese haiku, was intended for an audience of one person. Such poems serve as personal letters to mates, lovers, or friends. When you write a poem of intimate communication, publication or payment is far from your mind, and the poem is likely to be better written and, ironically, perhaps more enduring as literature for that reason.

Of course, the most important reader is yourself. Publication of a poem we deeply care about, even in the sense of enclosing the finished poem in a personal letter, may be an afterthought. We write for our own satisfaction. There is little we can learn from books, magazines, teachers, workshops, or editors about the demands of that audience, though the more we know about poetry, the harder we are to satisfy, and the poems we write primarily for ourselves become better as a consequence. Many good poets say that they themselves are their severest critics, which may be the one factor that links the poem to the ages. And being in touch with the immortal element in our private selves may produce a poem that is also immortal.

Yet it merely confuses or weakens you when you're working if you think you are writing primarily for yourself or for no one in particular. One of my correspondents said, "The imaginary reader was and is always real. I think this has much to do with poems. The good ones have, somewhere, a human target—not just the mob out there." What she means is, if you don't have an audience in mind, invent one—and the more specific the better, a subject I will return to in Chapter IX. Even though you may not be able to think realistically of publication as a goal, you will write better if you write *as if* you knew someone was going to receive and try to understand it. That will constitute a pressure to make your feelings intelligible, to shape sentences worthy of scrutiny by others, whether or not they are ever to be scrutinized.

Yoo-hoo! Is Anyone Listening?

People go to workshops like the one I have described partly for the same reasons others gather to play chamber music together—to share their talent, thought, and feelings in a sympathetic group. Moreover, they hope to improve their performance by comparing their work with that of others and by mutual criticism. Whether you ever attend a poetry workshop or not, you are likely to seek out friends or other poets for the most intimate, informal, and often the most rewarding kind of publication of all: letting others hear and read your poems and getting their reactions.

But given the relativity we have seen in the various purposes of poetry, what kind of criticism can we possibly give to one another on these occasions? Usually the poets themselves don't have a very clear idea why they are writing or for whom. How, then, can others provide them with relevant guidance or suggestions?

Faced with such awareness, listeners often freeze up. They don't know what kind of comments would be constructive, so they stifle their reactions with *hm*'s and *uh*'s. You may have experienced the frustration of getting such a response when you tried to get a reaction from a friend or member of your family. They just don't know what to say. They don't want to hurt your feelings, or they don't trust their own taste in poetry or their comprehension of the poem. You may yourself have responded that way to the work of others. That's why a good workshop, in which a spirit of trust and candor has been established, is usually so much more satisfying than informal sharing of poetry in unstructured situations.

Yet even in workshops some seem incapable of supportive participation. For example, a few poets don't seem to be able to take criticism. To one who responds to group comments, "I wrote it that way because that was the way I wanted it," the only possible response is a shrug. "If you know what you want," we implicitly say, "don't ask for our opinions." The truth is that the idea some have of "sharing" is simply getting others to listen to them. They don't really want any response other than adulation.

But, much as the comments may hurt, most participants want a searching discussion of what they have done. They may have written to please themselves, but now they want to view the poem as communication. The workshop provides a kind of implicit contract: We have agreed to use one another as audience and to articulate our responses.

Suppose you went to the doctor with a complaint, but he refrained from giving his diagnosis because he didn't want to hurt your feelings. Maybe he would mumble something about the relativity of physical needs and the uncertainty of science. Or perhaps he bathes you with a Socratic smile and asks, "What is health?" I doubt that you would appreciate his wisdom. As soon as we begin talking about one another's poems, we have to suppress our recognition of the fact that we will never know what good poetry is—or what it is good *for.* Judge and comment, we must.

And, when it's our turn in the spotlight, we must listen responsively to the reactions of others. If you are the poet whose work is being commented on, you have to remain quietly aware of the relativity of the source. The specific comments may not tell you what you ought to do about your poem. But they may nonetheless point up weaknesses. You recognize that something isn't working, though you may have to ignore the suggestions in discovering how to fix it. That process may help you understand why you wrote it in the first place. If your motive was, even in part, to share your inner self, the comments may help you see how and where—and maybe why—you failed to do so.

But one of the most basic factors in a writer's, especially a poet's, life is loneliness. Rarely does writing work as a group activity. (Remember the old definition of a giraffe as a horse designed by a committee?) Poetry starts in the perception of one's individual isolation—and it often ends there, too, at least for the poet. In later years, after you're gone, if your work has been preserved and made public, millions may discover that it speaks to and for their hearts also. But that is beyond your control.

I am reminded of a bitter winter, our family isolated in that same log cabin, when I was reflecting on the exciting experiences of the counterculture in the late sixties and early seventies. Many of us had felt in those days a brother- and sisterhood that promised somehow to make our society a less lonely crowd. We thought communes, such as the one where I lived, might serve the function of medieval monasteries, little pockets of culture in the Dark Ages. By 1978 all that seemed to have passed, and we ourselves, revolutionaries of the last decade, were scattered around the country settling into middle age.

MIDDLE AGES

Brethren, sistren, are we out of touch?
Rarely do barefoot members of our order,
begging and preaching village to village, come
bearing communication. Saints are silent.
The media have lost interest. Prophets no
longer bother to cry doom.
                                Are you
listening? I think you are there. Perhaps
you are not there. More likely, snug in your
monastic nook, you labor over looms
for the tourist market.
                                Here we are watching stars.
Fewer and fewer flying objects are
unidentified. For several years
running I forgot to renew my membership.
Last fall no one harvested hemp before
the frost, things got that bad.
                                Dark ages last
a thousand years. Scratching my hairy belly
through my robe, my feet before the fire,
I think there still is time. I think there will
always be time, always this now, always
this mote of urgency in the eye of God.
Messiahs trouble my dreams. I hope no more
messiahs come to save the world. The world
can only save itself—the cleansing fire,
fern growing fast on the charred land of spring—
if we will let it.
                                Now the winter sun
slices the slot of my carrel only a few
hours each afternoon, illuminating
old books, the practices which should be saved—
formulae, ceremonies, facts. Surely

these will be needed once the plague has passed,
the boundaries rearranged.
                        We were the cutting
edge, at every crossroads wild revivals
with eucharist of acid. That was no life
for children.
            Now in our scattered communes in
the crags we keep households where kids may grow
outside the law. I cannot keep those brawling
nations straight. There is only one weapon
against the state: indifference.
                        Stay in touch
and I will keep the record. Signed, your scribe.

To stay in touch, to record, to preserve what we perceive of value: That
is the underlying meaning and purpose of publication, though it may
have little to do with getting your poems into current books and magazines.

CHAPTER IV:
CURIOSITY,
CURIOSUS,
CURA,
CARE

We have considered some of the human anxieties and needs that find their expression in poetry. Those might be considered negative impulses which require some kind of outpouring of emotion. But there are also many positive impulses that cause people to write in broken lines. For example, we may be dazzled by the sheer abundance and diversity of life. In this chapter I'm going to take you on a personal tour of some of the ideas and experiences about nature that have dazzled me. Surely there are similar areas in your life waiting to flower into poetry.

I have talked about our uniqueness as a species stemming from our awareness of our own mortality. But we are also uniquely responsive to the intricacies, interrelationships, and the bounty of the world around us. Such responses generate poetry as surely as does our sense of isolation and awareness of our own mortality. Again and again I have found myself returning, in thought and poetry, to the mysterious throb of the life force. The French philosopher Henri Bergson called it *élan vital*, vital ardor, and he visualized evolutionary energy as a rocket bursting into many projectiles, each of which bursts again. As human beings we may be preoccupied with death. But we are also capable of understanding death as only one step of further bursting when life's umbrella of multicolored fire illuminates the night sky.

One term for our faculty for becoming engaged with the world is *curiosity*, which comes from the Latin word for "careful," "diligent," "inquisitive," ultimately from *cura*, the word for "care." Like innocence, curiosity is not something you can go out and get. It is something you have, and something you lose, to one degree or another, as you mature.

"Curiosity killed the cat," our parents warn, tucking away something not for children's eyes. Thus we learn not to be curious in the same way we learn not to be naïve. The model of adulthood toward which we are taught to aspire is one in which we restrain our natural impulses, including the insatiable desire to know, to experience, to test. Both phases of curiosity, of course, are necessary, as we discussed in Chapter II. We may relish, and certainly cannot escape, our artlessness. But to bring it into the social world we need art.

Kids Will Be Kids

I remember when we had seven baby goats which we separated from their mothers (so we could have the milk) and brought into the house as soon as they were born. Within an hour of birth, on their spindly, wobbly legs, they thoroughly explored their environment— the living room, then the porch converted to a greenhouse, then a small pen in the yard. They nudged and chewed each object, including available appendages of any human being who happened to enter the pen.

We thus had a good opportunity to observe them. Those kids would have made good poets if they could have kept their vital curiosity intact and had learned language (which can be an instrument of curiosity, just like a hoof or tongue). When they were a few weeks old, I was sitting out in their pen in the March sun reading proofs. I chose that unlikely place to work because I enjoyed having the little kids crawl over me. Like goats, I crave constant sensation. But I finally had to leave because they were eating the paper, along with chewing my hair and nuzzling my armpits and pulling things out of my pockets.

We thought they were cute, though pests, but a hardheaded observer might dismiss all that random activity as nothing but a search for food. Nothing but? One way of regarding the life force is as an eternal search for food, including food for the mind, the senses and other organs which, if they do not make music, desiccate and atrophy. Seven goats and one man in a pen. Doesn't that sound like eight chambers of a poet's brain?

To me it seemed that the goats lived in a world of perpetual metaphor. Of the fingers resting on my knee they think. *How like an udder! How very like an udder!* (I'll tell you later where that phrasing comes from.) Are they simply making an error in perception, or do goats, like poets, like to dally with comparisons?

How could they make comparisons at all, having had no experience with real udders? We brought them in before they had their first meal. I guessed that as they nosed into my pockets they were looking for the

Great Udder in the Sky. Tricked this way, they would not recognize real udders when we turned them loose to run with the grown goats. Like some people I know, they will continue to feed themselves on metaphors, oblivious to the Source hanging conveniently under their mothers, cousins, sisters, and aunts up and down the goat stall. We gave them grain and stole all the milk for ourselves. At that point the goats graduated to become mature consumers, conditioned to accept the surrogate gratifications available in the market (or trough), no longer questioning, as they did as kids, what other rewards might be available to the indiscriminate nose.

Curious Creatures

Nosey. That's a good word for many animals, including poets. Some seem to be nosey in a search for attention, which I am glad to give. I only take notes on what I've seen:

FLIRT

At dawn a nosey doe looked in
our window like she never meant
to pry. She quivered for a scent,

her lashes waxy with mascara,
silk ears swept up, a painted face
on a lightbulb head balanced in place

on an ungainly neck and narrow,
shivering shoulders. She, combining
the virtues of the hoyden, horse and sparrow,

appeared to be insulted when
we spied her, bolted feminine,
thick-thighed and little-footed—ten

rocking broad-bottomed hops and stopped
to see if we were watching for sure,
then—away! with a white jogging tail for a lure.

Surely she didn't imagine there was something in our bedroom to eat. What is it about our consciousness that drives us to the very edge of danger just to satisfy our curiosity?

SEALS . . .

. . . fluff white in the sun on barnacled ledges
as our boat draws near:

so many bags of flour dropped
with their corners in the air.

They flip themselves like legless pigs
or middleaged ladies at play.
Gracelessly giving a grunt, they dump
themselves into the bay

only to rise by the side of the boat
and individually peer,
each bald as a pickle, staring us down
like an affronted financeer.

Much poetry, like much of the busyness of the minds of animals or people, can only be explained as random play. I once had a job as an animal
man in a food research laboratory. Mostly I tended rhesus monkeys,
which were used for experiments in staphylococcus poisoning (commonly called ptomaine). Through rubber tubes forced down their
throats into their stomachs we fed the monkeys infected agar, then
watched them for five hours to see whether they got sick. Usually they
didn't, as most of the strains of staph being tested were harmless; but if
one vomited, our job was to record which monkey at what time—e.g.,
#53 at 2:14.

I had hours to spend each day meditating on monkeys, sitting there
in my lab suit, listening to some local disc jockey patter and platter his
way along Tin Pan Alley, watching the bank of cages for signs of nau-
sea. I learned much about myself and about the source of poetry. For
one thing I realized there for the first time that it is literally impossible
for them (or me) to do nothing. Confined to solitary metal cages with
about six square feet of floor space and just enough room to stand, they
were continually busy, exploring, examining, each chip of wood on
their cage floors, picking over their bodies, toying with the catches on
their doors (and sometimes creating excitement in the lab by opening
them and escaping). They would reach through the bars and around
into their neighbor's cage, trying to make contact. Anyone who passed
through the animal room provided them with a distraction and an occasion for noisy gossip.

Pick, pick, pick; play, play, play. Those tiny agile grey fingers, like
microbes, were into every corner, as though each miniature hand had a
bottomless hunger. Everything had to be felt, to be known, because it
was there. And what was I doing while my eyes methodically traveled
from cage to cage? I listened with dim attention to the radio, conversed
with anyone who passed through, doodled on the pad I kept on my lap

to record observations of vomit, tipped back and balanced on two legs
of the chair, hummed, made faces, scratched like a monkey. I, too, was
always busy, busy, busy, rarely doing only one thing at a time, rarely
concentrating, rarely governed by purpose. What is the meaning of all
this random energy, this eternal bursting and bursting again of the projectiles of attention? It amazes me that we are ever able to harness it into art.

An Imaginative Hornet

A poem is running through my head like a nagging tune, so I stop
to let it float up to consciousness. It is Robert Frost's "The White-Tailed
Hornet." I realize I borrowed something from it a few pages ago, as you
will see. Frost tells us that when he goes near the hornet's home in the
woodshed, the insect chases him more unerringly than a bullet, since
the hornet has the power to change direction in flight. But, complains
the poet, the hornet *is* in error: Doesn't he recognize in Frost "the exception / I like to think I am in everything"? The poet means no harm to
the hornet and his paper house.

When the hornet visits the poet's house, however, he is better be-
haved. At least he doesn't go after the man. Here he is hawking for
flies, yet still with persistent error:

> I watched him where he swooped, he pounced, he struck:
> But what he found he had was just a nailhead.
> He struck a second time. Another nailhead.
> 'Those are just nailheads. Those are fastened down.'
> Then disconcerted and not unannoyed,
> He stooped and struck a little huckleberry
> The way a player curls around a football.
> 'Wrong shape, wrong color, and wrong scent,' I said.
> At last it was a fly. He shot and missed;
> And the fly circled round him in derision.
> But for the fly he might have made me think
> He had been at his poetry, comparing
> Nailhead with fly and fly with huckleberry:
> How like a fly, how very like a fly.

That line came to mind when the goats mistook fingers for an udder.
The hornet's inaccuracies cause the poet to question the whole theory
of the infallibility of instinct:

> Won't this whole instinct matter bear revision?

Won't almost any theory bear revision?
To err is human, not to, animal.
Or so we pay the compliment to instinct,
Only too liberal of our compliment
That really takes away instead of gives.
Our worship, humor, conscientiousness
Went long since to the dogs under the table.
And served us right for having instituted
Downward comparisons.

The poet says that so long as we made our comparisons upward, to gods and angels, mankind had some dignity. He conceived of himself as beneath—but not much beneath—divinity.

But once comparisons were yielded downward,
Once we began to see our images
Reflected in the mud and even dust,
'Twas disillusion upon disillusion.
We were lost piecemeal to the animals,
Like people thrown out to delay the wolves.
Nothing but fallibility was left us,
And this day's work made even that seem doubtful.

Inquisitive Toddlers

I wonder whether Frost is, by popping into my mind this way, admonishing me for making downward comparisons—poets to kid goats, indeed, or rhesus monkeys, a hoyden doe and banker seal? Perhaps. But if we're going to sort out learned behavior from instinct, we have to look to creatures who are not so thoroughly conditioned as we ourselves are. We imagine that we can see what is essential and deeply rooted by observing animals.

Or babies. I began by mentioning the natural curiosity we have as children, which we unlearn as we grow up. That curiosity is sometimes difficult to contain. I know each of our children made it necessary for us to "babyproof" the house, putting everything out of reach that might be broken or ingested, making it secure as a goat pen. If something were within grasp, it would be grasped. The instinct involved is much more complex than a mere search for food. In insects, animals, and human beings there seems to be a perpetual drive to probe, test the limits, and even invent analogies. That's how I saw my daughters pushing their ways into consciousness:

INFANT WITH SPOON

Having learned to sit like a balloon full of water,
you have not learned all, daughter.

Be educated by whatever comes
in the fish grip of your gums

and seal your meditations in this school
with a slow tear of drool

on the kitchen floor. Before you ask what for,
ask *what*. Explore

plastic without plasticity, pure blue
you cannot see into nor through,

a straightness stuck to roundness, smoothly sheer,
not lollipop, but hemisphere

alleged to hold *1 tbs.* (or three
times *1 tsp.*)

Texture today: You twist your fist, intent.
Tomorrow, mysteries of measurement.

Regretfully, we find we have to impose on children a recognition of the
necessity of limits. Otherwise energy simply spills and dissipates or
even becomes self-destructive. A feeling running loose is a poem without a cage. I said this of another uncontainable daughter.

CAGES

First I was burst. My rib
(or wife) next swelled with life
which split her. Thus a daughter
we contained safe in a crib.
The crib grew small: like a rick
of blankets, dolls, its slender
slats burgeoned, burst before

the girl was three—a quick
climber and kicker, she,
who rocked crib like a carton
and made us fear her falling:
Of crib we set her free—
gave her a bed with bars
halfway. She could climb out

safely and in dark scout
for the door, come to the stairs,
where we had put a gate
to prevent her tumbling, half
sleeping, on down. The self
seems slow to save its pate.
Parents hypothesize

a girl's falls patiently.
Now she hates sleep, would
lie down never if her eyes
like cage doors never closed
her in, always at terminal
of tether like an animal.
Tonight, when I supposed

she slept, I heard a faint
scraping upstairs in the hall.
I went, and nearly fell
across her, trapped, and saint-
ly stretched on the hard floor,
arms like parentheses
around her head, her nose

making a miniature snore.
I carried her, moist and warm,
to my idea of comfort,
kissed her, left her under
covers: asserted the norm.
Asserted my love, that just
and outer cage, which she

will come to, certainly,
as sleepless daughters must,
in rage. The young must wage
hate on all bars. All bars
must be shaken, must be dared.
Fathers must bear the rage.
And she, at dawn, like fate,

will toddle to our bed, plead
that Papa wake. Indeed,
no love is sweeter than this hate,
nor hate so hard as age:
Dear child with touching hands,

night, day, age, youth, our veins,
our very ribs are cage.

And some of the cages most necessary—and most confining—are
purely symbolic, existing only in the mind:

THE NOTHING GAME

When my eighteen-month-old daughter pinches
with elaborate pains a bit of air
and toddles to you with it, you
should know what steps to take from there:

Bite it or give it back—with sweeping
courtesy—look it over long,
or throw it high (in which case she
will fetch another). Wrong

responses on your part induce
a fit of weeping only relieved
by peeking around a handkerchief
or some such elementary use

of fantasy, or symbols, I
should say, the signs which stay, although
the things they stand for go away,
or never were—the names we know

to use in games, handfuls of air,
mind-forged and finger-felt, which have
some distant relevance to things
(things that are there when they are there).

Thus will it be: Into the maze
of the symbol-world she will waddle,
gaining some grace, with greater dignity
losing her touch with the thing-world, her days

all clock-begun and ended, sun
improved upon. Already she
is name-bound: Say *Bottle* and her mind
(not stomach) cries a need for one,

repeating the Word with extravagant care,
"Bah-*ume!* Bah-*ume!*" (An empty one
will do.) In time her life will be
like mine, exchanging bits of air.

But, of course, as babies grow they learn to keep hands off. A polite adult visitor can be in a room for hours without touching a thing except the glass or dishes served him and the chair he sits in. He doesn't even scratch. His own body is invisible and shielded from contact and exploration.

In school we are taught such discipline with a vengeance. School sometimes seems a machine for destroying curiosity. Sit still. Shut up. In many respects the school cancels education, preparing children to live in a world in which babyproofing is unnecessary. They teach you to ignore your body, your friends around you, the colorful posters on the wall, the world flowering outside the window—everything except the one thing to which your attention is directed. Think about other things later. Do this now, and after school you can do what you please. After twelve years of such training one learns for sure that later never comes. This imposed tunnel vision is called "adjusting to reality." Maturity is catatonia.

Or so I reason in my more rebellious and romantic moods. Poets, I then say, are those who never learn that lesson—and so keep on learning. The elder Blackstone, the magician, once said that a child is harder to fool than an adult. When he points at something during a performance, the adult looks where he points, but the child may continue to watch his hand. That's the poetic knack—to ignore what's pointed at, to keep one's attention free from control by others.

An Instinct for Play

But, children—not to mention hornets and other creatures—rarely write great poems. The poets who write them usually have matured in society's ways. It may be argued that they learned to focus their attention, perhaps even to allow it to be directed. Their curiosity has survived, perhaps even benefited from schooling. Maybe in some respects curiosity is a learned trait—not the indiscriminate exploration of innocent animals and children, but a kind of tough and persistent inquiry, like that of the scientist, pursuing an objective single-mindedly, indifferent to distraction.

But Robert Frost (I say to the ghost with whom I'm carrying on this imaginary dispute), what kind of poet would you have been if you had stuck to your desk and ignored the hornet in the kitchen? Wasn't it you who stopped working on one poem to write another, "A Considerable Speck," about a mite crawling across your manuscript? Didn't you work all night on the long, tiresome satire "New Hampshire" and then, at dawn, knock off without forethought "Stopping by Woods on a Snowy Evening," which has come to be one of the best known and loved American poems?

But maybe I'm hearing Robert wrong. The whole instinct matter has indeed been much revised since (though not because) he wrote "The White-Tailed Hornet." I doubt that any scientist today other than a strident behaviorist would argue that the hornet dives only for some specific purpose, some reward of food or sex or other gratification essential to survival. That vision of a universe of reason and utility in which only people are subject to the inefficiencies of play and imagination has long been outdated.

Robert and I have reached a sly understanding. As fellow poets we knew all along that such textbook scientists and textbook hornets never happen in the real world. And we strongly suspect the hornet wasn't hungry anyway, goofing around the way he was with nailheads and huckleberries and missing the real flies. And if he felt he had a duty "To feed his thumping grubs as big as he is," what was to stop him from taking a little time off for target practice or sheer joy in power diving?

And those little goats. Am I to imagine they were so stupid as to think my proofs might be edible? It's more likely they just wondered what the big lunk would do if they ate his papers. And Jud—playing around with this book. Do you really think you're telling people anything about writing poetry? Or do you think that if we all just nose around a bit together, something artful might come of it, after all?

I hope poems come of it for you as they have for me. I can show you very concretely how mulling over these questions of how the mind works and how we relate to the natural world feeds into my own work.

Pigs Is Pigs

In 1968 I was swept up in the general reaction to the series of devastating events of that year: the assassination of Martin Luther King, Jr., and Robert Kennedy, the Soviet invasion of Czechoslovakia, the police riot in Chicago at the time of the Democratic Convention, the election of Richard Nixon. And like many others, I felt we were on the eve of a massive transformation of our society. There was a kind of joy in the air in the midst of tragedy. I began writing a series of poems which I called *Rumors of Change,* based on the premise that I was receiving telepathic messages from the scattered membership of the emerging new culture. Off and on over the next decade I added poems to the series reflecting changes I perceived in the social and political climate.

You've read one of these, from the late seventies, already: "Middle Ages" in Chapter III. As I mentioned, by that time I had moved to a commune with my family. I had "dropped out," resigning from my position as a professor at Antioch. But what seemed to have begun as a kind of cultural revolution had nearly fizzled out in the swamp of post-Vietnam prosperity, and I was reevaluating my own place in these events.

Meanwhile, with the emergence of the controversial field of sociobiology, the whole theory of instinct was once more being revised. One late fall day in 1978 I was feeding the two sows we were raising for meat, Swinella and Pigena, when I was reminded of John Ciardi's "Thoughts on Looking into a Thicket," a poem I had examined at length in *The Poet and the Poem*, In spite of having one of the most unpromising titles in our literature, it is one of those poems that function as reference points in my thinking—embodiments of ideas, experiences, attitudes, and definitive modes. Such poems help me name the world.

Before telling you about Ciardi's poem I'd like to comment on that function of poetry in our lives. I used the word "embodiment": A poem can seem like an idea in flesh and blood. Joseph Wood Krutch, the naturalist and literary critic, once used the term "the Long Discourse" to describe that timeless and continuing conversation in which the voices are works of intellect and art in our civilization speaking to one another, answering, qualifying, as though literature were a kind of soirée where the gods toasted their feet before some fireplace on Olympus. Ciardi's poem sits there and discourses—and it is so compellingly beautiful, clear, and strong that it demands some response.

"Life will do anything for a living," the poem says, a notion that is particularly graphic as one watches pigs eat. Ciardi uses as an example a species of spider that has learned the art of weaving a web that looks like a bird dropping. The spider sits in the middle, in imitation of the "more liquid portion," and waits for those butterflies that particularly like that sort of meal.

"If you," Ciardi warns, "will be more proper than real, that is your / death." We feed as we are fed upon. Each of us, as we think through these words, is teeming with microorganisms. He says,

> if there is an inch or the underside of an inch
> for a life to grow on, a life will grow there;
> if there are kisses, flies will lay their eggs
> in the spent sleep of lovers.

On that fall morning Swinella and Pigena seemed like voracious survival machines. But shortsighted ones, I thought, since the more they ate, the sooner they would be eaten. When I dumped slop in the trough, the pigs tended to knock the bucket aside, spilling it over their backs and into the surrounding mud. With yells and occasional slaps we managed to train the floppy-eared sow, Swinella, to back off until the slop was poured. But the one with straight-up ears, Pigena, was too eager for such niceties. While Swinella stood back being more proper than real, Pigena got the first gobbles, her head dripping slop I had to pour over her. She was showing me life will do anything for a living.

Except it's more complicated than that. In the first place, Pigena's bad habits wasted a good bit of food. They would both have had more to eat if she would only have waited a moment. Moreover, we were going to keep one of them for breeding, and there's no question, you may guess, which of the two would go first to slaughter. Was Swinella more intelligent—or simply more cowardly? Who knows? But for whatever reason, in our particular environment that characteristic had survival value. She was the one to perpetuate her DNA.

As Frost reminded us, we long accepted the dogma that other forms of life were programmed, but human beings are dependent on learning and socialization for survival. Denied any but the most rudimentary instincts, we were taught, we have to survive by our wits. At best that's an ambiguous advantage. Wit is more fallible than instinct (the truth behind Frost's wry statement "To err is human, not to, animal"). The very lowest, simplest forms of life, like protazoa, are the ones that have persisted the longest.

Yet in our relatively brief time on earth, our species seems not only to have survived but prevailed. We take a kind of pride in having pulled ourselves up by our own bootstraps, as it were. The controversy introduced by sociobiology centers on this issue. For years liberal orthodoxy held that nurture was far more important than nature in explaining human behavior. The sociobiologists are attempting to swing the pendulum back the other way with their argument that a great deal more than we have previously believed must be attributed to instinct in human behavior. To some this seems a challenge to our vaunted free will—our freedom to be wrong. The scientists are still sorting out how much of what we do is instinctual and how much is choice, but they seem generally to assume that, in either case, behavior is driven by the need for survival. That seems too limited a view of life for poetry.

God's Abundance

Contemplating the complexities of what would determine the survival of my two sows, I remembered a book that helped me expand my understanding of the life force, Annie Dillard's *Pilgrim at Tinker Creek*. Anyone aware of the stunning diversity of life forms and habits has to recognize how far we are—for all our science—from arriving at any understanding of the underlying principles of nature. Annie Dillard leaves one thinking, after considering with her the horrors and wonders of the world spreading around our feet, that surely life will do anything for a living, often more ingeniously than we could ever have imagined, but that may be just the beginning of what life will do.

As she points out with amusing and graphic examples, nature's "plan," if plan is the word for such a hodgepodge of contradictory principles, is no way to run a railroad. Nature thrives by excess—wild, crazy, tragic, wasteful, overwhelming, beautiful overproduction. We have heard enough of nature's wisdom and economy. What about its insane waste and wild abandon?

For example, no utilitarian explanation can account for so simple and common a phenomenon as beauty. The view of life as relentless and perpetual competition with the reward of survival going to the hardiest, most adaptable, most intelligent, or best equipped can't be upheld in the face of God's abundance. There is too much diversity for a purely pragmatic theory of evolution to explain. We miss the point if we limit ourselves to that view, a point I tried to make in this poem, another of the "Rumors of Change":

NO WAY TO RUN A RAILROAD

(after reading Annie Dillard)

Egoist, bloom, spreading your peacock plume.
Drench with your breath this thin and chill spring air.
Drunk on the liquor of earth, drug-drenched by sun,
sucking old snow, you open your petals like thighs,
exposing your tender pistil.
                              O soft explosion,
you invade my senses like sleep.
                              Your prodigal scarlet
is squandered on the fumbling bee, your bounty
could choke these acres with flowers, your roots could snarl
life from the loam with their infinite hairy extension.
Too much, too much.
                              Nature does nothing by halves—
for every egg a million willing spears
swarming the walls like bolsheviks, driven
by need, drowning all need in waste.
                              O God,
is this a sound economy? Is this
logical? Just? Has providence no sense

of careful planning? Fear of blind excess?
O drouth, O flood, O storm, O scorching sky!

So bombed by blooms blooms blooms,
                                    why then am I
so held in check, so cursed by body juices,
calculating, counting, regulating,
mounting my life
                    to ride with so tight a rein?
O bloom, most selfish when most generous,
most joined when most apart,
                                    why do I measure
my ebb and flow? Why close these valves? Why send
this hardhat down to engineer my heart?

Molecules Bumping

I left myself leaning on the fence, my boots in mud, considering the contrasting personalities of Pigena and Swinella and somehow being reminded of the leak in our truck's water system. At some unknown spot in all its windings there was an opening, probably no bigger than a pinhole, through which those clever molecules were finding a way out. No drip was visible, yet the level in the radiator kept going down. If the molecules weren't so clever, is there a chance they would not find the hole? No. Of course they're not clever at all, and there's no such chance. If they *were* clever, even a bit, perhaps they might overlook it, as intelligence leaves one open to deception. But their random action is a guarantee; if there's a hole anywhere, the molecules of water will squeeze out.

Ciardi's phrase "for a living" at the end of his line may mislead us. It is an analogy, comparing the life force to a person holding a job. But life doesn't have a job. Like molecules, life will simply do anything it can—randomly, without purpose. It will find any pinhole. No, we must put that more strongly. It's not that life will do *anything*. It will do *everything*. "Anything" implies some choice—as though the spider Ciardi mentioned, before weaving its deceptive blotch of web, thought, "I'll do even that, even make that disagreeable mess, if it will work, if it will lure a butterfly I can catch." The spider has no more thought of what will work than has the molecule, much less of whether his web is disagreeable or improper. The molecules that make up the cells of the protoplasm of the spider are as random as those of water in the truck's radiator. They do everything molecules can. They aren't even looking for holes. They don't want out. There is no goal, no intent, not even survival, though it's true that the life forms that develop patterns that permit or help in survival will, by definition, be those that perpetuate their strains. Swinella didn't back off from the trough so we would breed her and perpetuate her DNA, though that may have been one of the results of her backing off, and if her good manners are hereditary, her piglets may have had an advantage over piglets of less seemly sows.

As I sloshed back down the muddy trail to our cabin in the woods, a phrase came to me that seemed an illumination. It is not that life will do anything that will work, I thought. Rather, life will do everything possible—and will keep on doing whatever does not *not* work.

Much of the labor of biologists seem to be to explain the evolutionary, or survival, value of unlikely phenomena in the incredible array of nature's abundance. Maybe they are coming at it backward. The "explanation" of the beauty of the rose is not that it gives the plant some kind of edge in the struggle for survival. It's beautiful because its beauty does not *not* work. The bloom was a random product, but nothing weeded it out, so the flower kept on turning out more and more outrageous blooms.

There must be more to it than that, for these downward comparisons left me in a universe I don't recognize—one of utterly random matter and motion, all "Design" (see Frost's poem with that title) seeming to be mere afterthought, rationalization, projection, and comparison. Stare microscopically into the simplest cell, and that vision is denied. Certainly there is an ordering of the random, which we can perceive but not comprehend.

Okay, so I didn't figure out *every*thing. But I felt I had made enough progress to write the final poem in "Rumors of Change":

OUR RUMORS NOW ARE ENDED

I feed the pigs—Pigena with her stiff
ears and Swinella, floppy, coy, or calculating, standing back while her sister
nudges the bucket, spilling the slop on her head.
"Life will do anything for a living."—*J. Ciardi.*For her bad man-
    ners Pigena will go first
to slaughter. I ponder which is better
programmed to survive. They are so white
and fat.
        I watch the evening news. Their collars
are all too tight. The Mayor of Altoona
oinks treble with indignation after a Council
meeting. The girl who holds the microphone

doubles as Weatherlady. She has a twang
not all the speech courses at State College
could undo. Bold Bella nudged the bucket
once too often. The Shah is nudging the bucket.
They are all so barbered.
                          I hear few rumors now,
and change is loose in my pocket, random, or
like gradual frost line reaching down, two feet,
three, four, seeking our deep pipes. I have
grave doubts I ever spoke for any members.
I haul wood mornings, ashes evenings, teach
kids fix cars feed pigs play bridge watch news.
"A low dishonest decade."—*W. H. Auden.*
Full of our clever hopes and heady dreams,
so outraged were we by the Gulf of Tonkin,
we had no outrage left for Creep and Crook,
the blind machinery of power bull-
dozing indifferently. I feed the pigs.
I pay their taxes, ride their highways, eat
their bacon. My IBM Selectric sips
their blood. I share the Mayor's grief:
Surely we need a better County Jail.
Ten years have made me younger, candid, grey,
and brought my dizzy arias down to scale.

"Our actors melted into air, thin air."
—*W. Shakespeare.* Our revels ended, where
art thou now, Charlie Reich? Where is thy Greening?
Tim Leary (Peter Pan), where has thou flown?
And Eldridge Cleaver, with thy pants with cleavage,
dost thou hear God—and not thy people moan?
O Kesey, have thy Merry Pranksters nudged
the bucket once too often? Angela Davis,
now hast thou tenure, and so will not be budged?
Bob Dylan, art thou bloated now as Elvis?
Was it Reverend Jim thou once called Mr. Jones?
And Jud, sour Jonah who cried doom upon us,
hast thou left Nineveh to plow the stones?

Life will do anything that doesn't *not* work,
so beauty leaks like love, like water, through
the darkest soil or weighs the trees with ice.
We do what we must. We do a great deal more.

Excess of spirit, like our prodigal sperm,
sways in romance or madness, boils our dreams,
and swells the pupa till it bursts its seams
and wild imago crawling sticky out
stretches and airs its gaudy wanton wings
in the spring sun, so aimlessly to fly,
waver and bred in vanity, and die.
The throat that feeds is also the throat that sings.

This is the revolution, this slow turning,
this riding of the mountain round through winter,
these dormant seeds, this quiet compost burning,
this editing of copy for the printer,
this holding hands in silence round the table,
this tender loving that makes loving tough,
stretching our limits far as we are able,
knowing enough is enough—and never enough.

The poems in which we struggle to grasp and define our vision of what life is and how we fit into it with our curious minds should hold the mystery intact. They shouldn't explain—but carry us to the edge of more intelligent wonder. I hope your *élan vital* churns up such excitement for you as mine does for me—and better poems!

Chapter V:
LESSONS FROM THE BANDSAW

A poet who lived in a tipi at Downhill Farm for a couple of years was subject to spells of schizophrenia. Paul (as I will call him here) was a gentle and capable man, a close friend, but at times, without warning, a strange glaze would come over his eyes and he quite literally went insane. For example, he might attempt to stab himself, jump out of windows, hurl dishes or other objects at friends, or perhaps run naked through the snow.

But in his stable periods he was a good worker from whom I learned a great deal. He and I were the principal bandsawers for our communal industry making flowerpots out of oak logs. We both loved the work. Although it was very demanding, ever dangerous, and repetitive, we were attracted to it by the meditative state it induced. We had to concentrate so intensely that after a while we found that our minds were suspended. All sense of self was lost. It probably brought a strange glaze to both our eyes. I'll tell you more about bandsawing later.

But first I want to explore the allure of that trancelike state. Paul once told me that he experienced something similar when doing three other things: playing basketball (back when he was in high school), making love, and running mad. It was most delicious in his crazy periods—better than basketball, sex, or bandsawing. Once he came out of an insane episode, he hated what he had done and hated himself for having done it, but in the grip of one of those seizures he was in ecstasy (which literally means "driven out of one's senses"). Jangled as his behavior may have seemed, he was experiencing an inner peace which he found dangerously seductive.

But I'm surprised he didn't add writing poetry to the list of activities that induced this euphoria. Obviously, it is difficult or impossible to maintain such an intense level of concentration during the whole process of composition, but there are times when I'm writing that my mind drifts in a similar kind of trance, wholly in the grip of the poem. When I "come to" after an hour or a few hours, it feels like my spirit is returning to my body. I've been out of it for a while.

The Raw Encounter

Some time ago I was reminded of Paul and our discussion of bandsawing by a television interview with an attorney in Seattle who had scaled K-2, the second highest mountain in the world and one more perilous in some ways than Mount Everest. The interviewer was trying to understand what motivated the attorney to go back again and again to such difficult climbs. A tone of calm but keen engagement came into his voice as he described at length what he felt.

"The only sound is of your own breathing and the crampons on the ice, an experience so immediate you can't think of anything else," he said. It wasn't a thrill, exactly. It had nothing to do with delight or sensual satisfaction. He had to maintain absolute concentration on the goal in order to keep panic from rising. At the same time he felt utterly bonded to his companions on the climb. They worked together like organs of a single body. And when they reached the summit, they felt "elation—and emptiness, too." But the descent was the most dangerous part, for they tended to relax; they were emotionally if not physically wrung out, and it was hard to maintain the necessary concentration that had come almost intuitively on the ascent.

Well, writing poems is not so dangerous (or expensive!), I'm happy to say. But there are some risks and some comparable gratifications. For me the rewards are almost entirely in the writing process itself. Though I never regard a poem as really finished (Rainer Rilke said his were never finished, only "abandoned"), once it has reached a state fit to be published, I may be pleased with it, but I am like a climber on the descent: It's hard to remember the absorption in the experience and the escape from self that I felt while writing it. Imagine, if you can, the venture of getting this down:

PERHAPS AN OWL

"Did you hear that screaming in the night?" you ask
   me at breakfast. "It was probably an owl—
once, then again, again, not regular
   as an animal, not shrill, not quite a howl.

We were holding hands. I waited waited, thinking
you were hushed (it was so distant) waiting, too.
The dogs were still. Perhaps it was some cry
of mating, terror, pain, a screech to subdue
a quarry, I don't know. It wasn't human,
unless, of course, I thought, it was he alone.
(I remembered at dinner his eyes like dusty gems,
the scrape in his laugh. I thought I heard him moan.)
These warm March nights anything might be stirring
in the full moon, something on the prowl.
I should have turned on the light and read a book.
I'm sure it was nothing. Maybe it was an owl."

That time I slept, but I, too, have stared at the ceiling
or closed my eyes to witness bloody tableaux—
him stretched by his tipi fire, at last his knife
having found its way past ribs to sprout a rose.
Noises of birds and beasts still let one sleep.
On this dark and brambled mountain people are
what torment people—neighborly smiles by day;
by night mouse thoughts find bedded minds ajar.
People or fires—the fires that people cause—
these are the tongues that lick me to unrest.
Yes, better to read, to smoke, to have lights on:
If need be, meet the unknown fully dressed.
We lie so soft and naked in our darkness.
while madness stalks and in the doorway stands.
Better to sleep, but if you must lie waking,
I'm glad I was there, that we were holding hands.

The material of that poem is quite literal. What kicked it off in my head,
making me want to write a poem, was the casual way Marty, my mate,
dropped "we were holding hands" into her account of having heard
the noise. I liked the idea of her waking up in the middle of the night
and finding that we were holding hands. Thus, like many of my poems, it began with the last line.

Let me take you through what I remember of the process. The act of
holding hands itself, like Marty's mention of it, might be so casual that
it would pass by unnoticed. Therefore, I knew I wanted to slip it in casually first, then conclude with a repetition of the phrase in a rhyme
position to give it resonance, like a tonic chord. Okay, so that meant it
would be a rhymed poem, but the rhymes should be subdued. Since it

would be narrative, I wanted a fairly long, limber line—not too much *dah de dah*. I wanted flexibility, irregularity—poetry that felt like prose, with occasional simple, strong rhymes to set up that final one.

Notice that my thinking about a poem is likely to start with considerations of form. I have to know what sort of box I'm going to put the poem in before I can begin writing. In this case, having decided that much about the form, I could start at the beginning. I knew where I wanted to arrive and the poem's general pattern.

I wanted to follow the shape of the experience as accurately as I could. What do I mean by "the experience" here? The poem is not about Marty or about the sound in the night or about Paul. It's about what happened to *me* as I heard and reacted to what she said. The experience of the poem should take a reader through the stages of grasping what has happened, then feeling it and responding to it. First we hear Marty's voice recounting what *she* experienced. We follow her various efforts to explain the sound. In the midst of that account is buried the one tender little detail of our holding hands. The reader can deduce that the two people in conversation are mates. There is no indication that the speaker is a woman, or even that the couple consists of people of opposite sexes. That doesn't matter, though I will refer to the one whose speech occupies most of the first stanza as "the woman." The two people apparently sleep and eat together, and they seem to live in a wilderness setting. A third character, the shadowy figure of a crazed man, is introduced. He was present the evening before at dinner. Apparently he sleeps somewhere in the vicinity—perhaps in the woods?—if the woman speaking can imagine that he might have made the mysterious sound in the night.

The first stanza came out in four four-line groups, each of which might have been a stanza, but I preferred to run them together to give them the feel of a narrative paragraph. Notice that the language is entirely literal except for two touches of imagination in describing the man: "dusty gems" and "scrape in his laugh." Figurative language tends to heighten emotional response, so I used it sparingly. I wanted to keep the poem low-keyed at the beginning. The tone should be one of calm but tense reflection to characterize a person summoning reason and courage to face a threat.

The strategy of the poem is to let the mystery unfold and emotion grow gradually. I consider a poem like this as a little play. In this case there are three main characters, based, of course, on Marty, myself, and Paul. But I have to put the real people out of my mind and work with the fictitious characters in the drama: the couple and the madman. In additon there is a supporting cast of "people" who "torment people." The couple are especially worried about the madman, of course, but that concern is extended to a more general and pervasive fear. They feel isolated and vulnerable, "soft and naked," on the "dark and brambled mountain." Their security is being together and caring tenderly for one another, holding hands.

As I said, in order to work with the material of the poem I have to think of it as fiction—freeing myself from the actual experiences and actual people involved. If I were too concerned, for instance, about how Marty or Paul might react to what I was saying or whether I was representing them accurately, I wouldn't be able to build the structure the poem requires. This is a difficult separation for some poets to make, but I think it is essential. You have to take hunks of your life and use them just as a sculptor uses clay or a musician uses sound. True or not, the poem is fiction. Otherwise, you couldn't work on it, rearrange, enhance, or alter. Did Marty compare Paul's eyes to dusty gems? Of course not. The *poem* needed that language. That's why the act of writing resembles in some ways climbing a mountain. The poem, or mountain, begins to make demands, and the poet, or climber, must put ego and all personal feelings aside to respond to the immediate challenge.

The first stanza, almost entirely in the voice of the woman, provides a pattern for the man's response. Imagine a sixteen-line iambic pentameter box with no contents but two words, "holding hands," at the end. That's what I had to start with as I began work on the stanza. I knew also that the second line would rhyme with the fourth, and every other line thereafter would be a rhyme line. I didn't use quotation marks for the man's response because it doesn't matter whether he actually says these words aloud or merely thinks them. Quotation marks imply spoken words—a factor that can strain credibility. People don't talk in rhyme and meter, nor do they generally use vivid imagery. "Dusty gems" and "scrape" in the first stanza are risks because they make a reader aware that a real person wouldn't be talking this way. On the other hand, realistic, credible conversation can be terribly flat. Some readers might regard that first stanza as too prosaic, too realistic, to be interesting. A major challenge in the first stanza was to keep the language alive and yet convincing. Notice "again, again" and "waited waited." You can detect the trace of the poet's palette knife there. I set up the device of repetition, and then, when I used it again, I dropped the comma to increase tension and push the tone a little beyond flat narration. Similarly, compare "probably" at the beginning of the stanza with "maybe" at the end. I meant to dramatize the fact that as she talked, the woman became less certain of the harmless, natural explanation.

In the second stanza I hoped to heighten and generalize the tension. Now I wanted to stimulate the imagination of the reader by using somewhat richer language than the tone of the first stanza permitted. The reader should sense intimately the couple's dread as they lie there soft and naked. The man tells of the scenes of horror he has imagined, especially of what the crazed man might do to himself. I hoped the image "sprout a rose" for spurting blood would convey the ambiguity of the couple's feeling about the man—whom they both care about and fear—and also the ambiguity of the suicide's desires. Success would be ghastly, yet, in Hamlet's words, "a consummation devoutly to be wished."

But it isn't just that man who disturbs their sleep. Nor is it owls or animals. "By night mouse thoughts find bedded minds ajar" is a line so packed it's almost difficult to read. I considered combing it out, making it smoother and simpler, but I finally decided the poem needed that knot of congestion and the nightmare vision of mice creeping into minds as into open cupboards. The line stands out because in general the poem relies on relatively plain, straightforward language—and I hope it conveys a convincing tone of tenderness as we consider that couple, vulnerable and dreading, symbolic of many others who are probably lying equally vulnerable and fearful elsewhere. We never know when someone will run mad, stalk, and stand in the midnight doorway.

I hope this discussion has conveyed the kind of concentration on strategy to reach a specific goal that composition requires. Out of the morass of experience I selected something that seems significant—in this case a sense of dread heightened by that mysterious cry in the night and a compensating rush of tenderness for the frail security in a human relationship. Then I tried to design a dramatic structure that could evoke those emotions in a reader.

The job is to build that structure, to make it work, without being confused by either the details of the experience from which it was derived or the technical demands of the poem. A reader might never realize that my original motive was to write a love poem. I wanted to tell Marty how important her words about holding hands were to me. I wanted to set those words like a jewel in some enduring ring. Nor could a reader know that it was a time of great tension in our commune. Not only Paul but three other members were suffering severe and somewhat dangerous mental problems. Moreover, our mountain neighbors were none too friendly toward our hippie enclave in their midst. And we were, indeed, interlopers, green city folk trying to survive in a rugged and strange environment. Such factors inescapably resonate in the finished work, but they shouldn't be confused with the central structure. As your poem grows, it makes demands to which you must respond, and it has limits you must respect. Your life becomes so much clay, so much material to be reshaped. You hear only the sound of your breathing and the crampons on the ice.

The Goddess Necessity

At the beginning of this chapter I mentioned that both Paul and I were able to achieve a trance of total concentration while bandsawing. Our conversation about that—and about other activities that induce a similar state of complete focus, with utterly no sense of self-awareness—helped me understand better what was involved in the writing process. It especially taught me something about the balance required between passivity and control. I would like to explore with you the relationship between writing poetry and working on the bandsaw in some detail because I think it may help you see how various activities in your own life can give you insights into the creative process.

First you have to imagine the job itself. With a tractor-powered crosscut saw we made sections of log from four to seven inches long and four to about fifteen inches in diameter. Then we put each section on the bandsaw, cut in through the bark, made a circle, backed the blade out through the slit where it had entered, and removed the core. After that we nailed the rim of the hollowed log back together, top and bottom, sliced off a piece of the core for a base, nailed that in place, treated the pot with preservative, and sold it as a Hollow Log Planter. Hour after hour standing at the saw, we cut circles, circles (none quite a circle). Why were we so endlessly fascinated by the task?

To answer, I could rhapsodize on the transcendent pleasures of serving the goddess Necessity. Everything about that work seemed fierce with her presence. Yes, I could understand why the mountain climber scaled K-2. There is a powerful human yearning for situations in which no errors are possible, where everything counts, where need is sharp, clear, and implacable. Even for fun we seek out Necessity:

GULL AT PLAY

From the dune-crest I saw an idiot gull
bucking a squall on the fringe of a fretful sea,
awkward and suicidal, flapping for no good end,
fat, overcivilized, no windhover he,

but my heart stirred, for in my flapping jacket
I too had hurled myself for fun headlong
into a wind too big and had begun
to feel the cleansing chill. Who knows what fun

is any more? I remember pilgrims streaming
out of Boston to the sea, their autos heavy
with sacramental freight, their kleenex boxes,
innertubes and cameras, gazing, dreaming

of some salty absolution, bringing their young
to be blessed in the ceremony of the out-
of-doors. This Sunday morning sand-in-the-teeth
set has few libertines; they are devout,

wear hair shirts (blazing tropic blooms), submit
themselves, like pentitents to the salt and sun
not to the exquisite, artful agonies, but
to discomfort crude and pure. Since I am one

of such a holy breed, I can explain
somewhat what moves the gull and me. Suppose
in your pale condition, ignorant of the soil,
your hands no longer agents of your brain,

you woke on a desert island in a jock-strap.
With no tool but a pocket-knife, you devise
a gimcrack the city makes in plastic, sells
for a dime back home. Just think how you would clap

your rediscovered hands in celebration.
Similarly, if in the granite State of Maine
by the clear cold sea you wrest some campfire comfort
from driftwood, scrubby spruce and rocks, or rain

cutting around a stretch tarp does not quite
penetrate, or if, at Fundy, where
the headlands loom all shaggy in the fog,
the coffee perks, and in your duffle a pair

of dry socks waits your weakening, you know
my recluse ecstasies. Even the beach crowd
enjoys a form of flagellation, not
to feel the pain, but to feel after each blow

some measure of relief. Of course no pleasure
is more phony, more a sign of civilization
past the crest—when we feel pressed brutally
to sensitize our faculties, to treasure

our crude things, a rusty nail in a grimy hand.
But the need lies deep. Life lives a self-willed test,

or else that gull, fighting the wind out there
over the curling breakers, would welcome rest.

Even the games we play are self-willed tests, inventions to create artificial Necessity where it would not otherwise exist. But our work making flowerpots was no game. We bandsawed for survival. Each circle we cut was bounded not only by the necessity of supporting ourselves through some kind of industry, but by the momentary and detailed necessities of wood and machine, of co-workers and complex equipment, the physical needs of the workers, the aesthetic needs of the buyer.

Consider the machine: a hooded beast with yawning throat and some dozen inches of exposed teeth of the banded blade which spins on two giant wheels, each about a yard in diameter. As you push the wood into those teeth, you don't have a second or any fraction of a second to correct error. For error the punishment is instantaneous and irreversible as light. The sawyer must live in the presence of those teeth, not cringing, fearful, or uncertain, but with confidence and joy.

Writing a poem may seem less risky, but unless it contains an element of risk, the poem will be limp and flat on the page. The poet constantly has to reach into dark recesses of awareness, attempt new twists of technique, and reach beyond what can be easily grasped. Think of it as any other kind of work done on the brink. For example, a wise sailor never overcomes his fear—or his love—of the sea. The electrician may handle the deadly current with delight. The bullfighter is an artist who can dance only on the lip of death. Writing can seem like that, though few writers are gored except by critics.

The very danger sharpens one's awareness. One watches: the riding of the blade in its guide, its twist in difficult wood, its fierce sparks when pressed too hard against the guide, its instant chewing. One listens: to the hum of the motor, slowing with the strain, speeding when released, to the little whisper of the back of the blade when it has ridden out of the guide. One feels: sawdust welling up under until it jams and unsettles the pot, grain or chips under the log, unnatural heat of the bearings. One smells: the fragrance released from each new section of log (green chestnut oak) telling whether it is moist or dry, stringy or brittle, odor of the piling sawdust, the heated oil. Each signal tells something of the nature and mood of the beast and helps one anticipate its needs and capacities.

Moreover, just as within each idea or experience resides the essence of a poem, within each section of log resides the essence of a pot. What sort of pot it will be depends on the skill of the sawyer, of course, but, even more important, on the specific characteristics of the hunk of wood, its Necessity. The sawyer's job is to release the best pot he can from the available material. Novelists and sculptors have noticed the same phenomenon. Their best work occurs, not when they design, but when they perceive and respond to the design within their material. No matter how gnarled, slanted, oblate, or conical the section of log, within it is the best pot that log contains. The artist will release another pot, an approximation, near, nearing the best possible use of the hunk of wood. That is the fascination: the perpetual approach to the absolute. Similarly, each time you write a poem you will know that what finally comes out will never be quite the one you imagined you saw in the material. "Good? Maybe," you tell your friend. "But you should have seen the one that got away."

The Steady Hand

Though bandsawing seems to require surrender to all the circumscribing necessities, it actually requires consummate respect for and control of the tools and the task. Necessity can overwhelm you in an instant if you ever forget that. The work is hard for mind and body, requiring steady calculation, intuition, responsiveness, muscular force, and dexterous turning. It requires heightened awareness of all the demands and limits of the job from the shape and texture of the log to the degree of sharpness of the blade. All these conditions come to bear exactly at the juncture of teeth and wood, as the whole mystery of love focuses on flesh penetrating flesh.

And one of those conditions is that the lengthening line of the cut is steady and irreparable as time. What is cut cannot be uncut, and each minute variation, each falling away of a molecule of wood, limits the possibilities for the next. Though, of course, you can always blot out and revise when writing a poem, at each moment you are working there is a burning edge of your mind that alters your material irreversibly. Better moments may come, and better concentration. But each moment as it happens is unique, never to be repeated or recovered.

The key is respect, serenity, and joy. You need inner peace. If you hate yourself or your work, you will stumble on a means to destroy yourself. I made a hundred thousand pots, and the more I made, the less likely was I to get bored. The more I learned, the more I was aware of what I didn't know about the process. Much of the serenity has to do with minute arrangements: the way you lubricate the machine, stack logs to be worked, dispose of cores, stack the cut pots for nailing, clean out the sawdust. You want neatness, clarity, coherence, and satisfaction in the way you manage your work space.

And above all you need a happy relationship with Necessity—specifically, in this case, with the machine that ministers her will. You have to love its crankiness and peculiarities, its savage bite, its relentless, stupid intensity. I find it easy to be fond of that machine, which is older than I am—a massive, indestructible iron harp. Its bearings are bad; there's a wobble in the wheels; the blade doesn't track on center. You have to do all the thinking for the blade, sensitively and with concern and reverence for its blind power. Loving it is like making a pet of a rhinoceros.

You can't be jaunty, flamboyant, or flippant in your delight. You attain a high sweet seriousness of concentration and the steady, firm touch of a lover. Nor can you be a prima donna, demanding attention and solicitude, from either yourself or others. Your devotion is to the act of cutting, and self must be transparent as air. In your work, as in your products, you must achieve anonymity. Your serenity is the selfless delight of the surfer controlling his board so skillfully he seems to be controlling the irresistible Flow that is actually controlling him. He has learned to saddle and ride Necessity.

Romantic and Classic Pots

I've seen stacks of cut pots, like anthologies of bad poems, that spoke the torment, fear, panic, and impatience of inept workers—understandable but sad. The walls of such pots surge randomly to swollen thickness or skinny shaving. You can tell where the blade balked and nosed this way and that with a mind of its own. (Oh, beware that mindless mind of the blade!) It's not primarily a lack of skill these pots bespeak, but lack of serenity. Skill emerges from serenity, not serenity from skill.

But after they develop skill, some artists prefer to leave their individual stamp, like fingerprints, on their products. Look here, such an artist implies, there's no mistaking who did *that*. What he seeks is his personal immortality, some way to save that delicious sense of difference from others, that vibrant freshness of his youth. The effort is vain but spectacular. Such products stand as curios in museums like photographs in a family album. For me they are of more biographical and historical than aesthetic interest. In any case, that approach would never do for flowerpots.

At first I didn't understand that principle. When I was learning the versatility of the bandsaw I cut pots demonstrating great virtuosity and individuality. They had deliberate wiggly lines and shapes of hearts; innovation strained against the cage of intractable material. I think one inevitably outgrows such mannerism, not so much because it's bad art (though I think it is), but because the pursuit of Essence is so much more alluring, demanding, frustrating, and so much more endlessly satisfying. Pursuit of the Essence, of the best pot than can possibly be made from any given hunk of log, doesn't imply conformity—which means doing things the way others do them. One conforms only to Necessity, as sensitively as possible; the individual that emerges is that of the product, not of the artist. Anyone who sticks with art long enough becomes a Classicist.

One must develop what I call the Attitude, in the disciplined meditation before and during and after, in the readiness of spirit to submit, in flotation in the Flow. There are many tricks—for rescuing a pot from slight errors, controlling an unruly blade, or compensating for other problems that may develop. But ultimately, there are no tricks. You can't long outtrick Necessity. The trick is achieving the Attitude, and for that you have to renounce trickery.

The Attitude requires awe of the process. It is glad absorption in endless and futile striving for the ideal. You learn to respect things for being as they ought to be: blade always in its guide, held there by steady pressure, its path even and straight though constantly turning. And, as one eases the tiller in choppy seas and varying winds to hold a course that's never straight but approaches straightness, one learns to bear down firmly on the absolute, yet never to cross it. And finally, by becoming a complete slave to Necessity, by anticipating her least demands, one achieves freedom.

I remember once when I surged with self-confidence on making this discovery. Thinking I had found freedom within Necessity, I was singing at my work, twice in a minute swinging up a new section of log, studying it briefly, marking it with chalk, ripping in and around, shaking out the core, chewing across the core to cut a bottom . . .

TWANG! With a bone-chilling rip the blade broke and chattered noisily in the heavy, spinning wheels, sending me reeling (safe, though) back from the table, my heart pounding. It was as though a bolt from the deity had stricken my arrogance. "You think you understand, now, do you, Buster?" the slowing wheels rasped at me. "You still have much to learn. Neither mind nor muscle will ever really pacify me." I cowered like Job rebuked.

My particular error that time was simple enough. I hadn't steadied the core sufficiently as I moved its round side into the biting blade for a crosscut, so it spun the core round in my hands and whipped it like a twenty-pound boulder, snapping the blade. I knew better, but I wasn't paying attention. The books say you should never move any piece that doesn't have a flat base into the blade, but we take risks. I have used the bandsaw to make figurines, work that required holding the wood in at all kinds of angles prohibited by the books. I knew I could do it; I had done it a hundred thousand times. But now Necessity demanded I learn how better to maintain my concentration.

That was a lesson regarding Attitude. Again I was reminded to humble myself. I was never to think I was fully in command. To live with art is to live with reverence, yet with moments of muscle to meet an array of demands. Necessity forbids mere self-indulgence. The mature artist develops away from the tantrums children throw when things don't go their way. To love Necessity is to develop a kind of sensual passion for the grit and slap of her skin, her exudations and ravenous demands, her coquetry, her treachery.

Only the trivial or immature artist complains about conditions—wanting a different audience, different materials from those available, new equipment, or admiring attendance to his needs.

Releasing Ariel from the Oak

The art of poetry takes account of everything from mood to paper quality, from the demands of a bladder to news of the world. There are, actually, few conditions one can change. One has to learn to love the conditions. You'll never cure your ignorance, so carry on with what you know. Of course, you need six more dictionaries, but now, at the moment of engagement, the blade eating into the turning idea, use the paperback one on the desk. Your typewriter or word processor breaks, so you chew ahead with blunt pencil and tablet. You should have arranged everything meticulously, but you didn't, and now is when the great hooded beast is biting into the wood. You have dealt with the same idea in a thousand poems already, and you haven't yet got it right, yet you return loyally as to a mate with renewed ardor and infinite patience, snatching the moment of fusion from interruptions and obligations and personal tensions, finding joy in the spaces left by the necessities of boredom, exasperation, fear of, even disgust with, the material at hand.

And the blade cuts, bearing the weight and tension and buffeting of these forces, finding the true and best line to release the possible poem. It's in there—in any hunk of thought or experience. You have to learn how to respond, to let it happen, to exercise the sometimes almost violent force that delivers the latent ideal to the world in an imperfect image. Forget yourself. In Shakespeare's *The Tempest*, the magic spirit Ariel was trapped in an oak by the spell of a witch until the magician Prospero released him. Just so must you release the invisible, sacred, mysterious poem buried in the material of your life.

And, of course, the perfect poem will never emerge. You go back to it again and again, hypnotized by the possibility, sensing how close you sometimes come to perfection and yet knowing the tiny edge of failure that always draws you on to try again. Maybe it's a new poem you are working on (each draft is a new poem), or you're trying a new approach to the old subject or the old approach to a new subject. Each occasion provides a new intimation of possible perfection, a promise of inevitable failure. You strain for the constant goal without even wanting to reach it. It's like magnetic north, a perpetual, silent, invisible attraction, a yearning that sparks life itself. It's not something to reach, but to steer by, to be drawn by, to hold eternally present in the sensibility. It is love, which inevitably envisions the ideal and joyfully embraces the real:

THE ALCHEMIST

Your touch would Midas Midas. A daffodil
instantaneously in your palm is golder
trumpeting than bloom has been, or will.

Your fingers release perfection. Older
are antiques handled thus, newer new shoots,
shier the shy at your touch, and the bold bolder.

Higher the tree struts, curling its roots
like toes and digging. You, the cause,
leaning and loving there, stir attributes

of bark that stiffens stiffer, quicker draws
sappier sap up from the soul of soil.
The me of me wakes up and gladly gnaws

when I am brushed by but your eyes. I coil,
grow serpentine, when just your fingertips
trace the cheek of my cheek. My petals toil

to be touched. Change me, o palm that casually slips
into my handy hand. Oh gold and shrill
be the trumpeting of silence. Touch my lips.

PART II:
THE POEM AND THE READER

We have explored some of the sources of poems within the poet, and now we will look at the effects poems are likely to have on others. Whether they realize it or not, people wonder, as they begin reading anything, including poems, *Who's saying what to whom, and why?* They may also wonder *When?* and *Where?* These are natural questions, but poets often fail to ask them about their own work. As you will see, the answers make a lot of difference. A skillful poet knows how to communciate a personality through the voice of the poem and to hold the interest of a reader or audience. A poor one allows the words to drift untethered by either a strong sense of self or strong sense of purpose.

Let's start with what poems tell us about the "speaker." I will use that term to denote the voice of the poem, which may or may not be the actual poet. Some poems, for instance dramatic monologues, deliberately create a fictitious speaker, and it is important that the reader recognize that the poet is a completely separate identity. At other times no specific character is intended, but, as readers, we sense that it's not safe to assume that the words represent the actual feelings and thoughts of the poet. Most commonly, however, if a poem is in the first person, the reader will assume it *is* intended to represent the poet speaking in his or her own voice.

But aside from the specific strategy of the poem, there is a sense in which all good poetry inescapably communicates something about the personality of the person who wrote it. I have mentioned (in Chapter II) how Shakespeare the man seems to emerge irrepressibly from the tapestry of fictional characters in his plays. When you read the dramatic monologues of Robert Browning, you are bound to form some interpretation of Browning the man, though the words are attributed to a medieval duke or Renaissance friar. Walt Whitman wrote, in *Leaves of Grass*, "Camerado, this is no book. / Who touches this touches a man." It may be that the speaker of his poems is a kind of fiction, quite different from the actual Walt who lived and breathed, but the illusion is so convincing that the difference hardly matters; the poems convey an intimate sense of contact with a real person.

Don't you feel you can reach out and touch Myrtle Whimple, though her number is unlisted?

CHAPTER VI:
AN INTERVIEW WITH MYRTLE WHIMPLE

Who, you may ask, is Myrtle Whimple? Since she so often illuminates a view of poetry in healthy contrast to my own, I think I'd better introduce you to her now. Having seen her on talk shows after her splash into public attention in 1974, I knew I couldn't rest until I'd had an opportunity to interview her in person and share with readers something of the personality and opinions of the woman many regard as representing the new wave in American poetry. Actually, as she would be the first to say, she is not a new wave nor, she would protest, an especially old one.

"I'm kind of middle wave," she told me. "Kinda like, y'know, the mainstream." She thinks it is "high time your garden-variety poet got recognized."

Knowing her poetry, you would recognize her anywhere—or I might say everywhere. Success hasn't spoiled Mrs. Whimple. She greeted me on the front porch of her Guthrie, Oklahoma, home after wiping suds off her hands onto her apron. "Land sakes, no," she said, laughing, when I asked her whether fame had made any difference in her life. "I considered getting new drapes for the parlor," she said wistfully, "but no one uses that room anyhow, so what's the use?"

We sat in the kitchen, where she does all her entertaining. The cord to my tape recorder trailed across the floor to a double socket near the toaster. "It was different when the kids was home," she was telling me, "them and their friends all over the furniture, new slipcovers every other year. But now I try to keep it nice in there," she said, cocking her head toward the dark room at the front of the house, "and there just ain't the wear and tear."

I asked her what she thought of the remarks critics had made that she was the Grandma Moses of American poetry.

"I don't think it's proper to call anyone a grandma, even though I am one." She sniffed. "And I assure you I'm not of the tribe of Moses."

She did what she could, she insisted, to keep appearances up, getting to the beauty shop once a month and shopping in the department stores in Tulsa. "I don't like them implying I'm a dowdy."

I said I didn't think they meant that; Grandma Moses was a highly respected painter. "Well, I don't paint," said Myrtle (as she suggested I call her), "lest you count those saucers I do for folks at Christmas." She showed me one, then showed me the framed color photographs of her two married daughters, their husbands and children, her son in college, and her middle boy, obviously her favorite, in his "kaydet uniform." I couldn't tell what he was a cadet of. He looked mean. She apologized for not having one of her husband, who had died two years before. "He never would let his picture get took." I have a great deal of information on tape, which some future biographer may wish to transcribe, about how the various members of her family have been employed, how they did in school, and their chronic ailments.

I changed cassettes. "Let's talk about poetry," I suggested as the new one began to roll. Her response filled the tape, but I'll condense what she said.

"Well, I just write for myself, always have, since I was a little girl. It just comes over me, whatever I think I just got to put a rhyme to it, you know, like, 'Each year the spring brings its new crocus, / Though the winter nearly broke us.' Other people see the same thing, they just don't write it down. Mother said I was gifted and maybe so, but I think it was because I was sickly and plain and just didn't get out with the other kids and read too much: ever day I memorized the Edgar Guest poem in the paper and recited it at dinner. That made my daddy so happy. He drank a lot. He was a churchgoing man, but he worked so hard in the oil fields, he just had to relax a little before coming home, and he'd sit there relaxed, holding his fork and knife pointing straight up, before he ever touched his pork chop, listening to me recite, and he'd smile and say, 'You keep that up, Myrtle, and you'll be a schoolteacher one day.' Except for that, he hardly ever said boo to me. I think a person needs encouragement, no matter how different she is. Love and encouragement.

"Well, I never was no schoolteacher. I met Bert when I was sixteen and he just wouldn't stop till we got married and then you know how it is, kids, kids, kids. And Bert didn't encourage me in my poetry. I mean, he'd listen, but you could tell he wasn't interested. 'That's real fine, Myrtle,' he'd say, but you could tell. So it was mostly just a private thing I'd do at nights or even in the middle of the day when he was at work, just notebook after notebook of verses, verses, verses hardly anyone has seen, but maybe they'll bring them all out now. They can publish what they want, I don't care. I don't read 'em over myself, I can't tell the good from the bad. They're just what I felt at the time, you know. A lot of 'em are about God, how He helped me and showed me things when I was down, and I suppose they'll want to publish all those: Everyone's interested in God. But the ones they ask me to recite on TV are just about ordinary things and people no one knows. I don't know why they'd want to publish those unless they just like rhyming,

> Aunt Martha couldn't stand the way
>   Men wore their hair all oily
> And for each piece of furniture
>   Crocheted a little doily.

"Stuff like that. I mean it's common. But that's what people like when you're saying a poem on TV."

"How," I asked her, "did your poetry first come to public attention?"

"Well, there was a little insurance money when Bert died, and I thought what better use, in spite of the way he always felt about my poetry, than to get Display Press to bring out a little volume, including the memorial I wrote for Bert, you know, the one that starts:

> Another man has learned your route
>   And carries, now, the mail
> Since you at last checked in your pouch
>   And went beyond the pale.
>
> And yet all up and down the street
>   Our neighbors look for you,
> Though now you stand at Heaven's Gate,
>   Overweight, and postage due.

"Display done the memoirs of old Louella Arbuckle over in Henrietta about the early days of that town, and they did such a pretty job of it, photographs and all, and I heard she was right satisfied. Well, Display

said I had authentic talent and they'd be honored and delighted to
have such an original poet on their list, and it cost under three thousand dollars, even with my picture on the back flap, but, then, you
know, poetry don't take up the whole page, not like prose, so I reckon
that's why it was so cheap."

"And the book brought you to public attention?"

"Well, Display Press sent it to all the newspapers and critics and it
was reviewed very favorably in the *Guthrie Courier*, which said it was
the most important artistic event in our town since Silas Millicut painted the mural of a hog farm all around the dome of the courthouse, but,
as they pointed out, the sales was disappointing, and I had a chance to
buy up the extra copies. Land, I never *seen* so many books. I give 'em to
everyone I knew and then some. I thought libraries ought to have copies so I sent 'em out as far as Idabel. Then I had copies left over so I sent
'em to the TV programs I like. I sent one to *The Waltons:* I knew they'd
like it. And *The Price Is Right:* They could give it away, I didn't care. I
sent one to Walter Cronkite, though I don't always agree with him, and
Today, and *Tonight,* and *Sonny and Cher,* and Lawrence Welk, and *I
Dream of Jeannie,* but that came back since those are all reruns."

"Did you get any response?"

"Well, no, but I didn't expect any. Ever time I put in a personal letter
saying you don't know me but I always enjoyed your show or whatever and thought I'd like to share this book and you can just give it away
to a friend after you read it, you know, like that. I wasn't looking for no
attention or anything. You write poetry for the satisfaction it brings
you, not to get rich and famous, like I said in this poem:

ITS OWN REWARD

When I started writing poems
　It was just a thing to do,
　　Like embroidery
　　　Or a game of solitaire,
Then it got to be a habit,
　And I wrote 'em right on cue
　　In the kitchen, laundromat,
　　　Or anywhere,
Just to keep my fingers busy
　And to keep from being bored,
　　Since poetry's its own reward.

Then my folks all started seeing them
　And asking me for more,

And each read them
With a chuckle or a tear,
Then they said I ought to publish
And sell them in a store,
So each verse could be
A treasured souvenir.
Now you know I was delighted
To have struck a heartfelt chord,
Since poetry's its own reward.

I paid to have a book of poems
Bound up and stamped in gold,
And they sold
Like overcoats in the Sudan.
When the piles down at the bookstore
Began to flake and mold,
I paid to have them hauled
Home in a van.
Well, poetry is something
That it doesn't hurt to hoard,
Since, after all, it *is* its own reward.

Now a wave of generosity
Came welling through my soul.
I thought, "*Hang* the cost!
I'll *give* those books away!"
So I listed all my relatives
Of friends I made a poll.
I passed them out
At Joe's All-Nite Cafe.
I knew folks would appreciate
What they could not afford,
Since poetry *is* its own reward.

I mailed them to celebrities
And editors and such,
Gave them to bums
(I am so democratic),
And yet, for all my giving,
It still seemed I couldn't touch
The weight that strained
The rafters in my attic.
Sometimes I may have failed

To render thanks unto the Lord
  That poetry's its own reward.

And finally the truth dawned
  I'd been missing all along:
    My poems are much too good
      For all but me!
And if I write another,
  I'll protect it from the throng.
    I'll bottle it,
      And throw it in the sea!
Then maybe some poor castaway
  Stuck in an ice-bound fjord
    Will learn thereby it is its own reward.

"But what brought you to public notice?"

"Well, somehow this man on an interview show in Chicago got hold of a copy. I suspect my cousin Richard Bellknap sent him his: He never was very sentimental about keeping things. And they asked me up, to be on between one and two in the morning. Can you imagine people staying up to hear poetry at that hour? I, of course, never heard of that show, not staying up so late, and not getting Chicago anyway, but they sent me an airplane ticket and I went, and stayed over with Aunt Susie Bellknap in Evanston who I hadn't seen in a coon's age. She even stayed up and watched me and said I looked real good in color, only a little thick in the face."

"You must have made a big hit with the audience."

"They said I was real popular. They wanted me back the next night, but I hadn't left out enough cat food except for only two days, and you can't depend on the neighbors anymore, not like you usta could. People are so into their own ways."

"But, I gather, word got around."

"Land sakes, yes. I was no sooner home than they was calling me from New York. I said I didn't see why they made such a fuss, I was just your average poet, but they said that was the point. They said we hadn't had a really *average* poet in this country since Edgar Guest died. Can you beat that? Now I call that full circle."

Today, of course, the name of Myrtle Whimple is a household word. In millions of American homes there is one or more of her poems tucked away in a bureau drawer. Many tough men carry one in their wallets, and when their hearts are touched, among intimate friends, during commercials or half-time ceremonies at their local bars, they often pull out their tattered copies and stain them with fresh tears.

Fair Warning! As Anthony said to the Romans, if you have tears, prepare to shed them now. I have yet to see anyone get through one of her poems and retain his composure. As a poet you should be especially interested in this one which, Myrtle explained "I wrote for my granddaughter Patti Lorelei. She had an assignment to write a poem for her fifth grade English class and she said she couldn't think of one."

A RHYME IN TIME

If you've got to write a poem,
  And you haven't got a thought,
And your tummy's got the jitters,
  And your tongue in throat is caught,
And your brow is sort of sweaty,
  And your hand can't make a start,
There is just one place to find a pome:
      Child, look into your heart.

Sometimes a piece of paper can
  Seem blank and hard as stone,
And the pencil you pick up to use
  Seems blunt as any bone,
And the words that came so easy when
  You was talkin' on the phone
All scattered like the blackbirds that
  Left the king alone,
And you're sittin' there all bound and gagged,
  Your senses blown apart.
There's only one thing left to do:
  Child, look into your heart.

I know you are too big to cry
  And much too nice to curse:
Just listen to your quiet heart
  A-pumpin' out a verse.
No need to bite your pencil or
  To pout and make a frown.
Inside you is a ticker that
  Will never let you down,
That will straighten out your tangles,
  Put your horse before its cart,
And flood your emptiness with song:
  Child, look into your heart.

The Burden of Fame

The interview with Myrtle Whimple brought me no surprises. The personality of the woman is indistinguishable from the one that emerges from her work. In her case, more than any other I know, it is fair to say that Myrtle Whimple *is* her poetry. Of course, that was more likely to be true when she was writing only for herself. In the succeeding years of public exposure she has had to deal with the expectations of her audience, and she sometimes fears that may limit the full range of her expression.

"I don't wanna be typecast," she said when I met her again, ten years after our first encounter. She feared her fans might stereotype her in some limiting way. *People* magazine has called her "inspirational," but, she said, "I don't want to be known just as a religious poet, being compared with Dante and Donne and Esther Thelma Randolph," though she had to admit that her devotional poetry had done a great deal to bring religion up to date:

THERE'S ALWAYS GOD

In the depths of my depression,
  Which my pills won't touch,
    Feeling lonely and rejected and abused—
For instance, by the plumber,
  Who charges far too much,
    And I'll never buy another car used—
When my hair is grey and thinning,
  And it won't hold a wave,
    And my children haven't written since November,
Then I think about the government
  And nearly want to rave,
    But just in time I remember
That when everything is hopeless,
  Or at least extremely odd,
    There's always God:

Someone to comfort me and listen,
  And not tell me *His* troubles,
    Who feels about taxes like I do,
Who tells me not to worry,
  That a watched pot never bubbles,
    So I shouldn't work myself into a stew.
We dawdle over coffee,

And watch *The Eternal Light*.
  Down supermarket aisles I have a guide.
And when the drapes are drawn,
  And we settle for the night,
    I know that He will stay on His own side.
For when I need a Shepherd
  Who knows where to keep His rod,
    There's always God.

So if life's to you a mystery,
  An endless masquerade,
    And you have to play a part in this who-done-it.
If church is just a Bingo game
  Eternally played,
    And you always bought a card and never won it.
      If mankind just distresses you
  With wars and treachery
    And yet it seems to you you have no choice,
If you have put your two bits in
  On pollution and lechery
    Until it seems that you have lost your voice,
If yet you yearn to tread new waters,
  Waters never trod—
    There's always God.

"Pollution and lechery!" I remarked. "Myrtle, I think your vocabulary is changing. Are you *sure* fame hasn't gone to your head?"

"I asseverate that nothing whatsoever has gone to my head," she said. "But a girl has to improve herself. Isn't that why *Reader's Digest* teaches us how to enrich our word power? I study all the time. Poets have their responsibilities, though underneath it all we're still human. 'Hath not a poet hands?' Shakespeare said that. That's not all he said, but I don't remember the rest. I tell you, since I got all these personal appearances to keep up, I read, read, read. We poets have to be intellectuals, you know, and if you don't think that takes practice, you got another think coming. And we get weary, just like anybody. We can't always keep our mind on the poetry business."

"Well, Myrtle, how would you most like to be remembered?"

"As a *family* poet. I stand for the values of hearth and home. Like in this poem:

MOTHER'S LOVE

Now I have watched my children grow up and turn away
And oftentimes neglect me and hear not . . .

She stopped reading to comment, "I coulda said 'not hear,' but don't you think 'hear not' is more poetic?" I nodded as she resumed:

And oftentimes neglect me and hear not what I say,
But pout and sass and roll their eyes to God above,
And know it may take years before they value Mother's love.
But inwardly I smile and wait. In time they'll see
How right I was, how much they learned at Mother's knee.

First word I learned was *Nasty*, for my Mother taught
Us kids what not to put our fingers in. We fought
And disobeyed and thought our Mother was just mean,
But when we go to Heaven, God knows that we'll be *clean*.
We learned our manners, kept our bodies out of sight
For folks forgive most anything when people are polite.

But most of all a growing girl goes through a change
When womanhood descends, and her body gets all strange.
She needs her Mother—though advice is hard to take,
For then she's thinking time has come to make a break.
You bet I learned, although I chafed against the halter.
By sixteen I knew how to get Bert to the altar.

Oh Mother, I remember you caught me squeezing pimples
And slapped my fanny, smiled, winked and pinched my dim-
    ples.
I know you read my diary and found Sen-Sen in my purse.
And whatever I might tell, you thought the truth was worse;
But though you always seemed to me so harsh and cold,
I know you loved me, Mother, now that I am old.

"I guess I was just lucky"—she sighed—"being brought up right and all. I mean, you learn of love from those who love you. Like my daddy. Remember I told you how he listened and grinned when I read him poems? Well, he wasn't a man for many words when he was around women and children, but still he taught me things about love I never would have guessed:

A DADDY'S LOVE

How does a little girl learn to love?
  From her daddy, still and strong.
On Sundays he goes fishing,
  And he lets her tag along.

  "Why are you digging, Daddy?"

He never says a thing,
But scoops the worms into the can—
His way of answering.

"Don't stay out late," calls Mommy.
He lights up his cigar.
"Remember that child's bedtime!"
He simply starts the car.

He lets her watch him thread the worm
Wiggling on the hook
And cast the weighted, baited line
Into the dark brown brook.

And when the cork is floating free,
And all is under control,
He takes his bottle from his pocket
And lets her hold the pole.

But when the cork goes under hard,
He grabs the pole again,
Jerks, cusses at the naked hook—
For that is work for men.

Then when she has to wee wee he
Directs her to the bushes,
And when she tries to talk to him,
Finger to lips, he shushes.

All afternoon in silence they
Sit and don't scare the fish,
And though they don't catch any, it's
All that a girl could wish

To sit beside her daddy and
To help him home at night
And drift away to dreamland
Hearing her parents fight.

Learning that hugs and kisses are
Just not her daddy's way.
And you can be sure he loves you most
When he has least to say.

"I guess you can sorta tell that when I say *she* in that poem I really mean *me*. But times were different then, and I think people need to be reminded now of the glue that made families stick together. See, I grew up before the war. No, I don't mean Vietnam or Korea. I'm talking about the *real* war. The one when Keats said, 'Things fall apart.' "

"That was Yeats."

"One of them." A tear had welled into her left eye. "I ask you," she said, "what has gone wrong with the world? What ever happened to love and respect for Mommy and Daddy and old people? I know they call me old-fashioned, but I don't think these things should be a matter of fashion. Can you believe that when I read "The Funeral in the Rain" at the Tulsa Garden Club, one of those young wives, the kind that wear slacks out in public, actually said it was 'sentimental'?"

"I don't remember that poem," I said. "Could you read it for me?"

"I thought you'd never ask."

THE FUNERAL IN THE RAIN

All is forgiven Hilda Jean,
  As we lower you into sod—
The preacher and I in falling rain,
  Send you to God.

But I can see your spirit rise
  Above to greener pastures
And smile as I remember your
  Puppyhood disasters.

Born anew, will you again
  Chew on heavenly shoes?
And on those sainted carpets leave
  Your inimitable pooh-poohs?

How'd you like that 'inimitable'?" she asked.
  "Virtuositic," I assured her.
She nodded. "*Reader's Digest*," she explained.

Methinks I see the blazing light
  Around the golden throne
And hear from under it the crunch
  As you gnaw on a bone.

Perhaps Our Father takes you up
  To give you a manna-scrap.
Oh, Hilda Jean, I hope you won't
  Piddle in his lap!

I know the Lord has sympathy,
  Gives no unkind rebuke,
But even I sometimes got cross
  To find another puke.

But what a watchdog you will make,
  Relentless in your labors,
Wearing a path along the fence
  Yapping at Hellish neighbors!

The angels will watch over you
  When love begins to bloom
And, as your careful Mumsy did,
  Drive males off with a broom.

When you grew old and sick and whined
  And seemed to get no better
I put castor oil in your Friskies and
  Knitted you a sweater

To no avail: The hand of Time
  Throttled you in your sleep.
The silence now when friends arrive
  Almost makes me weep.

But in those blessed realms above
  You'll join the angels' choir
And howl throughout eternity
  Where terriers never tire!

"Well, Myrtle," I said, "people who didn't know Hilda Jean might not understand."

"Oh, that snip under*stood,* all right. She was just the kind to scoff at real deep feeling. That's why I think I have a mission, to bring all the good old values back into poetry. I want to remind them of the adventure in everyday life. I want to put poetry right smack dab in the middle of the living room like it was in the days of Beowulf and all them."

And so she has.

CHAPTER VII:
MELODIES
UNHEARD

When we write poems, we set out on a strange endeavor. A poem is a work of art made out of words. Words are primarily signals that communicate meaning to others, and though the words in a poem usually (not always) communicate meaning, they do so by drawing on qualities of language that apparently have little to do with denotation. Dozens of other characteristics of the words—from their etymology, symbolic value, connotations, sounds, and rhythms to their physical placement on the page—are involved in shaping a work of art.

For comparison, imagine carving a bust of Thomas Jefferson out of a baked Virginia ham. You would be using the meat for something other than food—and many people would not understand or appreciate that, or they might admire your ingenuity but consider the whole enterprise rather silly. That's just not the sort of thing one does with Virginia ham. Some people respond that way when we use words to make art.

You might explain that a poem, unlike a statue made of meat, can be consumed—again and again—and still be there to consume again, or that the artistic shaping of the poem is more profoundly related to meaning than sculpting is to food, or that words never rot, and the poems, unlike carved hams, often become more and more valuable over the centuries, that they can be endlessly reproduced and passed on to others . . . and so on. But all these justifications may fall on deaf ears. Making art out of words may still seem frivolous or even perverse to some people. They can understand using words to tell stories or make fictional dramas. But poetry demands a different kind of attention. Each word is set in the poem like a jewel, with judgments about its size, color, shape, and relation to other words. Many will always simply believe that that's not what words are for.

Thus there are two problems to deal with. We have to be able to respond to the aesthetic qualities of words in our own writing in order to make them into poems, and we have to understand and accept the likelihood that after we have so carefully shaped what we hope will be an imperishable work of art, others may simply read or hear the poem as they ordinarily respond to words, simply as signals of denotation.

Imperfect Pitch

If you expect others to hear your poetry, you first have to hear it yourself, which means you have to have what is called an "ear" for poetry. This isn't a talent test. If you don't have such an ear, you can develop one. And you may be able to write publishable poetry without developing an ability to hear it. Many do. But in my judgment they are missing the primary satisfactions of reading and writing poetry, and I think that it is only a cultural quirk that so much broken prose (I call it "proetry") is published as poetry these days. Poetry that endures is poetry that sings.

When I say you can develop an ear, I am reminded of a passage from John Holt's *Never Too Late* in which he discusses the director of his high school glee club:

> Someone had mentioned tone-deafness, and Mr. Landers interrupted to say that no such thing existed. We were astonished, having heard a lot about "monotones" and those who were unable to carry a tune. He went on to say that about one out of perhaps a hundred thousand or more persons had no pitch discrimination whatever, quite literally could not tell high notes from low notes, . . . [but most] who could not sing in tune could hear tunes as well as anyone else; they simply had not learned to coordinate voice with ear.

He explained how a person could eventually learn by trial and error to sing the notes a teacher was striking on a piano. After each note the teacher tells the student "higher" or "lower" until he hits it and finds out what it feels like to sing in tune. That process is similar to biofeedback, in which electronic instruments are used to help people learn to correct or control involuntary responses, such as the production or alpha waves by the brain or even blood pressure and body temperature. I wish I knew how to rig up a biofeedback device to teach people how to make their poetry sing.

We often forget that poetry is essentially an oral art. Because we usually encounter it in print, we need to be reminded that the written poem is rather like a musical score, or at least a dramatic script. Some musicians can "read" a score, in the sense that they can imagine the full richness of sound as they scan the printed notes. But for most of us a musical score conveys no more sense of that experience than blue-prints could tell us about the feeling and beauty of the Taj Mahal.

And when many people read a poem silently, they completely miss what I call (in *The Poet and the Poem*) the "isness of the art," its harmonies, rhythms, texture, and subtlety, its flesh and blood. They can't tell whether or not it sings, which is to say they can't tell whether it is a poem or merely a gray swatch of words in broken lines.

"Sings" is, of course, an inexact word for this essential characteristic of good poetry, but no more exact term exists. Saying a poem sings is something like saying that a dramatic script "reads well." That's a different judgment from determining whether the language is realistic or otherwise stylistically appropriate, whether the speeches are "in character" or suitably "dramatic." There are some cadences, sound combinations, and sentence structures that a good director recognizes as poor material for the stage, though they may be perfectly adequate or even effective in silent reading.

There are no rules to guide you in this area. It requires a seat-of-the-pants intuition which you have to develop by tuning in to aspects of language you are likely to ignore in ordinary reading. It is similar to the process Holt described of developing an ear for music by tuning in to how one's voice relates to piano notes. And it requires breaking the habits you use when you read primarily for meaning. Because we are all flooded in print, most of us learn to scan rapidly, looking for what we need, searching out the gist. But that's no way to read poetry.

I happen to be a relatively slow reader, which is a great disadvantage when I need to cover prose rapidly. But that disability helps me read poems. Most people have a hard time slowing their reading down. My brother, a fast reader, once told me that for him reading poems was like trying to hold quicksilver in his hand. He starts a poem, and *zip*, he's through. Knowing he didn't "get" it, he reads agin, but *zip*, there it goes again. "The damned thing just won't hold still," he said. He was talking about grasping the poem's meaning, and, true, you often have to slow down in order to understand. But he was also missing the "isness" of the poem, the elements of sound that make a poem art, not mere communication.

Good poetry or dramatic speech involves uncannily apt coordination of sound and sense. And the more closely these are coordinated, the harder it is to separate them in our minds. As a reader, you have no great need to separate them. You can let the words have the coherent intellectual and emotional effect on you that the poet intended. But as a poet you have to distinguish between these functions of words and be able to manage them separately.

John Holt's glee club—a group of adolescent boys—encountered the problem in a song that required them to sing, "Fa, la, lanky down dilly." The words embarrassed them because they seemed silly, but that chorus provided a good exercise in enunciating consonants sharply and clearly. It's tricky, but it does "sing well." But by concentrating on the music, the glee club was finally able to overcome discomfort with nonsense to work on the music. In separating sound and sense you may have the opposite problem—letting meaning (rather than nonsense) distract you from sound—but you have to overcome it just as those boys did.

As you concentrate on sound, you shouldn't associate the musicality of poetry with regularity, euphony, or sonority. Some poets—notably Algernon Swinburne and Sidney Lanier—wrote so musically that if they had anything to say, it got drowned in the lushness of their music. Swinburne parodied his own style in "Nephelidia" (the title means "cloudlets"), which begins:

> From the depth of the dreamy decline of the dawn through
>   a notable nimbus of nebulous noonshine,
> Pallid and pink as the palm of the flag-flower that
>   flickers with fear of the flies as they float,

When we talk about poetry singing, we don't mean singing like that! The rugged, muscular verse of Robert Browning—often difficult even to pronounce smoothly—is much more "musical" than poetry in which rhythms are too regular, the assonance and consonance too thick. Good music is rarely merely soothing, like the canned syrup of Muzak (which my daughter calls dentist-office music). Even a good barbershop quartet knows how monotonous unrelieved harmony can be. Rather, music—and musical poetry—involves discord, surprise, vigor, sharpness, and variety. That chorus "Fa, la, lanky down dilly" is not euphonious. It's good because it is difficult, not because it's simple.

Hearing the Beat

As you get more deeply into the technical study of poetry, you learn about such elements of phonetics as fricatives, plosives, sibilants, and glides. You learn whether vowels are back or front, high or low, rounded or unrounded. The terms are unimportant in themselves, but using them to analyze vocal sounds helps you sensitize yourself to phonic quality.

But one thing you cannot get by without is awareness of stress or accent. In this book I will not get into an extended discussion of meter—or measuring of lines, primarily by counting stresses or metrical feet—a topic I discuss in detail in other books. What I am dealing with here is much more fundamental, involving a skill you must have before you even begin to think about meter: hearing stress. ("Stress" and "accent" are interchangeable terms in this context.)

To my astonishment I have often met people who, given a word such as "perimeter," can't tell which syllable is accented or even how many syllables there are in the word. (Where to divide syllables, as at the end of a line of typing, has no relevance to poetry, as it is a convention of printing, not of speech.) You couldn't speak intelligible English if you didn't hear and pronounce accents correctly. You may automatically say *pe-***rim**-*e-ter* (four syllables, accent on the second), but blank out when you consciously try to locate the stress or count the syllables.

For practice, see whether this rhythm brings any particular song to mind. Imagine a rich bass voice rolling out the syllables slowly: *DUM DUM DUM da.* Try it over and over, singing it to slightly different notes. Maybe eventually you'll hit upon "Ol' Man River."

Here's an easier one, with a hint: It's associated with Christmas:

DUM DUM DUM
DUM DUM DUM
DUM DUM DUM da DUM

If you identify that,* try writing nonsense syllables for the rhythm of a familiar song, such as "D' ye ken John Peel," "Are You Sleeping, Brother John?" or "Row, Row, Row Your Boat." Or scheme out a few lines of a poem you know by heart, such as " 'Twas the night before Christmas, / And all through the house. . . ." Another good kind of poem to try is nursery rhymes, which provide some of the best examples of rugged, vital, irregular rhythms. Try "Little Miss Muffet," "Hickory Dickory Dock," "Pease Porridge Hot," or any other that comes to mind. Now flip back to the Introduction of this book and try some lines of "The Love Song of J. Alfred Prufrock," or some of the other poems you have found here.

Such exercises are easy for some and extraordinarily difficult for others. But if you become comfortable with the process, it can have immediate application in your writing. For example, I once wrote a long poem, "Hobbes and the Ghosts," most of which was in pentameter, like this passage in which the old philosopher is thinking about his young amanuensis (or secretary):

---

*"*Jingle Bells.*"

> My mind has never fumbled
> like my ancient hands: platonic hands, too old
> for loving, blurring the gesture, frightening her
> who loves me in the sunlight when I talk.
> We walk our walk. She stands all dumb with life
> while I am turning, deep in water toiling,
> head alive with trim moustaches, points
> of fire beneath my bushy head of ashes,
> then puts away my hand as though it were
> a wisp of hair that brushed her cheek, distraction
> in a maiden's summer morning. Our last years
> we hold the young ones by the ears. We want
> too much—that they should listen to our talk
> and bear our palsied touch.

But I wanted to break that rhythm up with something more intensely lyrical and casting about for a model, remembered a song (which has nothing to do with the subject of the poem). I wrote this:

> But time is unawed. Fraud,
> No more than a locked door,
> can baffle decay. Pray,
> cringe,
> subvert all your flesh love,
> devote your malign core,
> and squander your sense
> for God's recompense,
> for the long love, and the dry.

The basic rhythmical pattern comes from a Johnny Mercer song of the forties, "My Mama Done Tol' Me." Part of it goes roughly like this:

> From Natchez to Mobile,
> From Memphis to St. Joe,
> Wherever the four winds blow;
> I been in some big towns
> And heard me some big talk,
> But there is one thing I know:
> A woman's a two-face,
> A worrisome thing who'll leave you to sing
> The blues in the night.

The fit of my poem to that rhythm isn't exact, of course, but the song provided the basic beat.

Some think they can avoid the whole problem by writing free verse—but that's what's wrong with most of it that's currently published. Indeed, the lines above, "But time is unawed . . . ," are free verse. Like this passage, much of such verse is rhymed, and most uses identifiable metrical feet. The term "free verse" simply means that there is no set line length or pattern. Good writing in free forms requires extremely sensitive management of stresses. Here, for instance, is the opening of Ezra Pound's "The Return" (1912), which I'll accompany with *da-dums* to indicate where the stresses fall:

> See, they return; ah, see the tentative
> *DUM da da DUM// da DUM da DUM da da*
>
> > Movements, and the slow feet,
> > *DUM da// da da DUM DUM*
> >
> > The trouble in the pace and the uncertain
> > *da DUM da da da DUM da da da DUM da*
> >
> > Wavering!
> > *DUM da da*
>
> See, they return, one, and by one,
> *DUM// da da DUM// DUM// da da DUM*
>
> With fear, as half-awakened;
> *da DUM// da DUM da DUM da*
>
> As if the snow should hesitate
> *da DUM da DUM da DUM da da*
>
> > and half turn back;
> > *da DUM DUM DUM*
>
> These were the "Wing'd-with-Awe,"
> *DUM da da DUM da DUM*
>
> > Inviolable.
> > *da DUM da da da*

In 1914 W. B. Yeats said this was "the most beautiful poem that has been written in the free form, one of the few in which I find real organic rhythm." The word "organic" is thrown around a lot these days, but I think Yeats was using it carefully. The rhythm is governed by what the poem is dramatizing. As the poem talks about tentativeness, uncertainty, and wavering, the rhythm accordingly wavers. The "slow feet" plod slowly.

Free verse has sadly degenerated in this century, but the early modernists such as Pound had been trained in traditional meters. You may have heard pianists who can "improvise," just sit down and play nothing in particular, sometimes going on for long periods of time rolling out what sounds like good music, continuously varied, never playing anything that had ever been written down. They can do that because there are rhythmic sequences, chords, melodic scraps from here and there that can be endlessly combined, recombined, and varied by an accomplished pianist, making music like the colored patterns in a kaleidoscope. Such was the free verse of a poet like Pound early in his career, a constant, imaginative, and, indeed, organic variation of traditional rhythms and harmonies into something quite fresh and original.

But someone who tries to do that without the basic training will produce music rather like the noise I would make on the piano if I sat down and tried to improvise. And that is precisely the kind of noise a lot of poets are producing today because they literally haven't had the opportunity to learn the traditional harmonies and rhythms. By the time I started college in the early forties the traditional forms were no longer being taught. (I had to go to graduate school and learn them by studying Shakespeare, Milton, Dryden, and Pope—on my own because my professors knew nothing about prosody.) Young people being introduced to poetry read almost nothing but free verse, so how could they possibly learn the forms that good free verse varies? When they begin to write, they create only cacophony.

A free-verse poet has to give form to the poem phrase by phrase, line by line, and that's impossible without delicate control of stress. Since the rhythm of each poem is created specifically for that poem, there is no way one can "play it by ear." Rather, to hear its music you have to "sing" each phrase, and it may help to do that in nonsense syllables, those *da dums*, listening carefully to the number of syllables, stresses, the pauses, to see whether they cohere with what you are saying.

As you begin writing your own poem, one basic question is whether you have *enough* stresses. Prose can absorb as many as three or four unaccented syllables between accents (*das* between its *dums*), but poetry gets wobbly if there are more than two. That's why the lines of Pound's poem, quoted above, waver so: Three *das* in a row is a lot.

These are suggestions for sensitizing yourself to the musical elements of poetry. Analyze, *listen*, to poems that really work for you.

Don't let your ear be too distracted by the meaning of the poem, though of course you must think about that, too. If you have a tape recorder, read poetry you admire onto the cassette, emphasizing the stresses. Record some of your own poetry, too, and listen to it over and over, often enough that you no longer have to think about the meaning and can concentrate on the interplay of sound and rhythm. The road to the rejection basket is paved by poets who hope to be judged by *what* they say rather than *how* they say it.

I would also argue that poor poetry results from being distracted by what a poem *looks* like, too, but my ground here is shakier. In an excellent text with quite a different perspective from my own, *Writing Poems*, Robert Wallace says,

> *The rise of free verse in the twentieth century corresponds, I suspect, to the acceleration of the evolution of poetry toward the visual. . . . The visual will not replace the oral (poetry always relies on speech for its vigor) but will complement it, enriching and widening the poet's resources.*

Most people first encounter and learn about poetry today in the schools, and the experience is primarily visual. When you are looking at poems, and not hearing them, it is true that a whole range of devices, such as shapes, spaces, striking line and stanza breaks, balances in line length, and so on, become available and can be effective. Some excellent poems by E. E. Cummings cannot be read aloud at all, but they work because of their ingenious visual arrangements. I understand that but am impatient with such poetry, so habituated am I to regarding the words of a poem as a kind of musical notation, a score that is dead on the page until performed—either aloud or in the imagination. But you should know there are other points of view, and Wallace, in the book mentioned, explains very well many of the possibilities of free verse which I tend to disregard.

But whether you are considering your poetry as a visual or an oral experience, one question you have to answer honestly is, *Are you bored?* If there is genuine music and energy in the words, you aren't likely to be, and that won't be merely because of self-infatuation. Just as you can enjoy hearing favorite pieces of music again and again, one time after another, so will a good poem sustain itself as a listening experience. There is usually not much reason to reread prose over and over. We read prose primarily for meaning, and once we understand that, we can move on. But good poems, like good works of art in any form, only become better loved as one experiences continued or repeated exposure. I find most of the poetry of Ezra Pound unreadable or, when readable, detestable, but I have read "The Return" hundreds of times and find new beauty in it, new pleasure in reading, each time.

Incidentally, while you are practicing and listening, don't rationalize that you are a "poor reader." For one thing, you won't be if you really care about the poem—vowel by vowel, consonant by consonant, syllable by syllable, beat by beat. And if you *don't* care about it in that way, it's probably not a very good poem. But if it *is* good, you can't ruin it in performance. One of the worst readers of poetry I ever heard, especially of her own work, was Marianne Moore. She would squeak and pause and ramble and drift unemphatically away in the midst of a poem. I once heard her apparently try to destroy her magnificent "In Distrust of Merits" in this fashion, but, like a sinewy creature with a life of its own, the poem survived her reading. It was still thrilling to listen to because the music was written into it. By contrast, E. E. Cummings (at the same series of readings) tried to sing his poems, almost literally, reading them in a monotonously fluted tenor voice, giving too much attention to the sound and too little to the sense. But the poems popped up vivid, alive, and distinct in spite of his mistreatment.

You should, of course, learn how to perform your poetry effectively in public. For one thing, that's where the money is (or the little available for poetry): for readings, not publication. Ironically, one of the effects of poetry becoming a more and more visual art is that, once out of school, people often stop reading it. But they still turn out to hear it performed. One warning, however: If you happen to be a good performer, don't be misled by a favorable response from the audience. Some people can read the telephone book aloud and make it sound moving and intelligible, but that doesn't make the telephone book good poetry. The best reading is not one that necessarily makes a good show but one that lets the essential music of the poetry be heard.

What Do We Want?

Good poems will make themselves heard if anyone in the audience has an ear. But you can't depend on that. And there's no point in getting bitter about it. Though people turn out for poetry readings (a greater number than buy books of poetry), it's not always clear what kind of stimulation they are seeking. It probably has very little to do with the sound qualities I have been discussing in this chapter. The same cultural conditions that might have made it difficult for you to hear the music of poetry have made it difficult for them, too.

Notice that I'm not counseling you how to succeed as a poet but how to make good poems. "Success" is relative at best, and immediate appreciation by an audience may be one of the poorest measures of the kinds of success that matter most to you (and to me). You might create a tapestry of rhythm and sound as powerful as Pound's "The Return," and your audience could utterly fail to respond. Since the midcentury the poetry that seems to work best at readings has been closely related to the routines of stand-up comedians (a topic I will return to in Chapter XI). But such poetry has little to do with the values and views of poetry I have been discussing in this book.

If you seriously want to write good poems, you have to face up to one of the peculiarities of our art: that it often serves our own needs more than those of others. Not many really want what we make, or at least the poems we care about most deeply. I used to write poems as gifts for people on their birthdays and Christmas. (I'll share one of those with you in Chapter IX.) But I finally realized that many took my gift as a burden: I made them a captive audience. The recipient had to make at least a pretense of appreciation, and I was the one who was rewarded. I remember once giving a birthday poem to a woman I love. After a few days I had second thoughts and revised it and was going to throw away the original. But when I asked her for her copy, she was momentarily upset: Was the poem hers or not? And I was confused, too. Had it been a painting, I probably wouldn't have asked for her to replace it with a new version. And I realized that my awareness of a possible larger audience—a magazine sale or the ages—was distracting me from purely personal love.

It's always hard (as I discussed in Chapter II) to sort out our genuine needs and feelings from the art of poetry. This poem grew out of my experience as poetry editor for *Antioch Review:*

POETRY EDITOR AS MISS LONELYHEARTS

Round the horizon I see silhouettes
of sweet old ladies who live with their pets,
parents neglected by their children, scholars
bullied by schoolmates, men in starchy collars
whose daily wisdom always falls among swine,
girls who read on Saturday night, fine wine
merchants, inmates, shut-ins, neglected wives.
Acceptance is scarce as love. Their hope arrives
in bundles on my desk, these poems blest
with kisses, tears, stamped envelopes—self-addressed.

Since we want people to read what we write much more than they want to read it, perhaps *we* should pay *them*. I've considered attaching a five-dollar bill to each of my books, telling all who might pick it up that they could keep the money if they would read and think about the contents a little. But, of course, this would be like trying to buy love. The kind of involvement and attention we want from readers isn't for sale.

If you are like me, you may not be sure exactly what kind of response that is. Admiration, for instance, is sometimes a nuisance. Once I read to a small group a short story of mine that had appeared in *Partisan Review*, a surrealistic comedy which was ribald enough, I thought, to be at least amusing to an unsophisticated audience. But a friend—a laborer with little education or literary experience—was the first to comment. "Golly," he said, "I couldn't even *read* all those words, let alone write them down!" I was embarrassed. I hadn't, of course, intended to show off my vocabulary. And it wasn't his fault that his background hadn't prepared him for my story. I would much rather have reached my friend than to have impressed the intellectual editors of *Partisan Review*. His honest admiration only made me realize how poorly I had written if my goal had been to reach a wide audience.

Few are able to recognize skill in writing, especially in poetry, and those few are often the most supercilious readers, so insulated by their sophistication that nothing they read can touch them. When I think of my own response to great poetry, I realize that I value most highly those poems that changed my life. Coming back to those poems in later study, I may have been better able to analyze technical elements or evaluate the skill, erudition, energy, scope, or some other quality of what I read. That may have deepened my respect for the poem, but it wasn't essential for the initial experience. (One thing I've noticed is that the poems that deeply moved me once probably continue to move me every time I read them, no matter how much I have studied their technical elements.) Again and again when I was young, great poems struck me with salvational impact. That's what I want to happen to my readers. Admiration only gets in the way.

The Unspeakable Response

If, indeed, our work changes our readers' lives, can they tell us? You may yourself have a hard time pinpointing what your own work has meant to you. When it is "finished" to your (perhaps temporary) satisfaction, you have a flurry of excitement. You may read it to a mate or friend, but if your listener is enthusiastic, you may distrust that response: He or she is too close. You mail it out, and if, after some months of circulating, it's finally accepted by a magazine, you have another rush of satisfaction. Some editors somewhere thought it worth publishing. But did they really *hear* it? Were they moved? Did they care? Were their lives changed? The acceptance letter is uninformative on these points. In the pit of your stomach you realize that all the acceptance may mean is that the poem looked better than others recently received, or it fit space requirements, or perhaps it happened to be on a subject that the magazine considers interesting to its readers.

Interestingly, publication is the most anticlimactic experience of all. It is likely to follow acceptance by as much as a year or more, long after you have forgotten the excitement of composition. Your poem is a leaf dropped in a well. Ah! The magazine is out on the stands! You cock your ear for repercussions. Rarely do you hear anything at all. Maybe some buddy tells you, "Hey, I saw your poem in *Flaming Nostril.*" You reply expectantly, "Oh, did you?" And your friend says, "They certainly have improved their graphics." You grab his sleeve and ask, "But did you notice that sequence of open vowels and heavy beats in the third line?"

No, you don't ask that, do you? You know your friend is probably as embarrassed as you are. He may actually have liked your poem, may even have noticed that technical flourish, but he doesn't know what to say. What would *you* have said to Shakespeare had you met him in the lobby the first evening you saw *Hamlet?* Or suppose the kid down the block grew up, became tubercular, and, it turned out, was writing poetry. "Would you like to see some?" he asks. What can you say but "Sure"? So he hands you this poem which turns out to be "Ode on a Grecian Urn," and you read for the first time that "Heard melodies are sweet, but those unheard / Are sweeter." Or your uncle the insurance agent turns out to be Wallace Stevens, and one evening over brandy he hands you his latest: "Sunday Morning" (in my judgment the greatest poem written in English in this century). What would you say?

Although I've personally met many poets whose work has changed my life (e.g., Karl Shapiro, Archibald MacLeish, Anne Sexton, W. D. Snodgrass, Langston Hughes, Richard Wilbur, Richard Eberhart, John Ciardi), never once have I been able to blubber out my gratitude for their poetry. Though I heard him read several times, I had only one occasion to converse with Robert Frost, whom, since I am using superlatives here, I regard as the greatest American poet of this century. He was sitting in a straight chair at a reception, a glass of bourbon on the rocks in his gnarled hand—the year before he died.

Did I tell him that his poems, one after another, again and again, had changed my life, that, indeed, I owe much of the intellectual and emotional furniture I live with to what he has done? Of course not. I figured he would be embarrassed. Or maybe I was too embarrassed. I used our few moments together to ask a question about one of his least-known poems—I guess to show him I had studied his work in detail. "Is there really an orchid called *Calypso* growing wild in New England?" I asked.

"Yes," he said, and the conversation seemed to be dying, so I pulled out another obscure reference.

"In 'Masque of Mercy' you refer to Fundy Fault. I realize it makes a good pun, but is there indeed a fault up the East Coast like the San Andreas fault on the West Coast?"

He looked at me gruffly. "There isn't much in that book that isn't true," he said. That was the end of my interview with Robert Frost. Obviously I should have gone to the library, not to the poet, for those answers.

Meanwhile what I *wanted* to talk about was that I had discovered, in "Encounter," the poem that refers to the orchid, that he used a telephone pole as a symbol for Jesus on the Cross. The speaker in the poem was in search of Calypso (surely the nymph in *The Odyssey* as well as the orchid) when he casually heard and disregarded a revelation from the Cross: a rather astonishing twist from a poet generally regarded as irreligious. How *did* Frost feel about Jesus? But who am I to interpret his poem for him? I wanted to tell him how dozens of his poems had altered the very way I lived day by day—let alone the way I understood and practiced the art of poetry. But I knew no way to say any of that.

The Common Wages

I can only hope some readers' lives have been changed by my poetry, but I'll never know, or if they ever tell me I'll probably distrust or discount what they say. So we are all tongue-tied. Perhaps that's why we write poetry in the first place. Privately we distill and write; privately we receive. But few of us can accept these hard terms of our art.

The classical statement of this problem is Dylan Thomas's "In My Craft or Sullen Art." He probably uses "sullen" with reference to the etymology of the word, which means "alone, solitary," a reference to the fact that though we are gregarious by nature, we are solitary by calling. The first stanza tells how he labors, what he does *not* labor for, and the simple and unattainable reward he seeks:

> In my craft or sullen art
> Exercised in the still night
> When only the moon rages
> And the lovers lie abed
> With all their griefs in their arms,

I labour by singing light
Not for ambition or bread
Or the strut and trade of charms
On the ivory stages
But for the common wages
Of their most secret heart.

Had he been able to stick to the intentions expressed here, he might still be writing, but the real or imagined necessity to write for bread and, worse, to tread the ivory stages of American campuses in the early fifties destroyed him as a man and released the poet on the air. The second stanza returns to the same theme but is more precise:

Not for the proud man apart
From the raging moon I write
On these spindrift pages
Nor for the towering dead
With their nightingales and psalms
But for the lovers, their arms
Round the griefs of the ages,
Who pay no praise nor wages
Nor heed my craft or art.

Alas, though, he did write too much for the proud man apart—for the critics, the intellectuals, the arbiters of taste—and most of his work is consequently unintelligible and of little enduring value. He was seduced by or driven to seek fame, both cheap and highbrow, even notoriety for self-dramatizing, obnoxious behavior. He belied the pure, heart-rending vision of his poem, as many of us do our visions in our daily lives. He wanted wages and praise—and killed himself with his wanting. But this poem and a half dozen others, his play *Under Milkwood*, the essay-story "A Child's Christmas in Wales," and a handful of other stories and prose pieces of various sorts were sufficient to preserve his name in our literature. He will eloquently and passionately reach out from the bookshelves through the ages for those lovers who he believed would never acknowledge him; and here and there he will move one as he moved me, changing a life with imperishable phrases. He has humbled and transformed me repeatedly, long after his death. Were I to meet him on Olympus, I wouldn't know what to say.

But let's take a minute to listen to the music of that poem. First, can you represent the rhythms with *da-dums*? I'll help you with the first few lines:

In my craft or sullen art
da da DUM da DUM da DUM

Exercised in the still night
DUM da da da da DUM DUM
When only the moon rages
da DUM da da DUM DUM da
And the lovers lie abed
da da DUM da DUM da DUM

You should be able to find three stresses in each line, with the possible exception of "On the ivory stages," which may or may not be read with a stress on "On" (I stress it, guided by the pattern of the other lines). This is called "accentual" meter; the lines are measured by the number of stresses without regard to the distribution of unaccented syllables. Skillful handling of this kind of meter requires as much variety as possible within its limits. That second line is magical, with its whispering four unaccented syllables before the strong stresses of "still night."

Because of the powerful effect of our tradition of "alternating rhythm," *da DUM da DUM da DUM*, one concern of a poet using accentual rhythm is to keep his poem from falling into that pattern too often. If a reader begins hearing the lines as "regular"—that is, as alternating rhythm—he may hear the "irregular" lines as awkward variations.

Thomas shows great ingenuity in getting about as many variations as are possible out of his three-beat lines. Notice that all but three have seven syllables. The three exceptions, each with only six syllables, are in interesting places: the last line of each stanza and the line "On these spindrift pages," which sets up the rhyme for "wages," one of the three repeated rhyme words (the others being "art" and "arms"). Thus, most lines have three stressed and four unstressed syllables in ingeniously varied arrangements. He saves "regularity" for the climactic effect. The only *da DUM da DUM da DUM* lines are the last one of the first stanza and the last two of the second. These provide an effect something like that of tonic chords in music, a sense of resolution, as though the preceding lines in each stanza were looking for a pattern to settle into and finally found it.

Notice that almost all the words in the poem are of one or two syllables, and therefore the exceptions ("exercised," "ambition," "towering," "nightingales") ripple with simple eloquence. "Moon rages" is introduced in the third line, and the image is repeated early in the second stanza; he writes when the moon rages, and he doesn't write for the proud man apart from the raging moon. The lovers are introduced subtly in the fourth line of the first stanza: He writes while they are abed. At the end of that stanza it might not be clear that "their most secret heart" refers to these lovers, though that is the only possible antecedent for "their." This tactic sets up their dramatic emergence in the second, where the poet makes it emphatically clear that it is for them that he writes. He writes for the "wages" that, he finally says, they will never pay.

Thus, the poem is structured around slight, meaningful variations, very much like a musical composition. Key words are repeated, often emphasized by rhymes. Do you know how to describe a rhyme pattern? Assign *a* to the first word at the end of a line and all lines that rhyme with it, *b* to the second, and so on. Thus, the pattern for the two stanzas is *abcdebdecca abcdxecca*. I used *x* for the one word that has no rhyme pair: "psalms." Notice that both stanzas begin with the *abcd* sequence and conclude *ecca*. No detail of form was unimportant to Thomas, who took each of his poems through hundreds of drafts. If you look at the words that rhyme, you will often see associations in meaning. "Art, heart, apart, art," the *a* rhymes, almost summarize the poem in themselves. The *c* rhymes, with three occurrences in each stanza, are the only "feminine" rhymes (that is, ending with an unstressed syllable), and they seem to me a noisy group: "rages, stages, wages, pages, ages," and, again, "wages." What other associations and significant repetitions can you find?

Now consider again the paradox I have been discussing. As the poem says, the poet writes alone in a doomed endeavor. He will never reach the ones for whom he writes. Efforts to seek other "praise or wages" are merely destructive distractions from that unattainable goal. And yet the poem works after all, for you and me and millions more through centuries to come, an audience whom Thomas could never have known. It does exactly what the poet hoped. We lovers do indeed pay him the praise and wages of our most secret hearts.

I hope you have had the opportunity to hear a recording of Thomas reading this and others of his poems in what one critic called his "voice of blue thunder." But I hope even more strongly that by this time you are able to play the score in your head, and either by reading silently or aloud can fully experience its music. That's what I would call a poem that sings.

Though I would not like to invite comparison of my poem with Thomas's or with Keats's "Ode on a Grecian Urn," I want to give you another comment on reaching for unattainable goals:

NO SUCH

Poet, there is no such place
as in an orange spot of sun
a wooden tub (moss-slick, brimming)
catches the drip of the pump—

where the dog drinks, and the lizard
(pulsing his head) drinks and waits
and warms. Such pines never stand
in such hills. And that girl rinsing

her tin pitcher, flinging water
like jewels into the sunny air
or pumping with a round brown arm
or leaning to drink, her hair

falling, her blouse heavy, a blur
of the image of treetops and girl
when water drips into the still
tub—wanderer, there is no such girl.

I hoped to make the imaginary scene so "real" that it would seem to belie the poem's insistence that it fade away as illusion.

String Quartets

The unattainable goals of poetry seem to me worth working for, even with the frustrations of trying to reach a living, present audience. Perhaps the least satisfactory audience of all, in some ways, is the one most dearly loved, those closest to us. It is, of course, gratifying if they truly hear and are moved by our poems, but we can never be sure that their response isn't dependent upon their understanding of us as individuals.

And that response is never enough. That's one of the problems with love poetry, which ostensibly is written for an audience of one. Logically, if that one person receives and understands and appreciates, the poet should be satisfied. But the poem is also always a bit of a performance, which somewhat vitiates its value as personal communication, one to one, just as a kiss would be disconcerting if the kisser were aware as he made love that the ages were looking on. I meant this poem very sincerely and intimately, but I admit I was performing. (The speaker is tongue-tied at the beginning, which explains the jumble of the first line and the word "pantameter" later.)

THE SUPERIORITY OF MUSIC

Lang has no lovewedge. The world forgot
such courtly praise for neon eyes
as roused their hurricano sighs
in knightly years. I am not
like a yacht, nor dare I to
a harbor resemble thee. My tears
gully no landscapes. I have no fears
of chill disdain, nor wanly woo
pent in pantameter. My verse is ill
with marriage and commonsense
constraining conceit and elegance.
Shall I sonnetize the Pill?

Nay, wife, I still with clapper tongue
proclaim that you, like any she
belied with false compare, may be
with hyperbolic baubles hung:
I root my ropy route among
your petal hills; I pioneerly boar
my sow of despond, salty shore,
or, as spring from pikespeak sprung,
twist down melodically and clear.
I lick the jewels from corners, halt
midair nijinskywise, I sault
summerly and slobber, bucking near,

for you, my satin-saddle, gra-
vey grave, my scorching wine, my squirrel.
I love you like boiled onions, girl,
buttered. You suck my spine away,
soak me. You tenderize my twigs.
I think in orange. My tongue twitches.
till sundown. You invent my itches.
You look like music and taste like figs.
You are to be virtuo-solely played,
sweetly and with pizzicato,
ad libitum and obbligato,
my straddle-various, my fiddled maid.

No go. The mind in praise ties knots.
Yet when you lie there like a long smile
brownly smiling at either end a long while,
moon glazing your gullied landscape, thoughts

circling and settling like evening birds,
and you turn and stroke my skin with eyes
like tonic chords, and silence lies
as gently over us as music without words,
I would not then restore to love its tongue.
You are not like anything. No poet imagined you.
You are dreamed by the earth, wordless. You
are not to be described, but sung.

At best sincerity is an ambiguous virtue in poetry. Sometimes it ruins a poem. Often other considerations of craft take precedence, and the poet is left feeling phony in regard to relationships that may matter a great deal more than art.

Aside from family and friends, local writers' groups may be good sounding boards, though these, too, tend over time to be made up of friends, and the knowledge the participants have of one another's past work and personalities may confuse their aesthetic judgment. Some of the best exchanges about poetry are through the mail. If you write to poets whose work you find in magazines—especially if they are just breaking into print—you might strike up a friendship by mail which is relatively unencumbered by too much personal familiarity.

Some of the most rewarding experiences of sharing poetry I have experienced have been with comparative strangers at writers' workshops such as I described in Chapter III. When people travel some distance to get together for a week or weekend with the specific purpose of sharing their work, they develop a kind of implicit contract in their relationships: I will take you seriously if you will take me seriously.

I have compared these occasions to those in which amateurs (in the best sense of that word: lovers) gather to play music together. Proficiency is sought and valued, but awkwardness and inexperience are not condemned. Criticism is not so much the point as learning together. Evaluation is primarily for the poems not yet written: We learn from the poems discussed at the workshop things we can apply in those to come. No one scores. Nothing is "accepted for publication," frozen in time and form. And while there may be some technical discussion and analysis of craft, the most important reward each seeks is to know that caring people have heard and understood a little.

It hardly matters whether they think the poems are good or bad; but we do want others to have heard, and we want their comments to indicate an involvement with what is being said, what is being attempted artistically. You don't often get that from editors. (You get it more often in response to prose than to poetry.) You are lucky if you can get it from those close to you or those you meet with regularly.

Inescapably, our "real" audience is not yet born—or is unknown to us. Their aims are round the griefs of the ages and they pay no praise nor wages. The flesh-and-blood, immediate response of a living and present audience may be irrelevant and distracting. But in our craft and sullen art we all need that kind of warm feedback occasionally, at least a few times in our careers, and it's important to discover the people and the places where we can get it.

CHAPTER VIII:
ELUDING
THE
CENSORS

A strange and moving event occurred at one of our workshops. A sensitive fine-featured, gray-haired woman who had told us little about herself except that she was a nurse read several of her poems which stimulated very little response. They were too cryptic. We had no idea what they were about, so there was little we could say. There would be some polite, noncommittal remarks, then she would sigh delicately and go on to the next.

But suddenly there was a difference. What she was reading didn't sound like the other poems at all. There was a quaver in her voice. It was a passionate statement blaming parents and society for the crimes of the speaker . . . and then I recognized the words of Charles Manson, the leader of the cult that committed the Sharon Tate and other mass murders. At the conclusion there was some inconsequential addition from the poet, but the bulk of what she read was quotation. And she was sobbing. We were all deeply affected, but we still didn't know how to respond. Finally, because she couldn't speak, only sob, I crossed the room and embraced her reassuringly and said perhaps she would prefer to talk about whatever was happening privately.

But no. She was getting a grip on herself now, and she wanted to explain to the group. She was very worried about her son, who had left home and was wandering around the country as a hippie. He had an irreconcilable conflict with his father, who, according to the woman, was adamant, bullheaded, and prejudiced. She thought her husband was wrong on every issue he argued about with his son (including racism, Vietnam, consumerism, big business, marijuana, and a few more topics of the time). Her son's attitude seemed to her humane and reasonable, but his discussions with his father became explosive and at times nearly violent. Finally the son realized that his father was not open to change, that it was impossible to talk sensibly with him about these matters, and the father would not let the issues drop. So the son really had no alternative but to leave home. His mother didn't know whether he would ever return—and really couldn't blame him, though she missed him terribly and was desperately concerned for his welfare.

But she loved her husband, too, and wasn't about to break up their thirty-year marriage. His opinions on these matters were really no different from those of their friends and neighbors, even of their minister, and if her husband was vociferous in expressing himself, that was only because he couldn't bear the opposition of his son in the intimacy of the home. Otherwise, he seemed a good-natured, even tolerant man; he was successful in business and popular among their friends. She could not, at her age, change her whole life—her friends, her church, her job, her marriage—and yet she found it impossible to bear the separation from her son under these circumstances. She couldn't even *talk* to anyone about all this, for her views would be as shocking as her son's were to his father; and, besides, it wasn't the "issues" she cared about, but her family relationships.

So she wrote poetry. And if it was cryptic, that was because she didn't dare leave around the house anything her husband might find that expressed her real feelings. Then, when she read *Helter Skelter*, a book about the Manson case, she found this speech of Manson to the court which seemed to express much of what she and her son felt. She could copy that speech, because they weren't really her words, and no one need know her motive for copying them. But they reminded her of something her son might someday find himself saying.

Obviously, it meant a great deal to be able to share all that with us, a group of strangers at the poetry workshop. For once in her life she could get it off her chest, and our sympathy and understanding would, she thought, give her strength in continuing to bear what she could not change. We had no advice, and she really wasn't seeking any. Discussion of her poems was irrelevant. She needed only the confirmation that others, somewhere in the world, understood—and didn't think she was crazy. Now, she thought, she could go back home and be a good nurse, wife, neighbor, and church member and continue writing verses no one could understand.

I have told her story at some length because it helped me overcome some rather haughty attitudes about the function of poetry in people's lives. I realized there was nothing I could say—a wholesome and unusual experience for me. There was no way I could help her write "better" poems. She had no interest in publication—nor even in communication with the only audience available to her. Yet it was obvious that expressing herself in some way, which she chose to disguise as poems, was very important to her. And it was obviously also important that she travel some distance to find a group of sympathetic strangers to listen, however uncomprehendingly and helplessly, to her poems and her story. She didn't seem to need psychological counseling—yet. But if she continued to find her situation unbearable, she might find it helpful to consult a poetry therapist or join a poetry therapy group.

Poetry and Therapy

Poetry therapy has become quite a widespread practice in recent years. There are now national organizations of poetry therapists, conferences, publications, and practitioners working in mental hospitals, community centers, social agencies, and private offices.*

I first became aware of the burgeoning movement when I read a report in *Time*, March 13, 1972, which indicated that at that time there were "about 3,500 mental patients, prison inmates, troubled students and nursing-home residents . . . reading and writing poetry under the guidance of some 400 psychiatrists, psychologists, social workers and specially trained teachers" around the country. It said:

> *Patients in poetry therapy are encouraged to read verse, write it, or both. The technique seems to be effective in both individual and group treatment, probably because serious problems usually touch on deep, universal emotions. According to Yale Psychiatrist Albert Rothenberg, a patient who suddenly deciphers the message of a great poet may experience a flash of understanding similar to the dramatic insight that can come to patients in ordinary psychotherapy. By writing an original poem, an inhibited, repressed person may tell his doctor much that was previously secret. Poetry, says Rothenberg, "is even more revelatory than dreams."*

The professionals involved in this kind of therapy warn against its indiscriminate use. Jack Leedy, a psychiatrist, said that if poetry can predict suicide, it may also provoke it:

> *Reading somber verses with upbeat endings can help unhappy patients by demonstrating that others have been depressed and have recovered, but despairing poems may deepen the feelings of hopelessness.*

---

*For information, write the Poetry Therapy Institute, P.O. Box 70244, Los Angeles, CA 90070. Or you might want to read Poetry in the Therapeutic Experience, an anthology of professional articles on the subject edited by poet-psychotherapist Art Lerner.

Another psychiatrist says that if a patient merely gives vent to his feelings, relieving the pressure, without understanding and resolving his conflicts, the poetry has served little therapeutic function. But if it is well used, it has an advantage over the other arts (also used in therapy) because it encourages "verbalization, the life blood of psychotherapy."

I must say that I have been to poetry therapy conferences and talked and corresponded with poetry therapists, and, as a poet, I have been unimpressed. In fact, the whole movement seems to me to have very little to do with poetry as an art. I hope those I met knew more about therapy than they seemed to about poetry. But I wouldn't want to detract from a movement that apparently is offering genuine and profound help to thousands.

Of Fluttering Lashes and Limp Wrists

There's no question that reading and writing poetry has a continuous and generally beneficial function in promoting mental health, and though I have nothing to contribute to the use of poetry in professional therapy, I would like to comment on its therapeutic function for ordinary readers and practicing poets. You might think (I'm sure the husband of that woman at the workshop would) that poetry has more to do with craziness than mental health. There is an ancient association between poetry and madness. In the section called "Rivalry with Madmen" in *The Poet and the Poem*, I quote Plato on the subject. In the *Phaedrus* he comments on "the madness of those who are possessed by the Muses." This madness, he says,

> enters in a delicate and virgin soul, and there inspires frenzy, awakens lyrical and all other numbers, with those adorning the myriad actions of ancient heroes for the instruction of posterity. But he who, having no touch of the Muses' madness in his soul, comes to the door and thinks that he will get into the temple by the help of art—he, I say, and his poetry are not admitted; the sane man is nowhere at all when he enters into rivalry with madmen.

For this reason Plato excluded poets from his ideal Republic.

During the Romantic era (which has never really ended) there arose an idealization (or romanticization) of illness which seems to be related to social class. The "sensitive" person was presumed to suffer in this harsh world. Just as women, corseted and pallid, were (in the upper classes) considered too refined for hard work or even for exposure to the raw realities of the countryside or street, so upper-class men of an artistic bent sometimes unconsciously aspired to debility. Such literary figures as tubercular Keats and asthmatic Proust have become popular archetypes of sensibilities too delicate to survive in the brutal world.

It's fascinating to watch the change in taste in poetry from the late seventeenth and early eighteenth centuries into the Romantic period. Neoclassic poets such as John Dryden, Alexander Pope, and Jonathan Swift adopted the mask of sanity just as deliberately as later poets adopted one of insanity. Pope and Swift were both rather seriously disturbed men, but they disguised it in their literary work, presenting themselves in their poetry as brimming with common sense and solid rationality. A hundred years later poets were likely to present themselves as inconsolably tormented and irrational, even if they were, in fact, as emotionally and mentally stable as the dullest and most normal of us.

I am, of course, oversimplifying complex cultural changes, but it's good to remember that tastes (and self-images) do change, and what a poet (or patient) writes at any given time about his emotional and mental life may be deeply influenced by his concept of what it means to be a poet and what poetry is all about. Poetry may be useful in therapy today precisely because of a popular attitude that the poetic license is one that permits or encourages irrational statement. That attitude may be good for therapy, but I think it is very bad for poetry as an art.

And it may even interfere with cure. Sometimes the flamboyant behavior of Bohemians is meant to enhance, protect, or lay claim to a blessed state of unreason popularly associated with artists. In this frame of mind a person has no interest in getting well or adjusting. He is likely to believe that society is sick and his aberration is some kind of transcendental sanity.

Or a poet can develop an investment in craziness. One of the most brilliant and talented poets of our century was Sylvia Plath, who finally succeeded in killing herself at thirty-one after several attempts. Her suicide probably came as no great surprise to those who knew her, though on the surface she led a perfectly conventional life and was quite successful at school, college and jobs, marriage and motherhood. At one point she tried rather unsuccessfully to write slick-magazine fiction. But what she *was* good at was writing poems of craziness. Her elegy for her Polish father, who died when she was eight, depicts him as a hideous monster and a Nazi, though there is nothing in the biographical facts available about the immigrant biologist to justify lines like these:

I have always been scared of *you*,
With your Luftwaffe, your gobbledygoo.
And your neat moustache
And your Aryan eye, bright blue
Panzer-man, panzer-man, O You—

Not God but a swastika
So black no sky could squeak through.
Every woman adores a Fascist
The boot in the face, the brute
Brute heart of a brute like you.

But such poems flashed incandescently on the pages of the literary magazines of the 1950s. Rewarded for sensationalism, she continued to write sensational poems, including very explicit ones about suicide. One long one, "Lady Lazarus," says she dies every decade. When she was ten, it was an accident; when she was twenty, it was deliberate. Part of it goes:

Dying
Is an art, like everything else.
I do it exceptionally well.

I do it so it feels like hell.
I do it so it feels real.
I guess you could say I've a call.

It's easy enough to do it in a cell.
It's easy enough to do it and stay put.
It's the theatrical

Comeback in broad day
To the same place, the same face, the same brute
Amused shout

"A miracle!"
That knocks me out.

You might think that instead of congratulating her for what seemed to be desperate messages, someone would get her help. Maybe some tried. But her reputation was really based on these extreme statements, and I wonder to what extent her life was imitating her art when she finally put her head in the oven.

On the other hand, she might not have appreciated it if those who read her poems took them literally as cries for help. A fairly widely published poet once sent me a series of his new poems about the agonies of guilt he suffered because he felt compelled to seduce young boys. I wrote him that I didn't think the poetry was very good, but I felt great compassion for a man asking for help. I strongly advised him to get counseling, to do *something* about his sick and miserable condition besides write poems about it. What he was doing was obviously dangerous and destructive to others as well as himself. That was, as you might imagine, the last I have heard from that particular poet. He may have felt he had a poetic license to prey on unwary youths.

How Do We Help?

A poem "written by a fifteen-year-old boy two years before he committed suicide" is quoted in that issue of *Time* I referred to earlier. An English professor commented that had the boy been in poetry therapy, the poem's cry for help might have been heeded, and psychiatric treatment might have prevented his suicide. It doesn't require much professional analysis to see where the boy was headed:

TO SANTA CLAUS AND LITTLE SISTERS

Once . . . he wrote a poem.
And called it "Chops,"
Because it was the name of his dog, and that's what it was all
    about.
And the teacher gave him an "A"
And a gold star,
And his mother hung it on the kitchen door, and read it to all
    his aunts . . .
Once . . . he wrote another poem.
And he called it "Question Marked Innocence."
Because that was the name of his grief and that's what it was
    all about.
And the professor gave him an "A"
And a strange and steady look.
And his mother never hung it on the kitchen door,
Because he never let her see it . . .
Once, at 3 a.m. . . . he tried another poem . . .
And he called it absolutely nothing, because that's what it was
    all about.
And he gave himself an "A"
And a slash on each damp wrist,

> And hung it on the bathroom door because he couldn't reach
>   the kitchen.

There is a lesson here for the "professor" and all of us who read and respond to other people's poetry. I realize, for instance, my first impulse would be to tell the boy that the word "damp" is the best thing in the poem, that it brings that line alive, enables me to experience the young wrist just before the slashing, and it's a great relief from the otherwise rather tedious and flat language of the poem.

Just such responses may have helped drive the boy to suicide. He was no doubt trying to tell the professor something in that second poem about his "grief." It was apparently sufficiently revelatory that it evoked "a strange and steady look" in addition to an "A." The professor obviously got the message but considered his job was to judge it as writing (as I was judging it in the last paragraph), not as a personal statement.

But it's not easy to know what reactions are appropriate—for all the reasons I have been discussing. The boy may have trusted the professor *not* to respond in a personal way. He didn't show that poem to his mother, who would surely have been more interested in what it said than how well it was written. Was the boy seeking attention as a poet or as a person who needed help? By the time he wrote "To Santa Claus and Little Sisters" he was obviously asking for help—two years before his suicide—and anyone who received *that* one with no more response than "a strange and steady look" and an "A" would, indeed, be guilty of almost criminal aestheticism. But given the climate of celebration of literary sensationalism, as illustrated by the poems of Sylvia Plath, the training we all have to evaluate poetry primarily in terms of *how* rather than *why*, and a Romantic cultural indulgence of morbid sensitivity, a posture especially attractive to adolescents, one can understand how that might happen.

Untrue Confessions

As I have implied, there is danger to poets and poetry if poems are taken too literally as personal statements. A poet has to feel free to explore many depths of the human spirit without having loved ones or other readers become alarmed. If that woman at the workshop had felt free to speak more openly in her poems without disturbing her husband and others close to her, she might have been more successful in working out her feelings.

And we should remember that much of the great poetry of the world sounds the depths of gloom or searches in forbidden areas. Had

Robert Frost not fully explored his acquaintance with the night in his poetry, he would probably have been much less able to cope with the emotional storms in his life. Great poets (Shakespeare, Milton, Keats, Browning, Eliot, and Yeats are the first to come to mind) act out in their work the full range of sick spirit and tragic attitudes. And they often leave such work with the problems only dimly understood and certainly unresolved.

In the "play" of poetry we have license to search out extremes, to try all dangerous stances, and to transcend them by living through and beyond the most profound psychic disturbances. The poet gains mental health by being able to explore and survive; the reader is able to follow in imagination all dark promptings of spirit surging beneath sane surfaces, and though he learns no "answers" of much value, he exhausts his need to dwell in such realms. Even hopelessness, which no one can completely avoid, can be tasted and lived with. It won't go away. No "A" for a poem dispels it. But as we enlarge our experience with poetry, we gain perspective and recognize that even hopelessness is only one of the many avenues of mind. It can, of course, be tortuous, is sometimes inevitable, and it can also sometimes be strangely delicious and seductive. We are more immune to its dangers because we know it intimately.

I often wonder how I would have responded had I been Sylvia Plath's poet-husband, Ted Hughes, when she wrote those suicidal poems or, indeed, if I had been the "professor" who received "To Santa Claus and Little Sisters." I would try to remember that though such poets may be sick, they are perhaps a little less sick for having been able to express themselves in poems. That boy may have quite literally have written the poem about suicide *instead* of doing it, and had he been able to write another poem of comparable intensity two years later, he might have survived that impulse, too.

I would hope that whatever strange and steady look I might give a person who showed me such disturbing work would convey something like this: "I take quite seriously what you say here about yourself. I hope that, having said it, you feel better. If not, perhaps you'll want to talk about it—with me or with someone else. But I'm not going to panic and am certainly not going to try to force you into a discussion you're not ready for. Meanwhile, if you are interested, here's what I think about this poem as a poem."

Many of my own poems explore the illicit, and I am grateful that those who love me don't question too closely how much fiction and how much fact there is in poems such as these:

PHILANDER'S RAINY AFTERNOON

i

Soon I shall see your saffron hair
toss as you glance each way in the street
a block away. I wait at the sill,
standing, pretending to read. Oh fair
demolishment, oh bomb-bright sweet—
you fix me in your count-down still.

ii

Pick by the puddles, light step, light!
Nor seem to see my slitted door
until you veer, steal swiftly in—
for treachery, such discipline.
The neighbor's open eye is sore
Where you have minced upon its white.

iii

Door shut, inside, eyes flitting, you
assess this world you slipped into:
refrigerator's throaty noise,
a comb snarled dark with wifely hair,
a wad of diapers, clumps of toys
and me—made flexible by wear.

iv

What have these days done? Oh, I see
where they have cut you—here, and here.
Quick razor touches, two or three—
but twinging, slow to heal, I fear.
In public, in the broad sun—crime!
Yet day by day you walk through time.

v

When eyes see only eyes afloat
on face (but billows roll, we know,
and glint of blue should not obscure
that waves have mysteries below),
when signals over seas assure,
we dip, embrace beneath your coat.

vi

Having come this far, come upstairs.
The bed's not made—but that we can
forgive. The room is littered: Man
and mate make sanctuaries do

service as habitation, too.
Untidy though the altar, come upstairs.

vii

I drink the salty dew of joy,
bite lobes of flesh, breath fumes of birth,
feel blood collecting to destroy
with scalding surges of desire
all elemental water, earth
and air, and, finally, fire.

viii

Skin plump with languor, all my strength
spent fitfully upon your length,
I lie like a tuna, beached, aware
of the clock draped with your underwear,
sun speckling the blinds. Hurry—
dear, disengage this hook of worry.

ix

As a rag wrung, wrinkled, mops,
then twisted dry may wipe again,
my ardor kitchen-cleans. Depart.
I keep of you some dampish drops,
blonde whisking down the block, but then
absorb my home with ragged heart.

PHILANDER'S DOMESTIC EVENING

No words. I swallow this, as you,
no doubt, are swallowing last words, too,
but, dear, had you not known, I might
have juggled a dozen loves, delight
for you in being grasped and flung,
for me a game of staying young
by keeping all those shapes in air,
and if none knew, why none would care.

Knowledge is evil. Now what I know
of how you twinge behind your show
of ease and how you bite to cling,
contemptuous of the bitten thing,
unwilling, though, to let it go . . .
How can we love, with what we know?
How painful to shred all and then
laboriously build deceits again.

And you can imagine that one of the reasons Emily Dickinson tucked her poems away for posterity rather than showing them to family and friends is that she needed an outlet for thoughts she could not share, such as this poem:

> Rearrange a wife's affection?
> When they dislocate my brain,
> Amputate my freckled bosom,
> Make me bearded like a man!
>
> Blush, my spirit, in thy fastness
> Blush, my unacknowledged clay,
> Seven years of troth have taught thee
> More than wifehood ever may!
>
> Love that never leaped its socket,
> Trust entrenched in narrow pain,
> Constancy through fire awarded,
> Anguish bare of anodyne,
>
> Burden borne so far triumphant
> None suspect me of the crown.
> For I wear the thorns till sunset,
> Then my diadem put on.
>
> Big my secret, but it's bandaged,
> It will never get away
> Till the day its weary keeper
> Leads it through the grave to thee.

Of course these poems are not cries for help. Indeed, I regard them as expressions of almost embarrassingly healthy minds. The most shocking element in Dickinson's poem is not her adulterous but unconsummated love, but her comparison of herself to Jesus. Her confidence that her crown of thorns will be exchanged for a diadem in the afterlife gives evidence of an ego that is at least robust. But there is a defiant recognition, too, that not only her love but her pride is socially unacceptable. This is a poem that by its very nature cannot be made public while the poet is alive, for that would be certain to "disarrange a wife's affection" and probably put several other noses out of joint, too.

Poetry of Health

My own view is the opposite of Plato's. I think good poetry can only come from healthy minds, from balance of intelligence and feeling rather than from extremes of either. Seriously disturbed artists have, of course, produced great work, but I think that is the power of the life force burning through their derangement. Just as we are more likely to encounter heroism under conditions of stress, so may health burn more brightly when it is threatened by serious illness. To take an extreme case, I think a lesser person, a less healthy person than Sylvia Plath, might well have succumbed earlier to the forces that finally drove her to suicide, or a less healthy person might have developed some kind of zombie indifference that would enable her to survive on few cylinders. But it seems to me a fatal confusion to think she was great because she was sick. She was great in spite of that, and no doubt would have produced great cultural monuments instead of feverish lyrics had she been better able to cope with her torment.

And in may cases society is, indeed, crazier than the poet. The family experience of that woman at the workshop is the stuff of tragedy; it had reverberations like those of Creon's condemnation of Antigone, of Lear's exile of Cordelia. But aside from the question of whether she had the ability to use that material in magnificent creation, the sick society in which she lives forces her into a life of hypocrisy. Even her cryptic little poems, poor as they were, provided some means of healthy rebellion, some means of maintaining dignity. They come from and express health.

As these examples have suggested, poets are often isolated individuals surrounded by indifference, insensitivity, and ignorance, and their coded poetry is a way of speaking past those immediately around them to the scattered few, alive now or in ages to come, who may read and say Yes, I know. That's how it is for me also.

The first of my *Rumors of Change* opens with these lines:

> You are a member. (This message scrambles when grey people try to read it.) You are a member (you intersection in the network, capsule in the streams of change).
> We are the agents
>   locking
> eyes a silent instant, moving on.
> It is important we know we belong . . .

And my prediction has been confirmed. I have actually seen those whom I would call grey people read those lines and not understand a word, as though I were writing in code.

But the poem, indeed the whole series (and I might suggest, all poetry), is postulated on the assumption that the "members" will understand—that is, those of us who are members of one another. In a sense this assumption *is* crazy, suggesting a kind of mystic union which can never be verified. But to me it seems like health, as I tried to tell a society that was trying to cure me in another of the "Rumors":

THE THERAPEUTIC STATE

Doctor, I hear voices.
                    Tell me what
they seem to say.
                    Doctor, this is real.
Tell me how it seems.
                    I dream of tunnels,
walls of petal. Doctor, I am wading
in feathers.
            What kind of feathers?
                                    Black, and the air
is music.
        What kind of music?
                            Whale.
                                    You think
that you hear whales?
                    Not hear so much as feel
blunt throbbing of penetration, hemispheres
of brain knitting along their edges, glow
of lava, squeal of glacial scrape, the sear
of stars, the salt of flesh. Just listen, Doctor,
how rootlets munch the minerals in your veins.

And do you often have these dreams?
                                    Doctor,
I never wake, I only dream of waking.
And you are a disappearing smile in the air.
I can no longer hear, no longer read
the lines on your diploma. You are me
absorbed like sunlight in my balmy cure.

Even what seem our perishability and tragic isolation seem to me conditions of health. I believe that the freedom poetry gives us to explore the secret reaches of our hearts is in itself better therapy than the fashionable efforts of professionals to help us adjust to tomorrow:

PSYCHOLOGY TODAY

My belly joined the Belly Potential Movement.
My brain took est. My left eye last was seen
swimming with Swami Riva. My right was Rolfed.

I'm actualized, if you know what I mean,
transcending, getting ready for the future,
fulfilled with helium, unstressed, piecemeal.

My organs drift asunder above the circus,
each bulbous with capacity to feel—
eastward the nose and south the probing tongue,

each toe afloat and powdered like a clown,
aurora borealis genitalia
higher than acupuncture can bring down.

Why then this aching? Surely not my soul—
for none was found when all was picked apart.
And, strings all cut, who would expect such throbbing

from one gland left on earth—my leaden heart?

CHAPTER IX:
THE
IMPORTANCE
OF
YOU

Reading a poem can seem a little like picking up a phone and over-hearing an ongoing conversation. Who's talking to whom? And what, if anything, does it have to do with you? Whether or not you go on listening depends very much on your subconscious responses to those questions.

Notice that there are at least three parties involved. I'm going to assign them labels, which I will use in discussing poems:

I —the voice of the person speaking.

Y —for "you," the person presumably addressed.

R —for "reader," in this case the person listening in, of whom both **I** and **Y** are apparently unaware.

The people engaged in that conversation probably have no script, but when we read a poem, we know that still another person is involved:

P— for "poet," the one who wrote the words **I** is speaking, which are heard by **Y** and **R.**

This is the simplest of the various situations you will encounter in a poem. Let's look at a seventeenth-century poem by Richard Lovelace to see how it works:

TO LUCASTA, GOING TO THE WARRES

Tell me not (Sweet) I am unkinde.
  That from the Nunnerie
Of thy chaste breast, and quiet minde,
  To Warre and Armes I flie.

> True; a new Mistresse now I chase,
>   The first Foe in the Field;
> And with a stronger Faith imbrace
>   A Sword, a Horse, a Shield.
>
> Yet this Inconstancy is such,
>   As you too shall adore;
> I could not love thee (Deare) so much,
>   Lov'd I not Honour more.

The first question we might ask is whether **I** and **P** are the same person. Is the voice of the poem the real Richard Lovelace? Is he speaking to a real woman? In most poems you can never be sure, and it doesn't matter. Lovelace indeed went to several wars and had several mistresses to whom he might have had occasion to say farewell. His Lucasta poems were addressed to his betrothed, Lucy Sacheverell. But Lucy (believing Richard had been killed in battle) had married another man before the poet, in prison, prepared the poems for publication. You see, the facts of his life don't really affect our interpretation.

The poem is a valediction, a farewell—a conventional genre such as might be found in the Greek or Roman classics. Moreover, Lucasta is a name borrowed from Latin poetry. And since the soldier is talking about swords and shields instead of firearms, we think of him as a warrior of classical times. This tells us something about the poet's deeper intention. He wrote an English poem modeled on ancient literature. As such it is a "set piece," as when a painter chooses to do a still life of fruit, flowers, and a bottle of wine—an interpretation of a familiar subject offered to invite deliberate comparison with the classics.

And whatever the truth about Lucy, the Lucasta in the poem is fictitious. However, we can deduce a few things about her. He addresses her as "Sweet" and "Deare." He implies that their love is unconsummated ("chaste"). (The word "mistress" did not imply a carnal relationship in the seventeenth century.) She's his sweetheart or perhaps his intended. And she's capable of being jealous of the war that takes him from her.

But we don't know if she's blond or brunette, twenty-eight or eighteen, rich or poor, illiterate or educated—and none of that matters. She's an archetype who provides the poem with an organizing focus. She need not be characterized in greater detail because it seems obvious this is a heroic, martial, patriotic poem disguised as an intimate romantic scene. A real Lucasta, handed this poem in manuscript on scented paper, might respond, "Bug off, buster, I know what you'll be chasing in France." As a real man, the poet may not have been nearly so heroic as the **I** in this poem. And as a reader in the 1980s, I think the values expressed here are questionable: That kind of macho rationalization of honor has gotten civilization into a peck of trouble.

But as one who appreciates literature, and as a fellow poet, I value it as fiction—powerful, simple, yet with penetrating intellectual irony and exquisite lyric grace. I enjoy it as a little dramatic scene, with this swashbuckling bewigged gallant delicately kissing the fingertips of a perfumed beauty in lace and a hooped skirt. Accepting it as fiction, I am stirred by its eloquence and undisturbed by its ideological implications.

Now let's review what happened. The poet, **P**, wanted to present his cultivated contemporaries with an English version of a Classical theme. He did this by creating a little drama in which a fictitious warrior, **I**, takes leave of a fictitious maiden, **Y**. That's when I, Jud, picked up the phone and became **R** (the reader). All along **P** the poet knew, or at least hoped, that various people would eavesdrop on the intimate little scene he was creating, though I'm sure he never dreamed how many million **R**'s—readers—there would be over the next three hundred years. So **P** is really speaking to **R**, skillfully manipulating the fiction to engage attention and communicate—not so much the "message" about honor as his aesthetic values, his sense of what makes an enduring, beautiful set-piece.

Take One from Column A . . .

As I said, Lovelace's poem illustrates only the simplest of the strategies you can use. Consider the situation in this one of mine, which is more complex, but still relatively simple. One October I was looking out of my study, watching my son play with the dog in a six-inch stand of new winter rye. His birthday was coming up, so I was able to give him this:

FOR TOPHER AT ELEVEN

Like winter rye, you're pushing high
  cleanly, in tender rush,
and I look on in cautious joy
  with love that makes you blush.

Your spears of innocence stand keen,
  gleaming in autumn dew,
as though the frost and hardening soil
  were meaningless to you.

Sap pulses through your limber stem
as, pumping, unaware
you suck from matted, reaching roots
    as delicate as hair

and drink the lean abundance of
    antique October's sun
and suck in earthy chemicals
    that make your juices run.

While morning moisture blows away
    you point into your noon
and stand all night responsive to
    the bulging harvest moon,

flashing your feather blades that cut
    their way into the air.
The edge of Now is all you know—
    inexhaustibly rare.

As one behind a window watching
    foliage flame and fall,
warming his backside at the fire,
    his spirit growing small

in readiness for ice to come,
    I govern flesh with reason
while you spurt forth in naked green
    defiance of the season.

Your lips now turn from my dry kiss
    and your mind from what I know.
Hardest in autumn love is this:
    the gift of letting go.

Is I talking to Y here? Not really. Though the poem is nominally addressed to Topher, the language is more appropriate for an aging man's musing to himself. It doesn't sound like speech at all, but reflective thought. Topher, then, doesn't function as Y in quite the way Lucasta did. He provides a focus for the poem, but the real Y in this poem is also I. The man is talking to himself.

And I think any reader would sense that there is less fiction in this poem than in "To Lucasta." Though P and I are identical, it is, nonetheless, somewhat like a drama. On stage a man is giving a kind of soliloquy, though his words seem to be addressed to his son, whom he sees playing outside in high grass. Behind the footlights you, **R,** are sitting in the dark theater among all the other strangers listening in.

As a poet, though I was writing a personal, family poem, I was inescapably aware that there would eventually be other readers outside the family. You, dear **R,** might have more to do with the way the poem was written than did my eleven-year-old son, who probably didn't fully understand it at the time I gave it to him. In a sense, my gift to him was to write the best poem I could reflecting my feelings and our situation, whether or not it immediately made sense to him. (Incidentally, I didn't send that poem out to magazines. Some years after writing it I included it in my collected poems, its first publication, but I considered it too personal to be of much interest to a wide contemporary audience. It was meant for Topher and my immediate family and for a much broader audience even than **R.** It was written for **A,** the ages, the ultimate **R.**)

The two poems so far considered happen to use direct address as a device. That heightens drama. Suppose "To Lucasta" had been written *about* her instead of *to* her, the poet saying, in effect, "My mistress shouldn't tell me I'm unkind, because I couldn't love her half so much . . . ." It would have been a relatively flat poem. Moreover, it might raise questions the poet didn't want raised. "Who is this guy talking to?" we might ask. "Why is he telling someone else how his own girlfriend should feel?" But for other poems direct address might not be the most appropriate mode.

These poems also happened to be from a single speaker to a single listener, but **I** can be "we" (as in Francis Scott Key's "The Star-Spangled Banner"), and, obviously, more than one person might be addressed. You can see that there is a considerable variety of possible structures even for poems of direct address, depending upon whether the parties involved are fictitious or real, singular or plural, defined or undefined. For example, imagine a poem in which the speaker is an imaginary black woman addressing the actual Congress of the United States, or one in which we (very real) grey-headed men address the mythical goddess Venus, or one in which "we" an undefined mass of humanity address a typical (but fictitious) bag lady in the New York slums. A poem could be designed for each of the six varieties of speakers in the left-hand column below to address each of the six varieties of person in the right-hand column, a total of thirty-six categories. Can you dream up examples for the other thirty three?

Speakers	Persons Addressed
Singular, real I	Singular, real You
Singular, fictitious I	Singular, fictitious You
Singular, undefined I	Singular, undefined You
Real We	Plural, real You
Fictitious We	Plural, fictitious You
Undefined We	Plural, undefined You

Remember that these are only for poems of direct address. A straight narration, in which an omniscient narrator tells a story to unspecified readers, or other possible modes of poetry, aren't included.

Furthermore, that graph leaves out **P** and **R**, not to mention **A**, and, as we've seen, each of these can have a complicated relationship to the poem. It begins to sound like algebra when I say that in my poem to Topher, **P** spoke through **I** to **I** himself, right past **Y** and even **R** in hope of reaching **A**. But such complexities make for interesting poetry. You can use the whole range of possible strategies to create a structure appropriate for your aesthetic and philosophical intentions. The point is not so much to say outright, to an individual or group or to the world, what's on your mind. Rather, you use what you want to say in a work of art that can stand on its own, whether or not a reader happens to agree with your "message."

Look, now, at some of your own poems. Do they tell us who is speaking to whom? On what occasion? What has just happened or is about to happen? What does the speaker want as a response from the person addressed? You won't always be able to answer these questions. And sometimes setting, time, or the identity of the parties involved may not be important to the poem. But you might ask yourself in each case whether the poem would be fresher, more immediate, more dramatic, if there were some Lucasta or Topher implied—some fictional ears to hear the words, some implied play for the audience to witness and become involved with.

Friends, Romans, Countrymen . . .

When **Y** is plural, the poet may adopt the stance of public address. The reader is expected to imagine the poet mounting a platform and speaking to a crowd. One of the greatest and most materially successful poems in American literature does just that: Edwin Markham's "The Man with the Hoe," which, after it was first published in the *San Francisco Examiner* in 1899, was reprinted in newspapers all over the world and is said to have earned the poet more than $250,000 during his lifetime.

The subtitle, "Written after seeing Millet's world-famous painting," provides a kind of setting. Perhaps the speaker has been to a museum and begun his contemplation as he felt the powerful impact of the painting before him. The first words simply describe the painting, words addressed to no one in particular:

> Bowed by the weight of centuries he leans
> Upon his hoe and gazes on the ground,
> The emptiness of ages in his face,
> And on his back the burden of the world.

But the next line, and much of the rest of the poem, is in the form of rhetorical questions, implying direct address:

> Who made him dead to rapture and despair,
> A thing that grieves not and that never hopes,
> Stolid and stunned, a brother to the ox?
> Who loosened and let down this brutal jaw?
> Whose was the hand that slanted back this brow?
> Whose breath blew out the light within his brain?

To whom is the poet talking? The language and manner of the poem are those of the platform, the formal eloquence and grand impersonal phrasing that might ring through an auditorium. There is none of the intimacy here that the speaker in Lovelace's poem directed to Lucasta. Now the fictitious audience is massive and impersonal. We may imagine sweeping theatrical gestures behind the lectern under the gaslight glare.

And though the speaker in the poem seems to be addressing the public in general throughout most of the poem, at the end he directs his questions to specific people:

> O masters, lords and rulers in all lands,
> Is this the handiwork you give to God,
> This monstrous thing distorted and soul-quenched?

The finger now points out of the auditorium. After all, the masters, lords and rulers of all lands aren't sitting there with us—or even reading (and certainly not heeding) this radical protest poem. But still it warns them that in time the man with hoe and his male and female counterparts around the globe will rise up in revolution and strike down the powers of the state:

How answer his brute question in that hour
When whirlwinds of rebellion shake all shores?

This challenge to the rulers is in the form of another conventional rhetorical question. We can imagine the end of the poem followed by thunderous applause. The rulers would certainly not be applauding. And if the poem works as intended, we are united in opposition to those rulers. We're supposed to get up now, leave the auditorium, go out and organize resistance to them.

Such platform oratory in poetry seems dated. It reminds me of chautauquas (I have read about, not experienced), those programs of education, persuasion, and entertainment that traveling performers carried to rural settlements around the turn of the century. The chautauquas declined when radio and movies made a more intimate "fireside" mode of public communication the norm. It's ironic that though Lovelace's poem was written over two hundred years before Markham's, it seems more modern. We're accustomed now to the pretense that poems are intimate, personal messages (even when we know they aren't). I think we lost a great resource with the passing of the declamatory style in poetry, but you'd not be likely to have much success if you were to send a poem like Markham's to a modern publisher.

Soapbox in the Bedroom

Matthew Arnold's "Dover Beach" is an interesting blend of the intimate and declamatory:

The sea is calm to-night.
The tide is full, the moon lies fair
Upon the straits—on the French coast, the light
Gleams, and is gone; the cliffs of England stand,
Glimmering and vast, out in the tranquil bay.

So far we have no idea of who's talking to whom, but the setting is concrete. The I is in a specific place at a specific time describing a specific theme. Then a new character, Y, enters. I has to be talking to someone here:

Come to the window, sweet is the night-air!

Now we know the speaker is indoors with another person. We don't know who that is, but he's probably not talking to a business associate or butler about the sweet night air. It sounds like a romantic relationship. If we know the poet is man, we tend to assume that the **I** in the poem is also, and therefore it would be natural to think of **Y** as "she."

First he describes in lush lines the sound of the sea pouring on the strand and its roaring withdrawal. The tone of this first strophe is intimate, though hardly erotic (a tone we might expect in what turns out, nominally, to be a love poem).

In the second and third strophes the **I** takes a rather schoolmasterish approach, lecturing **Y** on what Sophocles thought when he heard the sea and discussing in grand, general terms the tidal withdrawal of the Sea of Faith from beaches round the world. In these strophes the tone is eloquent and declamatory, language more appropriate to the auditorium than to the parlor or bedroom. The fourth then brings these tonalities passionately, dramatically together:

> Ah, love, let us be true
> To one another! for the world, which seems
> To lie before us like a land of dreams,
> So various, so beautiful, so new,
> Hath really neither joy, nor love, nor light,
> Nor certitude, nor peace, nor help for pain;
> And we are here as on a darkling plain
> Swept with confused alarms of struggle and flight,
> Where ignorant armies clash by night.

At last we find out that she is his love. Truth between them is essential because all public faith seems empty and illusory.

As in the case of "To Lucasta," the poet uses a fictitious romantic relationship as a device to deal with a general, abstract issue. (Arnold spent two or three days at Dover on his honeymoon in 1851, and he may have written the poem then to his new wife, but, as in regard to Lovelace, the biographical details have little to do with an interpretation of the poem.) The poet says that as religious faith declines, personal relationships—based on faith in one another—become desperately important. What a topic to be discussing with a lady on a romantic moonlit night above the cliffs of Dover! If I were Arnold's "love," I don't believe this poem would move me to much romantic passion. Rather, it might evoke admiration and general thought. Nonetheless, the poem works powerfully, a perfect blend of the intimate and declamatory styles.

To Whom Am I Speaking

Consider the whole range of possibilities as you design the strategy of any given poem. Should the reader feel like a member of an audience in an auditorium? Like someone overhearing a conversation? Witnessing a private meeting? Reading someone else's mail? Or can you imagine other desired reactions? Sometimes poets address the reader directly, as I am addressing you right now. But remember that few people appreciate being lectured to, scolded, threatened, or instructed, nor do they appreciate too much familiarity from a stranger who can't even know whom he's addressing. If you give readers a fictitious setting and characters, they can fairly easily accept the convention that almost anything might be said in the course of the drama. The guise of a love poem, especially, can be used to say all manner of things, as does this one of mine, which has very little to do with love:

SCATTERSHOT

Never believe them: Receive my words, my dear,
as the world seals up man's campsite scar, as air
accepts the air age, as time endures its clocks.

I speak as a pouting child throws aimless rocks,
as a dog snarls at a wheel. My bullets flare
from a soldier raking the jungle night—for fear.

That poem is a general comment on the difference between the literal meaning of hostile words and their emotional source and intent. "My dear," **Y**, is no more than a device to provide an occasion for emotional intensity.

In one series of twenty-five of my poems, *Instructions for Acting*, the **I** is a director telling actors how to act. Of course, as the ambiguous title of the series suggests, the poems are actually as much about life as theater. The opening poem conveys that intention:

IMPROVISATION

We have no prompter for this show. In fact,
I have never seen a script, although, of course,
all surely know the general story line.
It gripped us young, continues to intrigue
in spite of its familiarity.
A kind of dazzle from the kleig glare makes
us unaware, performing, of the fact

that no one sits out there in the dark house.
No intermission follows any act.
No gun fires blanks. We laugh at our own jokes.
Although not many of us have studied lines
and almost none is very strong or wise,
the show goes on. The curtain already has risen.
Fear silence. Look alert. And improvise.

There is no defined Y in that poem, though the first person plurals (*we*, *us*) and the imperatives in the last line imply listeners, presumably the cast of a play, addressed by the director.

I intended to probe the relationship of illusion and reality, discovering how they interpenetrate. Often the poems leap right into the midst of an ongoing scene. Suppose that an actor is trying to pretend he is drunk by moving clumsily, and the director interrupts:

DRUNK SCENE

No, don't act drunk. No drunk acts drunk except
when soberly he wants to hug the world
like sun-warmed laundry off the line and blindly
tumble—or else he's young and thinks it's smart.
We drinkers stand much straighter than we can.

A tinkle tells us when we tilt too far.
We talk like alum-eaters, listen like
lip-reading lovers, hiccup man to man.
Our insight blurs our gaiety. We think
our underwater vista, wobbly, blue,

is somehow truer than landscapes of air.
We reconfirm the facts with each new drink.
As children play at seriousness, we are
more sober, drunk, than we know how to be.
Our life is acting, speaking lines we learned

uncaring, but, the curtain up, we *care*.
Just play the scene as though you cared too much,
as though the wall might shift beneath your hand
(which walls, you know, may sometimes do). Just play
at holding something you can never touch.

Sometimes I invented specific actors to receive the instructions. Here, for instance, the director tells Sally how to play a scene in a play, but he tells her even more about lust:

SALLY GIVES IN GRACEFULLY

Now scratching at the window, Sally, comes
your demon lover. Gather at the throat
your sheer white flowing gown. Your fingers fanned

at your lips, your shimmering hair undone, you float
to the casement and unlatch the shutter. Drums
trip at your temples; burning eyes expand

as Henry nimbly vaults across the sill.
A glance around the room, and he pulls you to him,
your spine bending. Your hands, like captured birds,

struggle around the face which snaps its fill
from mouth, cheeks, neck and shoulders. Still no words
as he darkly drives you to the bed and down.

No cries for help, for, after all, you drew him,
as petals ask for digging of the bee.
Accept his scalding crush—though fearfully.

Curtain—as Henry flings aside your gown.
Relax—they have done it this way time out of mind:
same set, same costume, no props of any kind.

And, having invented Henry, I gave him a tragic role to play to conclude the series:

NIGHTCAP

Peel off your beard, cream all the pancake off
before the mirror in your dressing room. The face
emerging slowly is more weary than
that of the king you played—who died. With half
your life gone, Henry, you are living
each evening one foreshortened life: Such pace
is murderous. That king, night after night,
drags down the sky upon his head. Your head
must throb as you lie dead beneath his crown.

I saw you back of the flats, waiting a cue.
A girl was taking stitches in your robe.
Your lips rehearsed your lines. Suddenly you
were on: The wasp buzzed nobly in the web,
but the web wound. Not once have you broken through.

How white you seem in the mirror now, a greasy towel
protecting your velvet doublet, your sleeves shoved back.
We wonder together how men bear up under
their artificial crowns, their final acts,
the poets blast of thunder, life condensed
(which is hard enough to take, God knows, dispensed
a minute at a time). Oh, art is a way
of making a living—sacrifice of kings
to charm the corn. We get what we are giving—
a nightly murder, life day after day.
Illusion, actor, sweetens as it sours.
Let's have a drink. It was a hard two hours.

I learned the value of starting a poem in the midst of ongoing action from John Donne, who often began his poems with dramatic, intimate direct address. Donne usually pretends to be speaking to a mistress or God. The tactic of beginning with an assumption of intimacy opens up possibilities of colloquial language, irony (the difference between what the speaker is saying and what the reader knows he means), wit, and intense emotion—qualities that might be hard to take or hard to understand if there were no explicit **Y** serving as a buffer between **I** and **R**. Donne was especially clever at sexual *double entendre*. He could make even his prayers sound like appeals to or wrangles with a lover, the constant sexual metaphor serving as a paradigm for all spiritual and personal union. Study of such poets will show you many ways to extend your repertory of techniques.

Though there are many very effective ways of setting up interesting relationships among the various parties involved in a poem from **I** to **A**, there is one wrong way for certain. If you seem unaware of who might be talking to whom and what it all has to do with a reader, the poem may become just a grey blur of words, words, words. We wonder, *Why go on reading?* A poem meant for no one is likely to find itself with exactly that audience.

Who's Talking?

We have considered the importance of the person or persons addressed in a poem, but what about the person speaking? Many who start writing poems don't realize how essential it is to draw a reader in by creating the sense of an engaging voice. After all, people don't usually read poems for information. Journalists, who *do* communicate information, use a "hook" to draw the reader in, some device or startling fact to grab interest. But in poems the most powerful hook is the personality of the speaker. The reader immediately, though subconsciously, begins evaluating the voice of the poem in order to decide whether he wants to listen to this person. As a poet, you have to anticipate this response by creating a voice people will want or be compelled to listen to.

One of the best ways to study this effect is by examining the openings of successful poems. Taking publication in a good anthology of modern poetry as a measure of success, I will choose a few poems at random and comment on the I. The first one I open to starts:

> I have met them at the close of day
> Coming with vivid faces
> From counter or desk among grey
> Eighteenth-century houses.
> I have passed with a nod of the head
> Or polite meaningless words,
> Or have lingered awhile and said
> Polite meaningless words.

Do you want to go on? What kind of person seems to be speaking? For one thing you know he is relaxed, informal—and somewhat self-deprecating, as he insists in a repeated phrase that his conversation on the street is polite and meaningless. Who are these people he calls "them"? You don't yet know, but you sense both his identification with them and a certain discomfort. On one hand, he knows where they work and live and he greets them in a friendly manner. On the other hand, he doesn't seem to know quite what to say.

Most readers can identify with such ambiguous feelings. I, for one, am drawn in. The easy, familiar diction, the casual, almost careless rhymes, the unabashed repetition, all these qualities of the poem develop an impression of a forthright and unpretentious personality. I'd like to know him better. I'll hear him out.

Those lines are from "Easter, 1916," by W.B. Yeats. It's an elegy for heroes of Ireland killed in the Easter Rising of the IRA in 1916, ordinary men, in Yeats's view, transformed by their dedication to the cause of rebellion. A lesser poet, attempting to write a memorial for patriotic fighters in what he regards as a noble cause, might have opened with drums and brass, pomp and circumstance, attempting to whip a reader into a frenzy of admiration for his heroes and indignation toward the enemy.

But Yeats chose almost to slouch onstage, deliberately placing the momentous among the ordinary. He invites us to see him as a fallible, uncertain man on the street. Just as his whole point is that from rather ordinary men, transformed by the political events of the time, "a terrible beauty was born," so from casual, everyday observations and speech, the poem rises to its terrible beauty, a much more effective strategy than promising readers a great deal with blare and banners and then disappointing them with platitudes.

Let's look at another opening. So you won't form any preconceptions, I'll wait to tell you the poet and title later. This one, like Yeats's poem, uses informality, repetition, unpretentiousness:

> A snake came to my water-trough
> On a hot, hot day, and I in pyjamas for the heat,
> to drink there.

The sentence structure is rather sloppy—perhaps an effort to make a prosaic description sound more like poetry. That's the beginning of "Snake," by D.H. Lawrence. Again and again in modern poems you will find that kind of easygoing narrator. For example, the next poem I open to starts:

> Once I am sure there's nothing going on
> I step inside, letting the door thud shut.
> Another church: matting, seats, and stone,
> And little books; sprawlings of flowers, cut
> For Sunday, brownish now; . . .

The tone is comfortable, almost chatty. Readers can identify with the speaker. We know the feeling of being curious about the interior of a church, but hesitant to enter until we know there is no ceremony under way. The phrase "thud shut" tells us as much about the speaker as about the sound of the door. He is willing to smile a little at himself and the scene. And one hears almost a note of sadness in his observation that the flowers are "sprawlings" and "brownish now" (here in midweek). That's Philip Larkin's "Church Going." Read it—and notice how that tone contributes to the total meaning and power of the poem.

In each of these random choices a person introduced himself as a rather likable, relaxed speaker. We have no idea, of course, whether Yeats, Lawrence, or Larkin was really such a nice guy. Who cares? The principle was recognized in classical rhetoric: The speaker is advised to portray himself as a common, approachable person. It is a literary device as appropriate to poetry as to advertising or political persuasion.

As we've seen, the most common technique for holding an audience is to present a "sympathetic" speaker, but another is to hold interest by creating a character who may be limited, obnoxious, pretentious, or insensitive. Such a speaker is called a persona, someone whom the poet wants us to see round, like a figure in a play. The intention may be to satirize the persona or reveal him as a villain. In other poems, such as Tennyson's "Ulysses," he may be admirable, even heroic. Such poems are called dramatic monologues. "The Love Song of J. Alfred Prufrock," discussed in the introduction, is an example, as is my "Instructions for Acting," in which the "director" is clearly a different personage from the poet. But even in dramatic monologues, the reader is aware of an affable, reasonable sensibility behind the fictitious character—the P backstage, behind the wings. No reader is likely to give his attention—except defensively—to a poet who seems alien, repulsive, or indifferent to the reader.

Many poems don't have an explicit **I**, but we know the words come from somewhere, and we're bound to make some assessment of the sensibility that generated them. The language of this opening seems objective and removed, the speaker faceless:

> Let me tell you a little story
> About Miss Edith Gee;
> She lived in Clevedon Terrace
> At Number 83.
>
> She'd a slight squint in her left eye,
> Her lips were thin and small,
> She had narrow sloping shoulders
> And she had no bust at all.

The colloquial style (notice the periphrastic "they" in line 6) and modern reference tell us the poet is of our time, though he is obviously imitating folk ballads. We know we may expect clarity, simplicity, a bit of humor, realism. Though an **I** never emerges in this long poem (W.H. Auden, "Let Me Tell You a Little Story"), the poet has clearly established a voice—to which that ironic "little" is a key. It is a voice of wry understatement with a cutting edge.

By contrast here is the beginning of another apparently impersonal poem:

> Clear water in a brilliant bowl
> Pink and white carnations. The light
> In the room more like a snowy air,
> Reflecting snow. A newly-fallen snow
> At the end of a winter when afternoons return.

These aren't even sentences—simply fragments of observation. What sort of person is speaking? Notice how he dwells on "snowy" and "snow," three times in two lines. Is the cadence that of a speaker trying to be very precise, to get it just right, coming at the idea again and again? Or is it just careless writing? There does seem to be a preciousness, a delicacy about the observations, a kind of passivity, as though the speaker were letting the details quietly sink in, attempting to capture an image of perfection, an exact moment at that season when the days are lengthening. But there isn't enough characterization of the speaker to enable us to be sure whether or not this was what the poet was trying to suggest.

This poem (Wallace Stevens's "The Poems of Our Climate") doesn't invite me to go on reading. These lines are too precious, static, too much absorbed in refinement. There seems to be some kind of snobbishness or assumed superiority in the tone. I find myself bored, thinking, "I don't know what you're getting at, but you're taking a long time doing it, and I have just so much patience for pretty-pretty pictures."

I think this example illustrates that it's better to make it clear who is speaking when you are conveying subjective impressions. (Notice how Auden, though he also doesn't characterize his speaker, avoids the problem of dangling, free-floating observations by using the recognizable voice of an omniscient narrator.) Stevens's point is to contrast external perfection with human need of disorder, as implied (the poem later says) by the "concealed / The evilly compounded, vital I." Maybe he meant the objective details, rendered without an I to observe them, as perfection; and he later brings in his evil self, with his need of disorder. But a poem that begins in hanging clauses and static observations unattached to any speaker is very nearly born dead. Had I not known it was written by a great poet, I probably wouldn't have read on, and that's a mighty poor reason for reading anything.

The Persona

Whatever judgment you make as a reader, notice that you *do* judge (though you may not be aware of it as you read). You can be sure that people are similarly unconsciously judging the sort of person whose voice they discern in your poems. It may seem manipulative to create the voice of a nice guy, but if you come across in your poems as boring, sentimental, preachy, dogmatic, trite, humorless, verbose, or obscure, there's no great virtue in simply being yourself.

In fact, when a poem gives the impression of those unpleasant qualities, it is usually not the result of honesty at all, but of ineptitude. When I have pointed out to poets how they sounded in their poems, they were often embarrassed. They weren't at all the kind of person the poem implied. But they didn't *listen* to their own poems. They didn't ask themselves how they would react to the same words spoken by another person. They may have imagined they were being spontaneous, presenting their unmasked selves, but they were misrepresenting and undervaluing themselves. They had better intentions than they had skill to carry out.

A tangle of self-consciousness results from the paradox of trying to achieve a natural impression of your own personality artificially. You can avoid that if you think of the speaker of the poem as a persona—a term I defined earlier as an invented speaker. Since the **I** is there in the poem, whether you mean it to be or not, make the most of it, treating it with the same care you would any other element of technique. Don't think of it as yourself but as a kind of thread running through the poem and holding it together. It's good exercise to make the speaker someone quite distinct from yourself—perhaps someone hateful, stupid, or pompous. Satirize that persona all you please. You'll be more careful if you are vividly aware that you don't want the reader to confuse the speaker with the poet. But remember that somehow you have to enable him to sense that there is an attractive, interesting, good-hearted, intelligent person in control of the material.

Here's an exercise in self-definition I had fun writing. The Peddler is doing everything he can to establish that he's a nice guy:

THE PEDDLER

I opened a stall in the market with many placards.
WISDOM I offered. Surely they need that
WIT NEW AND SECONDHAND for lighter moments.
FLATTERY should sell out in nothing flat.

HARD WORK I thought was something the world wanted.
HONESTY—spice for the discerning few.
DIPLOMACY for those with much to lose
For those with nothing I promised to be **TRUE**.

FACTS for skeptics, **FAITH** for mystics. **VISION**
for the undecided, also for the blind.
COMMITMENT for the serious, and for
the frivolous I had an **OPEN MIND**.

I had some **SKILL** and lots of **GOOD INTENTIONS**.
I knew **THE WAY**, but was **WILLING TO BE LED**.
I CAN BE HAD—a general sort of come-on.
Specifically, I added, **GOOD IN BED**.

IF YOU DON'T SEE HERE WHAT YOU WANT JUST ASK.
EVERYTHING MUST GO INCLUDING ME.
JUST MAKE AN OFFER. I scratched that out: **DON'T**
    BOTHER.
STOCK, SHOP AND ONE SHOPKEEPER ALL FOR FREE.

But all the traffic passed me by, attracted
to a scrawny fellow with a screechy yelp
and scrawly note pinned to his scrap of jacket
pitifully announcing **I NEED HELP.**

And then one day a gorgeous buxom maiden
pulled up in a Rolls. She'd found just what she sought.
She wheedled me with molten eyes of love.
"All I want," she said, "is everything you've got."

I hastily packed my cases, closed my shutters,
crouched by the counter, waited for darkness, to flee.
People aren't to be trusted—especially people
who show any interest in the likes of me.

The title tips you off that a persona is speaking. I hope you are aware of
P signaling from behind the Peddler, warning you that this clown is on
the wrong track entirely.

Starting Where You Are

Some people have difficulty managing the **I** in their poems because
they have gotten the idea that it is bad manners to write in the first person. My students have told me they were taught that in high school.
But their efforts to avoid the word "I" result in tangled structures,
weak passives, and a constant implication of evasiveness. When I
teach writing, I tell students to get that "I" in as soon as possible and
keep it up front—for *modesty's* sake. You can't tell us what is true, but
you can tell us what *you* believe, what you feel, what you have experienced.

And whether you mean it to be or not, the "I" is implied. No matter
what Myrtle Whimple writes about, she sticks out all over her poems.
What can you deduce about the person who wrote these lines (in the
American colonies in the seventeenth century)? Notice that no "I" is
expressed. The "he" in the first line is "man" in the generic sense; the
poem is about how "he" surveys human history and even prehistory:

Sometimes in Eden fair he seems to be,
  Sees glorious Adam there made lord of all,
Fancies the apple dangle on the tree
  That turned his sovereign to a naked thrall,
Who like a miscreant was driven from that place
To get his bread with pain and sweat of face—
A penalty imposed on his backsliding race.

Here sits our grandam in retired place,
  And in her lap her bloody Cain new born;
The weeping imp oft looks her in the face,
  Bewails his unknown hap and fate forlorn.
His mother sighs to think of paradise,
And how she lost her bliss to be more wise,
Believing him that was and is father of lies.

Now here's a test. Which do you think is the better of those two stanzas, and why? It may help you decide if you go back and circle the individual words that caused your interest to perk up (even a little: I grant the poetry isn't all that perky).

Let me guess. You circled words such as "apple, dangle, naked, bread, sweat, face, grandam, lap, bloody, imp." Whether or not our lists coincide, I bet there was one word on both your list and mine, and that if we had to pick the most striking word in both stanzas we would agree on "bloody."

That's a strong, almost sensational word, in any context, but it has a peculiar power here. The image seems to be of the baby unwashed, immediately after birth. Of course Cain committed a bloody act in later life, and the poet may have been alluding to that meaning here. But any reader is likely to be struck forcefully by the sense of experience in the words "In her lap her bloody Cain new born." What a way of focusing in on Eve! All the words above on my list convey a taste of life, but that line especially has the feel of intimate knowledge, making it stand out boldly from the rather grey words around it.

Are you surprised to learn that the poet was Anne Bradstreet, the earliest poet you will find in most anthologies of American poetry? Those two stanzas of her "Contemplations" illustrate to me that she knew a lot more about being a woman than about mankind in the abstract. And I think that were it not for the occasional flashes of definitively female consciousness, of emergence of individual self in her poems, we would not, three hundred years later, be reading Anne Bradstreet at all.

She knew what it was like to see an apple dangle, and she must have kneaded a lot of dough, getting bread by sweat of face. When she leaves her sometimes grandiose panorama of history and moves into family relationships, her sensibility comes fully alive. That word "grandam" has a comfortable humor about it, utterly lacking in "glorious Adam." Eve is put into a setting, a "retired place." And we are made to see her vividly, holding her bloody babe. There is nothing like that concreteness in the stanza on Adam. The poet is aware of the tragedy as well as the joy of birth, the dashed hope, pain, and dark foreboding that may accompany bringing children into an uncertain world. The word "imp" is affectionate and humorous, but it suggests that Mother is aware of the devil as of the angel in her child.

Unfortunately, Anne Bradstreet did not often write from her experience. She was phenomenally learned for a woman of her times, especially one living on a Massachusetts farm, but one unfortunate effect of her learning is to make her poems more literary and derivative than lively and fresh. Moreover, she could not suppress her Puritan distrust of art; she apparently sought to redeem poetry by making it endlessly instructive.

But the poems that are still anthologized are the exceptions. They are those in which, even if in fleeting moments, she expressed herself feelingly, concretely, as a woman. For example, most selections contain "Some Verses upon the Burning of Our House, July 10th, 1666." That poem's nine stanzas are, for the most part, a rather commonplace and tedious meditation on the theme of the vanity of earthly possessions. But her renunciation of material goods and joy in the wealth of God's love aren't nearly so convincing as her poignant, stunned imagining of life past in ashes present:

> When by the ruins oft I passed
> My sorrowing eyes aside did cast,
> And here and there the places spy
> Where oft I sat, and long did lie.

> Here stood that trunk, and there that chest;
> There lay that store I counted best;
> My pleasant things in ashes lie,
> And them behold no more than I.
> Under thy roof no guest shall sit,
> Nor at thy table eat a bit;

Do you feel the surge of life as the poem moves toward specificity? "Here stood that trunk, and there that chest." Compare that strong, moving line with the disappointing generality of "store" and "pleasant things." For three lines she drifts in abstraction, but the last two return to experience, her memory of serving guests, and the language is again concrete and charged with feeling, all the more so for the plainness of the words.

For me the remarkable quality of Anne Bradstreet's work is the way strong passages emerge in spite of her apparent efforts to repress them. No one taught her to be concrete, to express her personal feelings, to let her bare personality emerge, to believe that the details of her life were important enough to record. On the contrary, she must have assumed the opposite from the pious poetry she read: that she should leave herself out, teach upright living and sober tradition, be philosophical, abstract, and intellectual. But self kept emerging. Though most of her poems drone with piety and conformity, occasionally there erupts a flash of militant feminism, as in a poem praising Queen Elizabeth:

> Now say, have women worth? or have they none?
> Or had they some, but with our Queen is't gone?
> Nay Masculines, you have thus taxt us long.
> But she, though dead, will vindicate our wrong.
> Let such as say our Sex is void of Reason,
> Know tis Slander now, but once was Treason.

When she tells us where it really hurts or her lines warm with details of daily life (as of raising her "eight birds hatcht in one nest"), fresh observations of the countryside, or feminine insight into the anguish and love in family relationships, she prints her sensibility on the ages.

If you have learned anything from this discussion of Anne Bradstreet's poetry, what does it show you about your own work? Have you discovered the power and liberation of honestly saying "I"?

PART III:
INSIDE
THE
POEM

Now we can look more closely at the actual materials from which poems are made: words, phrases, sentences, and their arrangement into lines and larger units. Ezra Pound once said that poetry should be at least as well written as prose. That apparently simple statement comes as a surprise to many who think poetry might be their medium of expression. Somewhere they're gotten the idea that if you write in broken lines, the rules are suspended and anything goes.

At times it is, indeed, creative to confound a reader's expectations by using language in ways that defy convention. Poets, as we will see here, strain the conventions in every way they can. But creativity doesn't mean license. Unless a poet establishes a basis of understanding, firmly rooted in the principles of good writing, which apply equally to poetry and prose, there'll be no communication at all, and therefore no expectations to be confounded.

Since the advent of the Modernist movement, which made a wholesale onslaught on the conventions of Traditional poetry (see Chapter XV), that basis of communication has been severely undermined. Many people, frustrated by too many signals they couldn't interpret, have given up on poetry altogether. If we want to draw that audience back to our art, we will have to reexamine the very nature of our language to see how it works and what creative possibilities exist that are, indeed, fresh but that will strengthen rather than defy a reader's comprehension.

The intention of the Modernists in overthrowing convention was to increase the intensity of communication, and that goal is quite in keeping with the way good poetry functions. As I discussed in Chapter VII, poetry draws on more qualities of words than prose does, or draws on them to a greater degree. By arranging writing in lines a poet emphasizes the sound qualities, rhythm, suggestiveness, and dramatic force of language, with the result that more is communicated in fewer words.

This requires, in turn, a more intense, more sensitive response from the reader. John Ciardi once said that it's reasonable for a poem to require the kind of close attention one might give to a tough hand of bridge. But it's the poet's job to make sure his work evokes that kind of attention.

The poem, as the reader finds it, is lying there flat on the page. How can you, the writer, manage those words so they will stand up and take on the shape of a ghostly, multidimensional object in space? How can you wire them into the reader's nervous system so that he not only reads but *experiences* not merely words, but a living complex of meaning? That's the challenge—and it takes a lot of understanding of what words are and how they work to achieve it.

CHAPTER X:
THE ANATOMY OF ENGLISH

The phenomenal richness of English poetry arises from the unique blend of Germanic and Latinate elements in our language. Growing up with it, many of us don't realize what a curious amalgam of incompatible ingredients it is. The most obvious symptom of its chronic case of linguistic indigestion is English spelling, which outrages not only foreigners who try to learn it but our own schoolchildren. In other languages the written symbols more or less systematically represent sounds, but English spelling is likely to tell you more about the history of a word than how it is to be pronounced. Yet as a poet you learn to love it in spite of, or because of, all its warts. A language in which "though" rhymes with "blow" and "buff" with "tough" hath its own odd charms to soothe a savage breast.

In order to help you understand how the conglomeration of elements we call English got to be that way, I will take you through a little fantasy. Suppose our country were taken over by the Soviets. Suddenly we find Soviet officials in charge of the government offices, the industries, the institutions. Their conversation, correspondence, negotiations, contracts, rules, regulations—even their evening entertainment—is in Russian. They might translate into English some crude laws that apply to the rest of us, but for the most part we have to learn their language if we want to prosper.

That, after all, happened to the native Americans when English-speaking people conquered their land. The colonists and pioneers rarely bothered to learn the native tongues. They held the power. If the natives wanted to do business, it had to be in the language of the conquerers. In that case the native population was small, scattered over vast territory, and in itself was very diverse in both language and culture. Very rapidly English became the language of the main population centers, and the native American tongues disappeared into the wilderness.

Thus, if the Soviets were to conquer America now, the immediate effect would be linguistic layering. A relatively thin, but very powerful coating of Russian would float like oil on a vast reservoir of English water: We would simply be an English-speaking nation under Russian rule. But everything official, indeed everything published, would probably be in Russian. Nonetheless, if we were able to move ahead three hundred *more* years, English would still be the prevailing language. It wouldn't disappear the way the language of the native Americans did. Think how this might have happened. At first the Russians would have imported their culture, more or less as colonialists from Europe create little imitations of their home country in Africa or Southeast Asia. Perhaps adventurous sons of old Russian families would come over to make their fortune. But in time some might fall in love with American women, settle down, put in roots. They might even develop some fondness for the local culture, the folk songs and tales told by the natives in their ranch-style hovels.

After some years, without publication in the media, *pure* English would become largely an oral tradition, carried in the heads of elders and passed on in the home, as Yiddish still is by emigrant families of several generations past, though the young people speak English outside the home. But as the families of mixed Russian-English heritage became more established here, the -*ski*'s might drop off their names, and, indeed, intermarriage might bring many English names into positions of power alongside the Russian names.

At first the language appearing in print or in movies or even documents would show only traces of the subterranean language still spoken by the masses. But since the speakers of English would so vastly outnumber their conquerers, the basic structure of the language would persist, though the vocabulary, especially of words pertaining to state affairs, business, and higher society, might be heavily Russianized.

Many of the words in common use would now have Russian roots. The grammar might have changed. Spelling would have changed. Indeed, it would be a distinct language—let's call it Englussian, a language with identifiable strains of its separate English and Slavic origins. As Englussian developed greater and greater identity as a language of its own, it would be unintelligible back in the Soviet Union and to the older generations in the hills who still used English. In three hundred years most of the population would probably be able to trace only dimly, in genealogical studies, their connection with Russian heritage. (Place names would probably remain the same—just as we now retain native American words to name many of our states, cities, rivers, and mountains.)

Imagining those layers of language and culture intermingling to produce strange new combinations may help you understand some of the pecularities of what we call English today. The native Britons spoke Celtic. Romans conquered the British islands in the first century B.C., but they didn't integrate significantly with the native population, so they had little effect on the language. They built villas, walls, roads, cities, but they ruled the natives as the English later ruled Nigeria or as the Soviets might rule us in the first years of conquest.

In the mid-fifth century, however, long after Roman power had declined, tribes of Germans—Angles, Saxons, and Jutes—subdued the islands and imposed their own language, driving the Britons into Wales and Cumberland. (Modern Welsh is a Celtic language, derived from the language of those ancient Britons.) There was never any integration of the conquerers and conquered or of their languages. In the seventh and eighth centuries Latin-speaking Christian missionaries built monasteries and centers of learning, and Latin became, as for all of Europe in the Middle Ages, the language of scholarship and religion.

Furthermore, the priests began recording the native literature using the Roman alphabet (with a few additional letters from the ancient Runic alphabet), with the result that a specifically English literature flourished centuries before literature in the vernacular developed on the Continent. For some five hundred years a powerful and proud Germanic people held sway in what came to be called Engla land, the "land of the Angles," conducting their domestic life in their native tongue and relating to other nations in Latin. That's comparable to our situation before the Soviet invasion I asked you to imagine.

Now consider what effect all this had on poetry. The Anglo-Saxon period (as historians refer to it) occurred about the time that written poetry in the vernacular (that is, in native languages, other than Latin) was a relatively new phenomenon in Europe. As it happened, the Anglo-Saxons developed a rich culture with a very distinctive poetry far earlier than other European countries, largely because the Christian missionaries encouraged the development of their literature and transcribed it in an alphabet that could be widely read.

Though you cannot understand Old English, the language of the Anglo-Saxons, without special study, many words are recognizable.

Here is a passage from the Bible (Mark 12:1) as transcribed in Old English and translated into modern English by the linguistic scholar Morton W. Bloomfield:

> *Sum monn him plantode wingeard and betynde hine ond dealf anne seath and getimbrode anne stiepel and gesette hine mid eorthtilium and ferde on eltheodignesse.*
> *A certain man planted a vineyard for himself and enclosed it (him) and dug a pit and built a tower (steeple) and peopled (set) it (him) with farmers (earth-tillers) and went into a foreign country.*

Most of the words are recognizable if you use your imagination. For instance, *dealf = delved; ferde = fared.*

You may have studied, at least in translation, the epic *Beowulf,* the best known literary work in this language. The line of most Old English poetry was measured by four strong beats, divided by a central caesura (or pause), and linked by a careful pattern of alliteration. I imitated that form in this poem:

GRENDEL

Older than English: how evil emerges
on a moor in the moonlight, emotionless, faceless,
stiff-kneed, arms rigid, and stalks through the fog field
until finally its fist falls, forcing the oaken door
of whatever Heorot harbors the gentlefolk.

In the movies, a scientist, satanic, with a spark gap,
his power and intentions plainly dishonorable,
releases a monster with electronic instincts:
Hollywood's pronouncement on the nature of evil.
Whom shall we send for? How shall we meet it?

In dark times when warriors wassailed one another,
banged cups in the meadhall, then crumpled like heroes,
till Grendel (they called it) gobbled them, unwashed,
they stared in the daylight, dumbstruck, religious,
their hall all a shambles, their heads hurting,
and easily believed an evil wyrd
(generated in a fen not far from Heorot)
molested mankind. Such mornings we all have.

A blond boy, traveller, Beowulf, bear-boy,
sparing of word hoard, spunky at swimming,
arrived like justice (riding Old Paint),

had to be wakened to harry the hairy one,
grappled in darkness, grunted and clung
and unstrung the monster, as one masters a toy
by mangling the machinery. Men of the warrior-breed
approach the irrational rippling their muscles,
relying on wrestling to reckon with angels.

Grendel in our time goes by a new name:
Old Mushroom Head, the Mighty Bomb,
nightly distilled from seeping chemicals
in coils of our brain bed, composite monster
fashioned of guilt and our most fearful urges.
Blame it on physics: Feign that evil
is external, inhuman! We turn to our warriors,
hating all Science, harboring our mead dreams
hating intelligence, terrorized by instinct.

Send me no bear-boys when the brute crashes oak doors.
Although he goes howling, holding the socket,
bleeding and armless, back to his mother,
Grendel defeats us who fail of reason.
As the movies will tell us, tatters of bullets
rip Grendel's chest as rain rips a snowbank,
yet he comes plodding, impassive, stiff-necked.
Feeling cannot save us: Sober must we meet him.

For practice you might want to locate the caesura, or medial pause, in each line, then the two stresses on each side of it. The initial consonant *sound* (regardless of spelling) of the first stressed syllable after the caesura is the same as the sound that begins either the first or second stressed syllable before the caesura. All vowel sounds are regarded as alliterating with one another. I'll repeat the first lines with the initial sound of each beat in boldface caps and the caesuras marked:

Older than English: // how Evil eMerges
On a Moor in the Moonlight, // eMotionless, Faceless,
Stiff-kneed, arms Rigid, // and Stalks through the Fog field
until Finally its Fist falls, // Forcing the Oaken door
of Whatever Heorot // Harbors the Gentlefolk.

It is a pounding, emphatic form, well adapted to the chunky rhythms of the Germanic language, and it was used for a wide range of heroic and religious poems.

But Anglo-Saxon culture almost disappeared after the Norman invasion of 1066, the event corresponding to the Soviet invasion in our fantasy. The French-speaking Norman conquerers (who were related to the Vikings) became the new courtiers, businessmen, officials, and theirs were the wealthy and privileged families.

For some three hundred years the Norman kingdom spanned the Channel, with much traffic back and forth, but the Normans eventually lost their holdings on the mainland. Imagine our Soviet invaders being cut off from their mother country. They would go native, as the Normans did. And, as a result, instead of the language being a French layer on an English base, a new language, which modern scholars have called Middle English, emerged, and with it a new literature and new style of poetry. The colloquial language of the court in Chaucer's era—1350-1400—was more English than French, though with a decided coloring of Latinate influence, both from Latin and from French (which, of course, is a Romance—that is, a Romanish—language).

You can probably read much Middle English, though you wouldn't be sure how to pronounce it without special study. In Chaucer's day the dialects of Middle English (spoken in various parts of the island) were rather distinct from one another (as, indeed, they are today: There is a stronger dialectical variation within the small area of Britain than you will find throughout the United States). The language of the hinterlands differed from London English as Huck Finn's differed from Aunt Sally's—or from the language Twain spoke in cultivated conversation. We can see the difference when we compare a relatively folksy poem of Chaucer's time with Chaucer's own more courtly London dialect. Here is the opening of an anonymous poem of the period, "Alisoun,"

> Bitwene Mersh and Averil,
>   When spray biginneth to springe,
> The lutel fowl hath hire wil
>   On hire lud to singe.
>   Ich libbe in love-longinge
> For semlokest of alle thinge;
> He may be blisse bringe:
>   Ich am in hir baundoun.

In modern English that might be rendered:

Between March and April, when sprays [of flowers] are beginning to spring, the little bird has her delight in singing in her own language. I live in love-longing for the fairest of all things. She may bring me happiness: I am in her power.

The word *lud* is interesting. It seems to be a form of *leden*, which meant "Latin" and, from that, "language," "speech," "talk," and in this case the song of a bird. Note that "he" means "she," singulars mean plurals. Grammar obviously hadn't settled down. And you see words that look very German (*ich* for I), others that look very French (*baundoun*), while others seem to be confusing mixtures.

Chaucer also wrote about springtime in lines you may have had to memorize in school, the opening of the "Prologue" to *The Canterbury Tales:*

> Whan that Aprille with his shoures soote
> The droghte of March hath perced to the roote,
> And bathed every veyne in swich licour
> Of which vertu engendred is the flour;
> Whan Zephirus eek with his sweet breeth
> Inspired hath in every holt and heeth
> The tendre croppes, and the yonge sonne
> Hath in the Ram his halve cours yronne,
> And smale fowles maken melodye,
> That slepen al the night with open ye
> (So priketh him nature in her corages);
> Thanne longen folk to goon on pilgrimages.

Literally translated, that's (approximately):

> *When April with its sweet showers has pierced to the root the drought of March, and bathed every vein in such liquor of which power the flower is engendered, when Zephyr [the west wind] also, with his sweet breath, has breathed upon the tender crops in every plantation and meadow, and the young sun has run half his course through [the sign of] the Ram, and small birds which have slept all night with eyes open make melodies—so has nature roused them in their hearts—then folk long to go on pilgrimages.*

In some respects Chaucer is further from modern English than the more rural dialects, for his language is more Frenchified, more characteristic of the fashonable upper crust, than of enduring folk idiom.

But Chaucer created what became standard English prosody. I want to render a few lines of that passage phonetically, with caps to indicate accents, so you can sense the music of his verse. If you know any

Romance language, you will recognize that the vowels have their "continental" values: *ah, ey, ee, oh, oo* for *a, e, i, o, u,* and doubling them doesn't change their sound (except to lengthen it):

> Whan that Aprille with his shoures soote
> *WHAN thaht AHP-reel WEETH heese SHOO-ruhs SOHT-a*

> The droghte of March hath perced to the roote,
> *they DROHKT ohf MAHRCH hahth PEYR-sud TOH they ROHT-a*

> And bathed every veyne in swich licour
> *ahnd BAHTH-ud EYV-eyr-ee VEYN een SWEESH lee-COOR*

> Of which vertu engendred is the flour;
> *ohf WHEESH veyr-TOO eyn-GEYHD-rehd EES they FLURE*

Scholars will quibble (as, indeed, they do among themselves) with that representation of the pronunciation, but it will give you the general idea. Strange as the sounds may seem (in comparison to the way those words are pronounced today), I think you can probably hear in the phonetic rendering the basic verse form you are familiar with in poetry from Shakespeare to Frost.

Double Talk

The upshot of our foregoing discussion is that we are, in effect, bilingual, though we call both languages English. In Latin class I learned this saying, "Persons residing in crystalline structures should refrain from capitulating lapidary fragments," Latinate English for "People who live in glass houses shouldn't throw stones." Or try singing this:

> Propel, propel, propel your vessel
> Placidly down the liquid solution!
> Ecstatically, ecstatically,
>   ecstatically, ecstatically,
> Existence is but an illusion!

Similarly, you can find two ways to say almost anything, one way using words of Latin origin (which most likely came to us through French) and the other using words of Anglo-Saxon origin. The importance of this phenomenon for poets can be illustrated by these lists:

sweat	perspiration
spit	expectorate
house	residence

love	affection
food	nutrition
light	illumination

How many more can you think of? Obviously, the Germanic words on the left are those we ordinarily use in common speech (or parlance). Those on the right we associate with more formal, intellectual discourse (in Germanic that's stuffy, brainy talk). There are a far greater number of Latinate than Germanic words in our language, but the Germanic ones are more common. They're more quotidian, you see.

There is a strong built-in class bias in the distinction. One of the reasons that "Anglo-Saxon four-letter words" are in such ill favor is that they are used by common folk who are likely not even to know, much less use, such polite substitutes as "copulate," "defecate," and "urinate." That illustrates how censorship and standards of propriety function as instruments of social control, the means by which a dominant social class maintains its linguistic grip. The very poor (who have no hope of rising above their station) or very rich (and consequently unthreatened) and very literate (who are quite aware of the relativity of standards of usage) are likely to be less intimidated by these linguistic restrictions. All of these implications are important to poets, whose use of the language must be as sensitive as possible.

Predictably, those most concerned about standards of propriety and elegance of vocabulary are those with most to gain by conforming to the expectations of the powerful. A stock comic figure is the preacher whose speech is sprinkled with highfalutin vocabulary (including malapropisms)—usually one whose ministry is to the poor or the lower middle class. Or remember the Duke and the Dauphin in *Huckleberry Finn*, con men plying little frontier and river towns with little to offer but a carpetbag full of misused polysyllables.

I hope that by now you have a feeling for which words in English are of Germanic, or Saxon, derivation and which are Latinate. If you have ever studied French, Spanish, or Italian, you probably recognize the Latinate words as those having cognates in Romance languages. If you haven't studied one of these languages, you surely recognize the rather formal words—for example, nouns ending in -*ion* or verbs ending in -*ate*—which are characteristically Latinate. If in doubt, consult the etymologies given in any good dictionary. It's a distinction to which every writer should be sensitive. For example, we should recognize why legal documents, including the laws of the land, medical books, business contracts, and most other writing that communicates power and professional knowledge, are written in a language so Latinate that it is almost unintelligible to ordinary readers. Scientific prose uses terms derived from Latin and Greek almost exclusively. That helps international communication, but it also makes it seem almost a cult language, as of a priesthood, which puts its interpretation of Truth above nationality. The fancier words of social intercourse in English are often still traceable to their French roots; and, indeed, French itself, on menus or mixed with English in conversation, still carries a connotation of upper-class elegance.

But we should remember that the lifeblood of English is still, for all readers, its basic Germanic vocabulary. Latinate words in poetry at times seem precious, cold, removed—and sometimes humorous. Imagine a love poem using language like this: "Object of my affection, our relationship causes me to experience cardiac fibrillations and irregularity of respiration!" But some poets use occasional Latinate words with uncanny power. Here's a stanza from Emily Dickinson:

> The reticent volcano keeps
> His never slumbering plan—
> Confided are his projects pink
> To no precarious man.

The Latinate words "reticent," "confided," "projects," and "precarious" (not to mention "volcano") are strikingly used, twinkling with Emily's ironic wit. They are jewels, but notice how firmly they are set among hearty Germanic words: "keeps," "plan," "pink," and "man." The somewhat longer and rarer word "slumbering" is also Saxon in derivation—and notice that it seems more humorous than formal. And, of course, most of the "business" words of our language, such as *the, his, never, are, to,* are Saxon.

Poets have to be fluent in both branches of our language—indeed, in many of its dialects and other byways as well. But we shouldn't lose the throb of its Germanic pulse. Three hundred years after that Soviet conquest I asked you to imagine, "perspiration" might be replaced by some Russianized synonym. But we poet folks will still be sweating.

Of Horses and Carts

The blending of Germanic and Latinate elements into one language had as profound an effect on grammar as it had on vocabulary. Both the Germanic languages and those derived from Latin are heavily inflected languages. (Inflections are changes in form which make differences in meaning.) If you have ever studied Latin, German, or any of the Romance languages, you probably groaned under the necessity of learning all sorts of declensions and conjugations which have no counterpart in English. Old English had four main declensions of nouns, and several minor ones, each declension having separate forms for nominative, genitive, accusative, and dative cases, strong and weak verbs in three moods (indicative, imperative, subjunctive), and, of course, singulars and plurals of all these (and, for a while, a third number, a "dual," used when two people were referred to or addressed, as distinct from one or three or more, but this mercifully died out). Latin had an even more impressive array of inflected forms (with, for example, six cases for each declension of nouns), and though there were fewer inflections in French than in Latin, there were still more than we have in modern English.

You can imagine what happened when these rivers ran together. First there was a lot of muddy confusion, then most inflections disappeared altogether. The words of English have remarkably few forms compared to those of most languages of the world. Watch what happens to the word "cool" in these sentences:

> **Cool** my beer.
> Is the beer **cooled**?
> You **cooled** it yesterday.
> Beer **cools** quickly.
> It's **cooling** now.
> Have a **cool** beer.
> Is your beer **cooler** than mine?
> His is **coolest**.
> She **coolly** picked up her purse and left.
> I work in the **cool** of the morning.
> But I don't like those morning **cools**.
> The **cool's** dew gets my feet wet.
> She went to Arizona to avoid those **cools'** dews.

That will give you an idea of the flexibility and simplicity of our language. The same word can serve as a noun, verb, adjective, or adverb. As a verb it has four forms: *cool, cools, cooled, cooling*. As a noun it also has four: *cool, cools, cool's, cools'* (but the last three are all pronounced alike). As an adjective, three: *cool, cooler, coolest*. And as an adverb, one: *coolly*. That demonstrates almost the full range of inflections in English. We have some irregular plurals (*children, men, sheep,* etc.), some irregular verbs (which also happen to be the most common ones), such as *give, gave, given*. And we have a large number of pronouns with different forms to indicate gender and number: *he, him, his, she, her, they, them, their, theirs, who, whose, whom,* etc. But most changes in meaning of English words are indicated by context—the way the words are used in sentences.

How does that affect our writing? One factor of crucial importance in poetry is word order. The more highly inflected a language is, the more flexible can be the sequence of words in a sentence. It doesn't matter whether you say "Brutus necavit Caesarem," "Caesarem necavit Brutus," "Necavit Brutus Caesarem," or any other order of the three words, you're still saying Brutus killed Caesar in Latin. But try that in English! One can imagine contexts in which "inversions" might be intelligible: "Whom did Brutus kill? Caesar Brutus killed. Brutus killed whom? Brutus *Caesar* killed," and so on, but they are awkward and not very clear. English and, I've been told, Chinese are unusual languages in that they are almost totally dependent upon word order for meaning. And since we have a less flexible word order than most other languages, fixed forms (such as the villanelle) are more difficult, which is to say more challenging.

The second factor that is supremely important in conveying meaning in English is stress. The following sentences all mean slightly different things:

I don't want too much money.
I **DON'T** want too much money.
I don't **WANT** too much money.
I don't want **TOO** much money.
I don't want too **MUCH** money.
I don't want too much **MONEY.**

A difference in stress can totally change a word from a verb to a noun: We ob*ject* to an *obj*ect. In other languages such subtle shadings in emphasis or changes in meaning are much more likely to be made by rephrasing, using different words, adding additional syllables or words, or rearranging word order. But stress is the soul of the English language, and poets must be especially sensitive to it.

For one thing it provides the basic measure of the line. We saw that the Old English line was characterized by four pounding stresses. Measurement by stress was to become a central feature of later English prosody. The lines of French and Italian poetry, for instance, are measured by syllable count, stress being relatively unimportant. However, when Chaucer began writing his Frenchified English poems, often in imitation of French or Italian forms, a decasyllabic (ten syllable) line became, in practice, a five-*beat* line. Since stresses usually alternate with unstressed syllables, the lines were likely also to have ten syllables, but because stress was the basic factor, he was free to drop or add an unstressed syllable here and there. (Can you find examples of both of these variations in the lines quoted above from the "Prologue" to *The Canterbury Tales?*)

Because we have few inflections, fewer English words have identical endings, which makes it a greater challenge to find rhymes. Moreover, because of the peculiar spelling resulting from the melding of languages, English rhymes are inherently more interesting; they seem subtler and less mechanical. We have a variety of ways of constructing words with various prefixes and suffixes, each with a slight difference of nuance, as in such a cluster as *doubtful, dubious, doubtfulness, dubiousness, dubeity, doubt, dubiosity, dubitation, dubitable, dubitative,* not to mention *doubtless, indubitably,* etc.

Still another characteristic of English that resulted from the blending of languages is a vastly enriched vocabulary. There are simply more words in English than in any other language, and new words are easily added. Some are made up from existing words, and others are borrowed from other languages. We freely use words for various parts of speech, with minor adaptations.

For example, Bikini is a little Pacific island where atomic bombs were tested in 1946. Designers borrowed the name for a skimpy bathing suit that had an "atomic" impact on viewers (perhaps they were also referring to the tiny size of the atoll). We can easily imagine a bikinied girl (using the word as a verb) or a bikini pattern of untanned skin (using it as an adjective). You would know what I meant if I said a girl was dressed bikinily (using it as an adverb). At our house we play a poker game called bikini (high-low crisscross with middle card and all like it wild), notable for explosions at the end. And I can imagine all sorts of poetic applications:

> The telephone with lighted dial
> Stared with a stark bikini smile.

The possibilities are limitless!

Plain and Fancy

Poets are bound to stretch the limits of the language every way they can, but you do well to start from a solid base, a good understanding of the peculiarities of your language and their implications for good writing. In this respect I was interested in a list of "20 Rules for Good Writing" published by the Writer's Digest School. They were intended primarily for writers of prose, but they contain some useful reminders for all of us:

1. Prefer the plain word to the fancy.
2. Prefer the familiar word to the unfamiliar.
3. Prefer the Saxon (i.e., Germanic) word to the Romance (i.e., Latinate).
4. Prefer nouns and verbs to adjectives and adverbs.
5. Prefer picture nouns and action verbs.
6. Never use a long word when a short one will do as well.
7. Master the simple declarative sentence.
8. Prefer the simple sentence to the complicated.
9. Vary your sentence length.
10. Put the words you want to emphasize at the beginning or end of your sentence.
11. Use the active voice.
12. Put statements in a positive form.
13. Use short paragraphs.
14. Cut needless words, sentences, and paragraphs.
15. Use plain, conversational language. Write like you talk.
16. Avoid imitation. Write in your natural style.
17. Write clearly.
18. Avoid gobbledygook and jargon.
19. Write to be understood, not to impress.
20. Revise and rewrite. Improvement is always possible.

I am amused by #15. Grammarians instruct us to say "Write *as* you talk"—those same grammarians who were outraged by the advertising slogan "Winston tastes good like a cigarette should." They tell us that "like" is a preposition, not a conjunction. That is, it can be used to introduce a noun, pronoun, or gerund ("like a charm," "like me," "like talking") but not a clause in which a verb is expressed, like the second sentence in #15. If the verb is unexpressed ("I slept like a log"), it is acceptable to most of our guardians of purity; but if you put in the verb ("I slept like a log sleeps"), you should use "as" instead. Or so they say.

But it's a schoolmarmish distinction, and it serves as an example of how skeptically you must regard such pronouncements. "Like" is used as a conjunction not only in everyday speech but in good literature (and not only when speech is represented). Here are some examples quoted in *Webster's New Collegiate Dictionary:* John Keats, "they raven down scenery like children do sweetmeats"; Norman Mailer, "middle-aged men who looked like they might be out for their one night of the year."

So I am glad to see that whoever wrote those "20 Rules" practiced what he preached: He wrote like he talked. Nonetheless, given the prejudice of the grammarians, I probably wouldn't use "like" as a conjunction, especially in a poem, unless I were deliberately representing colloquial speech. I realize that what might be called "Editorial English," a dialect never spoken but fiercely enforced in publishing houses, often takes precedence over common usage.

One limitation of the "20 Rules" is that our "plain, conversational language" is likely to be very trite, dull, and vapid. Turn on a tape recorder sometime when a casual conversation is going on, then try transcribing it. You'll probably get mostly *ah*s and *uh*s and colorless, lifeless, repetitive, inexact, vague, and general language, exactly the sort of thing an editor would strike out (see rule #14).

Nonetheless, rule #15 is a good one if properly understood. Learning to write means unlearning a lot we were taught in school. Poets should discover their own idiom, find, isolate, and preserve those hard nuggets of conversational language that are as much a part of them as their posture and voice register. This is especially true for those of you who were brought up speaking a rural or an ethnic dialect: We need your influence in expanding the range of our literature, especially now, when a homogenizing mood seems to have settled over editorial offices.

That's because a prejudice has developed against dialect verse, the kind that used to be most popular in the United States (written by James Whitcomb Riley, Eugene Field, Edgar Guest, and many others). Such dialect verse fell out of favor as a reaction to racial and class stereotyping, the sort of thing that used to be popular in minstrel shows, ethnic jokes, and that sustained movie stars like the comedian Step'n Fetchit, who let himself be used as a gross characterization of a lazy, ignorant, cowardly (but delightfully sly) black.

Though some correction of linguistic stereotyping was in order, it can be carried too far. Where would English literature have been without its rich tapestry of Cockney, Yorkshire, and other dialects? Robert Burns wrote in both conventional English and his Scottish dialect. His English poems are dreadful, and they have been mercifully forgotten, while his dialect poems remain a revered part of our literature. Not only black writers such as Langston Hughes but also many white writers have used Negro dialect to great effect. Unfortunately, the tales of Uncle Remus (by the white writer Joel Chandler Harris) would probably not be published if written today, and modern publishers would surely deny us what is probably the greatest American novel, *Huckleberry Finn*, for reasons I will discuss in Chapter XV.

As I say, poets are bound to try the limits, which is what I was doing in this poem protesting prejudicial limits to my use of language:

TINKIN BOUT DE DOG

You wanna know why I look dis way? You wanna *know?* Well Baby I ain givin you
my full attention, das why. I got my
mine on de dog.
     You don know what I mean?
Jus spose you had dis dog. Now I don gotta
dog, *you* don gotta dog, but spose you did.
An here you was, dis guy you really groove on,
you gettin air, *get*tin air, when you hear dis howl.
You *know* dat howl—like the voice of de man you love.
Dat was *your* dog. Why she howl? She hurt? She scared?
She fine some fella down de block and she
pleasured? She *pleas*ured? Ooh.
      Well, *you* don know,
and dat guy don know *nuth*in bout no dog.
His mine strickly on his monkey.
       Why,
he ask, you got dat funny look? And why
is cause yo mine is on de dog.
       Now ize
distracted, tinking *poet*ry. You say
some somepin bout dose melodies unheard.
You got me tinking Keats. He *here*, he coughin
blood on dese sheets, he in dis *bed*.
      Who *Keats?*
How you say melodies unheard you don know Keats?
You dint in*vent* it. Maybe you heard it an
forgot, but you dint make it *up*.
      But what
I was sayin was, you come on wit dis poetry
shit an my mine jus drifs away like steam
from a pipe, jus like I heard my dog howl. You
holing a limber carrot in yo han.
Baby, when you use words flashed from de tunder,
you gonna have me tinkin bout de dog.

 Ah, this is a poem I'm not allowed to write,
 its melody unheard because I'm white.

Though the language may be stereotyped, the characters and the subject of conversation are not. But I think the poem demonstrates above all just what it says: that it doesn't work to flout convention too broadly.

A subtler stretching of the possibilities of language and defiance of expectations can be seen in Robert Frost's way of capturing the exact flavor of speech, including its vague, ungrammatical, and awkward characteristics, and somehow lifting it whole into poetry. One of his finest poems, "Directive," begins with the line "Back out of all this now too much for us." It is almost impossible to paraphrase, though I think its meaning is clear enough. He is talking about escaping from the world, which has become too much for us, by going back in time, back into the hills, to find the site of a house, now no more than "a belilaced cellar hole." (How about the word "belilaced"—surrounded by, decorated by lilacs—for an example of the possibility of fluent linguistic invention in English?) But, to return to that haunting opening, one is reminded of Pope's comment about bad poetry, "And ten low words oft creep in one dull line." Astonishingly, Frost's line *isn't* dull. It dramatizes the confusion and exasperation we need to escape, just in the way we might put it when too wearied and frayed to be precise. (Compare this with the discussion of Wordsworth's "The world is too much with us, late and soon," in Chapter XII.) And the poem takes us to a kind of communion, with cold brook water and a goblet ("like the Grail") from a children's playhouse. There we may "Drink and be whole again beyond confusion."

In this case it's not regional or ethnic dialect, but ordinary informal American speech, that he has captured. If a poet listens to the common speech about him with a sharp ear and selects those truly distinctive, pungent phrases that convey thought, insight, meaning, humor, these can be the material of poetry. The other day I heard a woman say quite casually, "I can tell up from down—when the sun's out." That's a line of poetry I'd like to use someday.

Those rules urging common, plain speech upon us are valid and helpful, though they aren't always the best guidelines for poetry. It depends on what you want to do. Milton seemed never to use a plain word when he could find a fancy one, or a Germanic word when he could find a Latinate equivalent. Who but Milton could refer to "the maculate giraffe?" I don't know that the word "maculate" was ever used elsewhere in English, but we can figure out what it means from "immaculate," which means "unspotted." A maculate giraffe has spots! Yet Milton was often most powerful when most simple, as in his description of Adam and Eve leaving Paradise:

The World was all before them, where to choose
Thir place of rest, and Providence thir guide:
They hand in hand with wandring steps and slow,
Through *Eden* took their solitarie way.

The words in that passage are mostly Germanic (what the "Rules" call Saxon) and conversational. Would you believe that some critic with a grammarian's mind objected to the use of the word "solitarie" here. *How could they be solitary,* he asked, *when there were two of them?*

At best anyone's "rules" provide only a general guide. Once you can write effectively and clearly, you will be better able to follow inspiration when it surges in directions no rules can prepare you for. In Pope's poem that I quoted earlier, "An Essay on Criticism," such moments are described:

. . . Pegasus, a nearer way to take,
May boldly deviate from the common track.
From vulgar bounds with brave disorder part,
And snatch a grace beyond the reach of art

"Art," as Pope uses the term here, means "artifice" or "craft." He illustrates deviation with the very word "deviate," which throws a radical (for Pope) variation into the meter. Also the off rhyme of "take" and "track" is quite outside Pope's normal practice. He does indeed snatch a grace beyond the reach of his normal regularity, and it works because his verse is overall sufficiently regular to make the variations significant. Otherwise, they would emerge as no more than sloppiness.

At various times in my career I have thought of Eve as the quintessential poet (and Adam as the quintessential scientist). In this poem she discovers imagination as a form of rebellion against the tyranny of language.

EVE: NIGHT THOUGHTS

okay so the wheel bit was a grinding bore
and fire a risk in the cave never mind the dogs
he brings home and cows and I can endure
his knocking rocks for sparks and rolling logs
it's his words that get on my nerves his incessant naming
of every bird or bug or plant his odd
smirk as he commits a syllable taming
Nature with categories as though the Word were God

okay so statements were bad enough
and accusations crossing spoiling digestion
but then he invented the laugh
next day he invented the question
I see it he's busy building a verbal fence
surrounding life and me but already I
counterplot I'll make a poem of his sense
by night as he dreams I am inventing the lie

Language is perhaps the greatest gift of our human heritage, but as poets we mustn't let it become our destiny. It's such a powerful force of conditioning that it can begin to govern, not merely express, our thoughts and feelings. I agree with Eve. We have to learn to lie our way out of it.

CHAPTER XI:
PROSE
POETRY
AND
PROETRY

I have a proposition that might save much of the Canadian forests. It would save not only paper but postage. Literary journals could be mailed first-class in their new reduced size. Yet these lightweight journals could print more poets, more poetry, than ever before. You might get your collected works—in perfectly readable type—into a slim pamphlet.

This revelation came to me as Sandy read poems to me from a poetry magazine that had just arrived. She liked several that she read, and so did I, but since she didn't particularly emphasize line breaks, and I was lying back on the bed and couldn't see the page, I heard the poems as little paragraphs. Why shouldn't they be printed that way? At a rough guess, that would reduce the size of the magazine from twenty-eight to four pages!

Of course, this wasn't an original idea. The form I am suggesting originated in the early nineteenth century when the French poets Aloysius Bertrand and Maurice de Guérin began publishing poems in prose. The *Princeton Enclyclopedia of Poetry and Poetics* describes it thus:

PROSE POEM (poem in prose). *A composition able to have any or all features of the lyric, except it is put on the page—though not conceived of—as prose. It differs from poetic prose in that it is short and compact, from free verse in that it has no line breaks, from a short prose passage in that it has, usually, more pronounced rhythm, sonorous effects, imagery, and density of expression. It may contain even inner rhyme and metrical runs. Its length, generally, is from half a page (one or two paragraphs) to three or four pages, i.e., that of the average lyrical poem. If it is any longer, the ten-*

*sions and impact are forfeited, and it becomes—more or less poetic—prose.
The term "prose poem" has been applied irresponsibly to anything from the
Bible to a novel by Faulkner, but should be used only to designate a highly
conscious (sometimes even self-conscious) artform.*

Charles Baudelaire popularized prose poetry and Arthur Rimbaud
used it for his major work. The *Encyclopedia* says that from Rimbaud
and Stéphane Mallarmé

> *. . .direct paths lead to such important literary phenomena as free verse,
> the stream of consciousness, surrealism, James Joyce, and, indeed, modern
> literature's emphasis on private metaphor and* mélange de genres. *. . .
> By the end of the 19th c. the p.p. is firmly established, and even to list its
> major European and Am. practitioners would be impossible here.*

Prose poems turn up regularly in the literary magazines today, but
so far as I can remember the last use of the form for a major work in this
country was Karl Shapiro's *The Bourgeois Poet* (1964). Here is a sample
prose poem from that book:

> *Lower the standard: that's my motto. Somebody is always putting the food
> out of reach. We're tired of falling off ladders. Who says a child can't paint?
> A pro is somebody who does it for money. Lower the standards. Let's all
> play poetry. Down with ideals, flags, convention buttons, morals, the
> scrambled eggs on the admiral's hat. I'm talking sense. Lower the stan-
> dards. Sabotage the stylistic approach. Let weeds grow in the subdivision.
> Putty up the incisions in the library facade, those names that frighten
> grade-school teachers, those names whose U's are cut like V's. Burn the*
> Syntopicon *and* The Harvard Classics. *Lower the standard on classics,
> battleships, Russian ballet, national anthems (but they're low enough).
> Break through to the bottom. Be natural as an American abroad who knows
> no language, not even American. Keelhaul the poets in the vestry chairs.
> Renovate the Abbey of cold-storage dreamers. Get off the Culture Wagon.
> Learn how to walk the way you want. Slump your shoulders, stick your
> belly out, arms all over the table. How many generations will this take?
> Don't think about it, just make a start. (You have made a start.) Don't
> break anything you can step around, but don't pick it up. The law of
> gravity is the law of art. You first, poetry second, the good, the beautiful,
> the true come last. As the lad said: We must love one another or die.*

The rebellious spirit of that poem—in both form and content—obviously reflects the mood of the sixties, of *Howl* and *Hair*.

But, then, all important literary innovations stem from rebellion. As the *Encyclopedia* indicates, prose poetry began in the nineteenth century as a protest against the strictures of the French Academy. The metrical requirements for poetry had become so precious and confining that poets began turning to prose, writing novels, imitation translations (that is, original works that the author claims to have translated from another tongue), and other works that were poetry except for their avoidance of line breaks. (James Macpherson's *Ossian* is probably the best-known example for readers of English.) The modern counterpart of the French Academy, then, is the Culture Wagon Shapiro refers to: the literary Establishment, the New York Boston publishing axis, and the professor-poets who head the committees and award the prizes.

He had good reason to rebel. The literary climate created by the Establishment can be stultifying. But it's a shame that with our growing ecological awareness the rebellion isn't extended to include an effort to stop wasting paper. My point about saving space isn't facetious. Imagine how much would be used if Shapiro's poem were in free verse—such as this:

> Lower the standard: that's
> my motto. Somebody is always putting
> the food out
> of reach. We're tired of
> falling
>   off
>   ladders
> Who says . . .

and so on. It would take pages. Shapiro was full of his subject. He had a lot to say—and packed it in. One might ask, Why didn't he write an essay? Well, for one thing, he has written many—essay after essay, book after book, carrying this essential message; and, for another, the writing gains enormous intensity from its prose-poem form. It wouldn't pass as prose, anyway. It lacks the connectives, the transitions, the logical development an essay would require. It is rhythmic, forceful, fresh, and rich with wordplay and imagery. (Incidentally, many of the other selections in *The Bourgeois Poet* are, in my judgment, better poems, but I chose this one for its relevance to the subject of this chapter.)

I imagine there are many poets with a lot to say who are simply frustrated by their line breaks and by space requirements of magazines which make it difficult to get a poem of over twenty lines published.

How much can they say in twenty short lines? Perhaps they should follow Shapiro's example.

Invading the Left Brain

There is always something to rebel against. I'll suggest one influence to which poets might give more attention: advertising. For years I
have been trying to understand the popularity and prevalence of free
verse, and it occurs to me that it may be a subconscious imitation of advertising. If so, poets might well consider rejecting that model. Advertising copy, like poetry, is composed line by line, with much attention
to visual impact, juxtaposition, compactness, sensationalism, forceful-
ness, suggestiveness, and bypassing of logic. Just as we worry about
kids being conditioned in their choice of breakfast foods by the boob
tube, we should worry about poets unconsciously slipping into the
mode of copywriters. It would be natural—indeed, almost inescap-
able—that we be influenced by all the advertising we are exposed to,
and perhaps we should make a greater effort to resist. If we forgo the
dramatic effect of line breaks, perhaps we will put more emphasis on
other techniques and qualities of good poetry.

You do it. I don't want to write prose poetry. I don't want to write
advertising copy, either. I don't even want to lower the standards,
though I am as exasperated as Shapiro with the literary Establishment.
I'll stick to metered poetry and wish, vainly, that other poets would either do the same or write prose poems. The problem, as I see it, is that
the Establishment has already lowered standards about as far as they
can go—much further than those for national anthems—by fostering a
spirit of "anything goes" in poetic form and content.

Am I exaggerating? To check myself I opened at random a copy of
one of the major Establishment journals, *The American Poetry Review*, to
new work by one of the major Establishment poets, James Dickey (also
author of *Deliverance,* a highly successful novel and motion picture).
Now, Dickey is a good ol' Georgia boy who can talk English as plain as
the next fella, but these days he writes like this:

> Roots out of the ground and on-going
> The way we are, some of them—
> Spokes earth-slats a raft made of humped planks
> Slung down and that's right: wired together
> By the horizon: it's what *these* roads
> Are going through: fatal roads,
> No encounters, the hacked grass burning with battle song—

That's the opening of a poem called "Craters—with Michel Leiris." There's no way of telling who Michel Leiris is or what "with" means in that title, but it hardly matters, for the poem obviously wasn't meant to be read anyway—just published, chewing up the forests of Canada. It is arrogantly incomprehensible in both form and content. Many in the literary world accept such journals as *APR* as arbiters of taste, assuming that knowledgeable and responsible editors have exercised some judgment in deciding what to print, but judging by this random example, what the editors are really interested in publishing is the *name* of James Dickey, and they'll use any nonsense to which Dickey attaches that name. If printed as a prose poem, those lines would at least take up less space.

Though such poetry dulls all our sensibilities, if free verse poets switched to prose poetry, they might be able to invade the left side of the brain. By now most readers are familiar with the discovery that the two halves of our brain respond differently to stimuli. The left brain (which controls the right hand) is associated with logical, rational, connected thought. But the right side of the brain is more responsive to aesthetic and emotional effects. Good poetry, of course, speaks to both sides of the brain, since in part it is coherent, logical communication and in part it is aesthetic enhancement of that core of meaning.

Line breaks announce that a piece of writing is intended as art. Hence they are an invitation to the reader or listener to turn on the right brain. But for many readers poetic lines may also be an invitation to turn *off* the left brain—to follow the advice I once heard a professsor give his wife: "Don't think, honey; just react." Unfortunately, so much unintelligible poetry has been published, such as those lines by Dickey, many no longer expect poetry to make sense. Prose poetry might be a way of reawakening their sleeping left brains.

The effect of poetry on the two sides of the brain was discussed in an important article in the August 1983 issue of *Poetry*, "The Neural Lyre: Poetic Meter, the Brain, and Time," by Frederick Turner and Ernst Poppel. I hope you'll look it up in the library, as it explains in great detail (much too complex to summarize here) what has been learned about human cognition as it relates to poetry. The authors make a scientific case for the value of metered poetry and the culturally destructive effect of free verse. They establish that in all cultures and languages, throughout history, the poetic line has consisted of a unit that averages about three seconds in duration. The evidence they offer from a comparative study of poetry in a wide variety of languages is related to physiological facts about how we discriminate sounds and process auditory information. We can receive only about ten to twelve syllables (each taking about .3 seconds) before our brains cut off for a microsecond while the information is relayed to the memory.

For that reason the three-second line is emphatic and memorable—something our prehistoric ancestors all over the world intuitively understood. The authors further argue that metered poetry—that is, poetry with a fairly regular rhythmical pattern in those three-second lines—speaks simultaneously to both halves of the brain, thus involving the whole consciousness in response. Other aesthetic characteristics of poetry, such as emotion, imagery, sonority, and repetition, reinforce the poem's aesthetic communication (to the right brain), but above all, it is the regular pulse of meter that creates that stereophonic effect. Using terms of information theory, the authors explain that meter sets up a "carrier wave" or constant medium of communication like the band of a radio signal: "The rhythmic stimulus entrains and then amplifies natural brain rhythms, especially if it is tuned to an important frequency such as the ten-cycle-per-second alpha wave."

On the other hand, free verse undermines that stereophonic communication. It jolts and disrupts thought, speaking primarily to the more emotional, intuitive, artistic right side of the brain. Poetry, then, has much the same effect as slogans, mottoes, poster messages, and advertising.

> *The consequences of this new understanding are very wide-ranging. . . . It would suggest strongly that "free verse" . . . is likely to forgo the benefits of bringing the whole brain to bear. It would also predict that free verse would tend to beome associated with views of the world in which the tense-structure has become very rudimentary and the more complex values, being time-dependent, have disappeared. A bureaucratic social system, requiring specialists rather than generalists, would tend to discourage reinforcement techniques such as metered verse, because such techniques put the whole brain to use and encourage world-views that might transcend the limited values of the bureaucratic system, and by the same token it would encourage activities like free verse, which are highly specialized both neurologically and culturally. . . . The effect of free verse is to break down the syntactical rhythms of prose without replacing them by meter, and the tendency of free verse has been toward a narrow range of vocabulary, topic and genre—mostly lyric descriptions of private and personal impressions. Thus free verse, like existentialist philosophy, is nicely adapted to the needs of the bureaucratic and even the totalitarian state, because of its confinement of human concern within narrow specialized limits where it will not be politically threatening.*

That's pretty rough—in effect calling free-verse poets the tools of bureaucrats and even fascists; and you and I know they probably don't *intend* to be any such thing. But, as I mentioned, the polluting effect of advertising may have influenced them in ways of which they were unaware. Moreover, prose poetry suggests a way out of the dilemma.

Historically, poetry has always been an oral art, and Turner and Poppel quite rightly base their arguments on the physical facts of spoken communication. But today poetry tends to be read more than recited. It is, then, often the poem on the page, not the poem that strikes the ear, with which we are concerned. Written communication that comes in paragraphs usually speaks to the reasonable left side of the brain—carrying information, argument, business, narrative, and connected thought.

Suppose, then, that more free-verse poets were to convey the content associated with the brain's right side with the form associated with its left—the paragraph. Because readers would see what looked like prose, they would switch on their left brains. But the poets would have planted their little paragraphs with buried rhythms, harmonies, images, dissociations, and other devices to enhance emotional intensity. These have the effect of awakening the right side of the brain as well. Prose poetry might then have something like the effect of metered poetry in speaking to the whole consciousness.

Proetry

Poets aren't very likely to give up free verse in favor of prose poetry or metered poetry in the near future, though the literary Establishment has created an orthodoxy as stifling as that of the French Academy in the eighthteenth century—an orthodoxy in which free verse is practically the only recognized mode. In recent years this is changing a little as more and more poets recognize how, in spite of its apparent "freedom," free verse is, as Turner and Poppel indicated, actually a very confining and limited medium, especially weak in longer and more ambitious works. Poetry has come to mean almost exclusively short bursts of lyrical expression of very slight appeal to general readers. And some poets are beginning to protest.

For example, X. J. Kennedy described the tyranny of our present climate in his essay, "Fenced-in Fields" (in *Claims for Poetry*, edited by Donald Hall, University of Michigan Press, 1982). He discusses the influence on modern poetry of Charles Olson, a poet who promulgated a variety of free verse that he called "Open Form," or what Kennedy describes as a "theory of breathing as form":

> *. . . to claim that white space and indentations counted with the spacebar on a typewriter can possibly denote with any accuracy the subtleties of the human breath process is like claiming that a bucket of housepaint can capture the blush of the rose. [But] Olson's revolution has succeeded. In fact, so thoroughly has it overpowered the crumbling empire of the New Criticism that it is in danger of giving way to a police state, with an orthodox church every bit as doctrinaire as the Empire's used to be. Here and there, it is true, you see pockets of elder conservatives still in power. But it is open form (whether derived from Olson's thinking or from elsewhere) that prevails among most citizens. It has become practically an act of civil disobedience to write a sonnet. Opt for the villanelle and you cringe, waiting for the tap of the nightstick at your door.*

Kennedy's comment is an indication that since the early days of the Modernist movement (which will be discussed in Chapter XV) there has been a steady deterioration of the idea of poetic form. When free verse was written by poets deeply imbued in the metrical tradition, the old music persisted even though their line lengths were irregular. But by now poets are imbued almost entirely with free verse. They imitate the irregularity but are deaf to the music. As Kennedy says in the same essay,

> *We are cautioned by the new orthodoxy that the old measures no longer correspond to the nervous, staccato rhythm of our civilization. Perhaps there is truth in that assertion. But why poets should want to be faithful to the cadences of this particular civilization anyhow, is more than we can see. Kooky as it may sound to affirm this, there are still, after all, rhythms perceptible in the seasons and tides, in the succession of daylight and dark, in the beating of the blood against heart-valve and artery. Such facts make us wonder whether, in identifying the irregular with the natural and organic, proponents of open field poetry aren't taking a limited view.*

The result of this deliberate cultivation of irregularity is poems that are simply prose broken into arbitrary lines.

Anyone can do it—and generally does. Such a cultural situation certainly lowers the standards with a vengeance, but it has some value in liberating expression that might otherwise be repressed. For example, my friend John Holt—author of many bestselling prose books, primarily on educational reform and letting children learn outside of schools—occasionally sends me some of his poems, which he makes no effort to publish. Here's an example (which has no title):

The people in the TV ads
Laugh all the time
Those teeth, those white shining teeth!
Everything shines, eyes shine, bouncing curly hair shines
Soft parted red lips shine (lick them once again, please).
Oh, God, it's so great to be young and handsome and pretty and
    sexy
And laugh, laugh at anything, everything
And life is wonderful,
Sitting on the deck of a million dollar yacht
A little tired (all that sailing!), but not very,
Watching the great red (shining) sun go down in the West
At least five times as big as life.
Who wouldn't want to live forever, living like this,
Drinking our Miller or Schlitz or whatever it is
With the shining white foam sliding down the sides of the glass,
Laughing, laughing,
And bedtime
(eyes, lips, teeth, everything wet and shining in the dark cabin),
Barely an hour or two away.

Whether one calls it poetry or not, it's an interesting and effective piece of writing. John sent me three earlier drafts as well as this one. Thinking of it as a poem rather than as prose probably helped him focus on the process of revision and made him look at it more closely, word by word and phrase by phrase.

And you certainly couldn't classify that piece as an article, as journalism, as an essay or story. What is it, then? It's a kind of lyrical satire for which we have no name, material such as appears in the fiction of Kurt Vonnegut or Richard Brautigan. We call it poetry by default. I wish we could somehow get beyond *poetry by default*. I suggest we call such writing *proetry*. That term, used without pejorative intent, enables us to look at it freshly without distracting comparison to poetry by, say, Yeats, Eliot, or Frost.

Here's another example of what I would prefer to call proetry—by Ronald Koertge:

HAPPY ENDING

King Kong does not die. He gets hip to the biplanes,
lets them dive by and ionizes them. Halfway down
the Empire State he leaps to another skyscraper,
then another and another, working his way North

and West until people thin out and he can disappear.

Fay's boyfriend is sure she is dead OR WORSE
but just as he is about to call up the entire U.S.
Army, a scandal mag breaks the story. The couple
has been seen in seclusion at a resort somewhere near
Phoenix. Long lens telephoto shots show them sunning
by a pool. There are close-ups of Fay straddling
the monster's tongue and standing in his ear whispering
something Kong likes. Look, his grin is as big as
a hundred Steinways.

I love it: It's fun, fantasy, a richly told joke—and the image of Kong's teeth at the end leaves a powerful afterglow. Moreover, it's roughly metrical, written in what I take to be a five-beat accentual line, except for the last short one. One might even call it a sort of sonnet. The great thing about proetry is that it breaks through the limitations of conventional free verse. It needn't be so intense, so self-consciously poetic, as most free verse has been, yet it can use the radical line breaks and spacing of free verse for dramatic effect. On the other hand, it can use techniques associated with formal poetry, such as meter and rhyme. The one demand I would put on this genre I am inventing is that it have the clarity and speed of relaxed prose. It should rattle right along, a good rap.

Though "Happy Ending" superficially resembles poetry, I'd rather call it proetry. It gains little by its line breaks. The rhythm is so arbitrary it does not differ much from that of good thumping prose. The sound echoes, internal rhymes, the surprise in diction, the figures of speech—all these are as characteristic of good prose as of good poetry. Again I think of Brautigan, whose short pieces of highly imaginative, amusing, and surprising prose have a similar effect.

And like the prose of Brautigan, this poem invites the reader to enjoy more than to appreciate. But the mere fact that it is printed as a poem has the curious effect of diminishing enjoyment. It seems pretentious, a dare. The form asks us to appreciate a work of art rather than merely enjoy an imaginative escapade. The form invites us to look closely, to discover the intricate order of art—and that's not really to be found. Its resemblance to blank verse, even to the sonnet form, suggests comparisons with the blank verse of Milton or sonnets of Keats, and it simply doesn't stand up to that kind of scrutiny. It seeks to play a game it can only lose.

Or consider the proetry of Steve Kowit. His "Lurid Confessions" starts:

> One fine morning they move in for the pinch
> & snap on the cuffs—just like that.
> Turns out they've known all about you for years.

The proem goes on to explain that "they" have your whole life on film, tape, files, recording from a mike they plugged into one of your molars, catching "your least indiscretion & peccadillo." Suddenly, in this surrealistic fantasy, we are at a trial:

> Needless to say, you are thrilled
> tho sitting there in the docket
> you bogart it, tough as an old tooth—
> your jaw set, your sleeves rolled
> & three days of stubble . . .

But it turns out that the evidence "they" have collected doesn't reveal exciting criminality at all, but "a life common & loathsome as gum stuck to a chair,"

> Tedious hours of you picking your nose,
> scratching, eating, clipping your toenails . . .
> Alone, you look stupid; in public, your rapier
> wit is slimy & limp as an old bandaid.

As the trial drones on, we hear of unsuccessful sex and a bored audience. The poem concludes:

> You leap to your feet protesting
> that's not how it was, they have it all wrong.
> But nobody hears you. The bailiff
> is snoring, the judge is cleaning his teeth,
> the jurors are all wearing glasses with eyes painted open.
> The flies have folded their wings & stopped buzzing.

> In the end, after huge doses of coffee,
> the jury is polled. One after another
> they manage to rise to their feet
> like narcoleptics in August, sealing your fate.
> Innocent . . . innocent . . . innocent . . .
> Right down the line.

> You are carried out screaming.

The writing is cadenced rather than strictly metered, but there is some poetic form, almost subdued by the breathless pace. It's not merely broken prose. There are occasional touches of imagination ("gum stuck to a chair," "an old bandaid"), but otherwise the language is plain, straightforward—a well-told fantasy that manages to be both funny and insightful. I think it's wonderful—if we can call if proetry instead of poetry.

That, too, is the term I would use for the best work by a friend of mine, Jim Hall. Jim has told me he was influenced by the poetry of E. E. Cummings and Edward Field and writers of fiction such as Brautigan and Flannery O'Conner (to what he calls "the glorious funny deadly seriousness" of her work, as well as her "richness of detail and visual imagery").

His comment reminded me that, indeed, Cummings was the granddaddy of this genre. For example, you may know one of his poems which is an extended analogy between breaking in a new car and a new girlfriend. It begins:

> she being Brand
> -new; and you
> know consequently a
> little stiff i was
> careful of her and(having
>
> 'thoroughly oiled the universal
> joint tested my gas felt of
> her radiator made sure her springs were O.
>
> K.) I went right to it flooded-the-carburetor cranked her

And so on. It's hard to stop quoting because the proem pushes on so unswervingly. The humor and meaning are locked into the form, which is as visual as it is auditory—too swift, kaleidoscopic, and clever to paraphrase. Look it up—and also Cummings's "nobody loses all the time" about "Uncle Sol," who failed at various kinds of farming until he finally drowned himself in the water tank. The coffin was lowered:

> (and down went
> my Uncle
> Sol
>
> and started a worm farm)

I asked Jim Hall what he thought of the poetry of Kowit and Koertge. He said he'd read a little of their work—but it looks "too easy." That's a common reaction to proetry, but Jim should know it looks easy because so much effort has gone into hiding the effort. It takes great skill and a sense of timing to achieve a relaxed, casual-sounding patter.

Sit back and enjoy this proem of Jim Hall's as an imaginative, humorous excursion. Hear it, as told by a storyteller. Trying to classify it will only detract from your pleasure:

THE MATING REFLEX

On his way out the branch
the young man says to himself
I know better than this. This is certain death
He leaves a slime trail, where his hands are
praying sweat on the bark.
His nose wiggles. He is moving so slow
nothing seems to be happening.

On the tip of the branch a 1,000 facet-eyed green bug
is sleeping. It has eaten the last ten men who edged out
to touch it, and now is
digesting.
God, life is hard, it dreams.
God, men are mostly the same, it dreams.
God, men are less than bugs, it dreams.

The man is only a foot from the bug now.
He is bowing forward toward it, clutching a sprig,
worshipping.
I've given up my scholarly studies for this, the man says.
I've left a nest full of eggs. I've lost
my retirement fund. Forced my wife to shout.
But look at that bug, look at how it is perched,
how it could burst into bloom or flight,
if I made an awkward move.

Man, dreams the bug. I could snip off a batallion of men's
heads, and be half starved.
God, men are pitiful, the way they stream out this branch
like bugs.

The man feels the branch bend, arching like his wife before
she wheezes and hugs him each time.

He is an inch from the green tightly wound bug.
It has taken me a semester to get this far. This will be worth it,
    he says. This one will be worth the lost
fellowship, the summer grant money returned.
This one is as green as the footprint of an ivy vine.
This is my secret questions answered.

Here comes another one, dreams the green bug. Here
comes another drooling feeb. Given up a pretty bug
wife and a teeming larva to have a chance
at me.

The man waits a weekend before reaching out.
He takes a school week to move his hand above the green
bug's back. He waits for some response:
an antenna flick of recognition, acceptance.

I'm prepared to be very slow, he says. I'm ready
to be as restrained as the best lover could be, under
these circumstances.

God, she dreams. Here we go again.

Decapitation, so the naturalist says. Decapitation even
seems to stimulate the male's mating reflex.

Though I find myself rolling in the aisles, it is painful laughter. I recognize the instinct. I have slimily crawled out such branches for just such bugs.
    And it would have Abe rolling in the aisles, too. Jim wrote to me about Abe when he was describing the sources of his poetry:

> It all began in a little town in Kentucky. . . . Actually, I guess my earliest influence was my hometown barber. I always thought this guy, Abe, had terrific taste. He knew which of the kids in my crowd were blowhards and which ones (like me) were authentic. I've always wanted, and always pretended to try, to write poems that people like Abe would like. . . . I thought I had a greater connection with Abe than with T.S. T.S., in fact, got me thinking when I was a freshman in college that perhaps the world could use a little less obscurity and a little more downhome openness . . . Of course, I always wanted to please that little old gentleman in the back of the hall who bears a remarkable resemblance to you, and John Nims, and Peter Meinke, and those others who spend their life with poetry. I don't want too much, right? Just what everybody else wants, that's all.

Jim's discussion of his aims in poetry has a consistently theatrical frame of reference. For instance, notice his language as he acknowledges the influence of Frost:

> . . .*in whom I found and still find the rippling power of the seemingly un-strained natural sentence, hoisted over a very careful construction of meta-phor, rhythm and structure. He's the kind who could give them what they wanted in every row. Please the old gents up front (the chattering teacup crowd, the oh, how beeyooutiful crowd) and the dark young man in the back of the room who was counting syllables.*

He confesses:

> *I like jokes. I like funny stories. And I love to give readings and have them laugh at the good lines. I've found that at some places if I start with a couple of funny poems they'll often laugh at everything, even the depressing stuff. Amazing, and not totally desirable, but still it's better than dead silence for fifty minutes. I guess that's my bottom line. I believe in the poet as enter-tainer. The court jester with a sting in his jest. I like that role and I'm glad that most other poets don't. I wouldn't want to have to compete with a lot of would-be comics. Are the Poconos ready for this goy? Jimgoy.*

As is probably true of Koertge and Kowit, Jim has considerable knowl-edge of poetic form, and many of his poems subtly employ it. But the techniques we associate with poetry (as opposed to prose) have almost nothing to do with the effectiveness of "The Mating Reflex." Maybe they're there, but they're incidental. To the extent one notices them they may gum up the act rather than enhance it.

The Borscht Circuit

Jim's allusion to the Poconos is, of course, a reference to the "Borscht Circuit" of resorts, catering mainly to Jews, which has nur-tured so many of our stand-up comedians. And it's interesting to me that much of the best proetry I have seen has the flavor of sophisticated nightclub comedy. Each poem is a script for performance. But these po-ems are effective on the page, too, and it may be that line breaks help. Proetry is not the same thing as prose poetry; it's not as intense, indeed not as poetic as most good prose poetry. It requires a relaxed, almost slack style—and, printed, needs those breaks and spaces to suggest timing of delivery. While I don't think highly of it as poetry, it seems to me a delightful and effective novelty genre. I've tried my hand at it my-self, using a loose pentameter line:

UNCLE MORTIMER'S THEORY

Uncle Mortimer has a theory there's nothing sacred
which he set out to prove.
                            Ate his way like a weevil
through family business law church the Masons and three
wives before I got to know him.
                            I don't trust you
Uncle Mortimer I said and he said I had good reason,
laughing and returning my pewter ashtray from
his pocket to the table. Don't turn your back he said
I like you.
            Then get your hand out of my crotch I said,
is nothing sacred?
                    I suppose that you're inviolate?
Very nearly I said at least selective.
                                        Values said

Uncle Mortimer philosophically are all
subjective you show me any real reason to
refrain from anything or for that matter to
do anything I'll show you a game the rules
like fences in your head Blake's mind-forged manacles
he said blowing his nose on a flag he carried for that
purpose.
          I couldn't live without those fences I told him.
More likely you couldn't die *I* have nothing to die *for*.
People are always making contracts you poets for instance
twist everything you want to say to make it fit
some arbitrary form people are always building
altars to sacrifice their Isaacs on people
are always organizing clubs to keep other
people out of always drawing boundaries
saying MINE well property is theft if you
really want to end war crime racism injustice
just remember one man's sacred cow is another's
beefsteak.
            It won't work I said.
                                    Well you just tell me
what does? You think if we just keep on pulling up
and putting in fences we'll finally get it right?
                                            Well
what about your theory that nothing's sacred? I

asked him.
                    What about it?
                              I mean suppose it's wrong
suppose I went over to that bureau drawer and pulled
out something sacred and you saw it and knew right then
it really was?
                    He watched me warily.
                                        Don't worry
I said I wouldn't I don't trust you and besides
the bureau drawer's not where I keep it but suppose.

You're lying! he screamed
                    and clutched his sacred theory close.
I don't trust you! he screamed
                              and fled into the night.

CHAPTER XII:
PRESERVING
THE
MOMENT

The reasons we have for writing poetry can be so overpowering that they blind us to the quality of the language we pour out in response. We have momentous feelings or thoughts and somehow imagine that if we can just say them, the resulting poem will be momentous, too. Wordsworth wrote, "Poetry is the spontaneous overflow of powerful feelings; it takes its origin from emotion recollected in tranquillity." Those two clauses seem to contradict one another, but I think he is implying that unless one has sufficient tranquillity to permit some perspective on the emotions, the "spontaneous overflow" will wallow in artlessness.

But "powerful feelings" are always somewhere at the core of the experience. A woman who had given up writing poetry for many years once wrote me about hearing that her son was going to Vietnam:

> . . . when my youngest, childlike son (just a kid to me) called me from Washington D.C. to say he had just had his shots for bubonic plague . . . in my mind's eye I saw his young beauty and strength destroyed by fire, or poisoned stakes in the woods, etc.—a sort of collage of all the news-pictures and movies and TV reportage I had ever seen, something in my mind gave way like a tight wall and all the toughness, ambition, reaching-out qualities burst through. I became another person. That same day, I picked up a book of Spanish poetry of which I am inordinately fond (Jiménez) and found there in polished crystal clear greatness the only answer I could find anywhere for the immediate confrontation of death itself. And right then and there I assigned a value to this particular human effort of writing poetry. Days went by and slowly I began to know that after decades of playing around with jobs, work, marriage, intellectual tomfoolery I knew from the bones out that if I could have said "I wrote this" [Jiménez's/prose poems] I

would have felt my life to have been justified. . . . My deepest self began to work on turning me into a poet, to save sanity and really, though it sounds pretentious, to save my life. In other words, no turning back and no question of "if I have talent" or "if I succeed," simply throwing myself in the cold water and learning to swim, or else—

I think we can all recognize the impulse. I wouldn't be writing this book, or you wouldn't be reading it, if somewhere in our lives there wasn't a comparable development of commitment.

It has nothing specifically to do with her son's going to Vietnam or the prose poems of Juan Ramón Jiménez (a Nobel laureate Spanish poet who died in 1958). It need not even be an experience of dread or grief, as it was in her case. As she reports what happened to her, it hasn't much to do with what Jiménez may have said in the passages she happened to read. There are two essential elements of the experience. The first is that something happens that makes us get serious about life, deeply recognize its preciousness and perishability. That can be an almost paralyzing experience unless the awareness is accompanied by the second element: a sense that something can be done about it.

What is that "something"? It is not necessarily, of course, writing poetry. But it is the discovery that one can use one's creative force in a valuable way. What Jiménez said was apparently less important to that woman than the fact that he wrote imperishably. I don't happen to respond to the work of Jiménez as she did, but he was noted for a "naked" style in his mature work in which pure, classic ideas were expressed "unadorned," a retreat from the heavily decorated sentiment of his youthful work. He was obsessed by a fear of death and wrote a great deal about the strength and perspective needed to face "nothingness" (often symbolized by the sea). Apparently, something he said along these lines struck a chord one woman needed to hear at a time of personal crisis. It mobilized her creative force. She could see at least one thing to do about an overwhelming consciousness of death. She would try to write something that might endure and mean to others what the words of Jiménez had meant to her.

I happen to have a copy of my response. In part I said:

Poetry at its best moves us to those perceptions. Poems don't tell us how to live, for sure, but they change our lives. The news from your son changed your life in just the way a powerful poem does. It didn't tell you what to do. But if you were to live in a universe in which the possibility of destruction existed, a possibility you suddenly recognized, it would be madness to go on living the way you were living. The only sanity was the craziness of de-

termining to write poems, to feel in your life some glimmer, at least, of the worthiness you found in Jiménez. Right? Again and again poetry works like that, and, amusing as much of even the best is, it is always grounded in tragedy, or tragic perception, always recognizes (and struggles against) some disastrous limit, always says, well, if that's the way it's going to be, allow me at least the dignity of articulating my awareness. If the Universe is doing a job on me, let it not have the satisfaction of thinking I don't know.

To make a poem, then, you try to render experience so vividly as to incorporate (not to tell, but to show) significance of comparable magnitude.

But for whom? First of all, for yourself. It is staggering to demand of your own poem that it change your life, and yet that, finally, is the only criterion that really matters. Great poets have changed my life again and again, not because they wrote to please their contemporary audiences or me or the ages, but because they wrote to change their *own* lives. They wrote as though their lives depended on it—and their lives did.

Frost, for instance, describes the impulse to poetry as the necessity of combining vocation and avocation, need and love united.

> As my two eyes make one in sight.
> Only where love and need are one,
> And the work is play for mortal stakes,
> Is the deed ever really done
> For Heaven and the future's sakes.

That is the abstract conclusion to a very concrete poem, "Two Tramps in Mud Time," in which he reluctantly gives up a task he was richly enjoying, splitting wood, so that two tramps can earn a meal. "My right" to the task "was love," he says, "but theirs was need. / And where the two exist in twain / Theirs was the better right—agreed." But one can imagine him, after turning over the ax, settling down to unite love and need by writing a poem about the experience, a poem that no doubt changed his life as it did mine.

You might want to look up that poem (which is in most anthologies of modern poetry) for a vivid review of what I have been saying here. First there is the heightened sense of life's preciousness and perishability, in this case half-humorously rendered through observations of the ambiguous weather on the edge of winter and spring:

The sun was warm but the wind was chill.
You know how it is with an April day
When the sun is out and the wind is still,
You're one month on in the middle of May.
But if you so much as dare to speak
A cloud comes over the sunlit arch,
A wind comes off a frozen peak,
And you're two months back in the middle of March.

He observes a bluebird singing in such a way "as not to excite / A single flower as yet to bloom," the water in the wheel ruts and hoof prints, which, he knows, will have "crystal teeth" as soon as the sun sets. He enjoys:

The weight of an ax-head poised aloft,
The grip on earth of outspread feet,
The life of muscles rocking soft
And smooth and moist in vernal heat.

It is a delicious and delicately balanced pleasure that he must surrender in view of the tramps' needs. But that sacrifice evokes the response of the poem, a way of preserving the transitory in enduring lines, a strong statement of renewed commitment.

Memorable Phrases

We need to remind ourselves of those moments that bring love and need together in poems, lest we get lost in the details of the craft. At one of those workshops in our log cabin I piled anthologies on the coffee table and asked the gathered poets to leaf through them and find (to read aloud) some single poem that had been very influential at a crucial time in their lives. I suggest you do that yourself—asking what connection the poem had with your experience.

You may find that it's not the whole poem, or even whole lines, that seemed so significant. One of the basic units of a poem is the phrase. Nuggets of language implant themselves in your memory because they seem to define something otherwise inexpressible. In that letter quoted at the beginning of this chapter the woman says, "in my mind's eye." I wonder whether she realized that she was quoting *Hamlet*. As the poets at the workshop read the poems they had selected, I was struck by how many familiar phrases rolled past—phrases whose source I had forgotten.

An insurance agent from Connecticut didn't use the anthologies but recited his choice from memory. If I told you the first line, you would know the poem immediately, but let me quiz you by starting elsewhere. Surely you remember the phrase "his wreathéd horn." Whose wreathéd horn? Maybe the whole line comes back to you: "Or hear old Triton blow his wreathéd horn." Could you now go to an anthology and find the poem it comes from?

That's the last line. Just before it we see "Proteus rising from the sea." Maybe that jogs your memory. How about "A Pagan suckled in a creed outworn"? Or "a sordid boon"? "Getting and spending"? "We lay waste our powers"? If you are like me, these phrases are familiar as old friends, but I would still not have been able to identify their source without help. I'll stop teasing you. It's William Wordsworth's sonnet:

The world is too much with us; late and soon
Getting and spending, we lay waste our powers:
Little we see in Nature that is ours;
We have given our hearts away, a sordid boon!
This Sea that bares her bosom to the moon;
The winds that will be howling at all hours,
And are up-gathered now like sleeping flowers;
For this, for everything, we are out of tune;
It moves us not.—Great God! I'd rather be
A Pagan suckled in a creed outworn;
So might I, standing on this pleasant lea,
Have glimpses that would make me less forlorn,
Have sight of Proteus rising from the sea;
Or hear old Triton blow his wreathéd horn.

The poem contradicts many of the pronouncements I customarily make about good poetry. I warn poets against indulging in abstractions, preachiness, and vague generalities—yet this poem is full of those. The imagery is blurry and weak. The sea baring her bosom is a relatively easy metaphor, and while the idea of a still day being one in which the winds "are up-gathered now like sleeping flowers" is ingenious, it is neither very vivid nor strong. "Pleasant lea," if not exactly a cliché, is very near one. The poem doesn't actually make me *see* Proteus rising from the sea or *hear* Triton's horn (or even imagine it clearly). I'm not sure I even believe the poet would like to have those myths renewed. I can feel the anguish of too much getting and spending in "the world" (which here means the social world, as opposed to the natural earth). But what have these myths to do with a greater responsiveness to nature and freeing ourselves from economic slavery? Yet, in spite of these weaknesses, the poem endures as a great work of art primarily because of its resonant, memorable phrases.

Who was it "amid the alien corn"? That phrase is familiar to many Americans who don't even know that "corn" refers to wheat, not to what the English call "maize." Some may associate it with the story of Ruth from the Bible, and others may remember that the phrase occurs in Keats's "Ode to a Nightingale," but the phrase has a life of its own. The combination of that particular adjective with that particular noun is strangely powerful in a way that can't be explained by the sound, its literal meaning, its effectiveness as an image (practically nil), or its emotional association with Ruth, the nightingale, or the ode.

Some have tried to explain why certain phrases are memorable on the basis of their sound: alliteration, assonance, or rhythm. And it's true that some phrases stay with us because of sound quality. "Out of the cradle, endlessly rocking" creates itself through rhythm: *DUM da da DUM da// DUM da da DUM da*, a cadence very characteristic of Walt Whitman. Some may remember Milton's "with ivy never sere" (from "Lycidas") because of its sound, though they haven't the least idea what the image means. Some phrases are vigorous or dramatic: "Let me not to the marriage of true minds / Admit impediments." Here heavy alliteration combines with authoritative tone to stamp the phrases in our minds—whether or not we figure out exactly what Shakespeare was talking about in that sonnet. What's a true mind? One that isn't plastic?

John Ciardi used the word "irreducible" to describe the staying power of certain phrases, but that, too, seems only a partial explanation. Surely there are shorter ways—and more precise ways—to say "The world is too much with us," for instance. I believe the power of that phrase arises from the curious emphasis it throws on "with," which, it happens, also alliterates with "world." A simple preposition is given concrete force: One almost feels that "with" as physical trammeling. It sounds colloquial, reminding one of the twists of ordinary speech Frost so often made memorable, yet I doubt that it really is or ever was in common parlance in this kind of usage. Would anyone ever say the children are too much with us? That worry is too much with us? It seems unlikely. Are we to take "late and soon" as a common locution for "too late and too soon" or for a preoccupation with time? Would one say, "I'm always arriving at meetings late and soon"? Or "He's late and soon worried about his unpaid bills"?

What I hear in Wordsworth's opening two lines is a great deal of emotional weariness that takes the form of simple speech twisted out of shape a bit by its effort at emphasis. The feeling is too strong for precision. Some pedant might complain that it would be more logical to say we waste our powers than that we lay them waste. The latter phrase suggests cutting a swath, leveling, as a conquerer might lay waste a countryside. Is that the appropriate connotation for a leakage of energy in getting and spending, late and soon? The pedant would be wrong—not in logic, but in his failure to grasp that driving, homey, exasperated intent that Wordsworth's words capture.

Meaning and Form

All this fussing about sound, rhythm, synonyms, imagery, irreducibility, and other technical elements misses the simple majesty of a statement of universal emotion. Consider another memorable statement, "To err is human, to forgive, divine." Pope certainly put a great principle succinctly, with effective parallelism, with remarkable ingenuity, but the essential power of the sentence is the thought itself. The strength of Wordsworth's sonnet is that it eloquently expresses a common feeling of world-weariness. It takes neither learning nor high intelligence to know what he's talking about. But if the feeling is so common and simple, what is the difference between this statement and one that consists merely of clichés?

Frozen Phrases

"Cliché" is simply the French word for "stereotype," which literally refers to a metal cast of type but metaphorically means language or thought that has been rendered rigid, fixed, unchanging. Clichés tend also to be trite—literally "worn away," overused, banal. Imagine a head filled like a printshop with slugs of type already composed in phrases: "golden morning," "willing ears," "twittering birds," "silver notes," "scattered coins," "glad tidings," and so forth. Now imagine trying to write poetry using only these fixed units. The resulting poem would be, like Myrtle's, a jumble of conventional ideas. Rhyme and meter won't save them. They were born dead. (Though I would also have to admit that Myrtle's innate force of personality gives them a certain sprightliness.)

Getting rid of clichés in a poem is not simply a matter of going back and eliminating a few unoriginal phrases, as one might correct minor mistakes in grammar. Clichés in language are symptoms of clichés in thought, a disease that eats deeply and cannot be cured by Band-Aids on the surface. "The Raising of the Flag" doesn't need plastic surgery; it needs psychoanalysis.

First, though, the symptoms. Clichéd writing is almost always disconnected. One phrase has little to do with the next, as the trumpets of the second line have little to do with the bosom of the first or the coins in the next stanza. Sometimes one image sets off a train of association—as golden in the first stanza might have summoned up the silver in the second—but no real coherency. You don't get anywhere trying to relate golden trumpets to silver coins, diamond-bright announcements to dew-bejeweléd lawns. Sounds like a pirate's treasure chest, but it's really an indulgence in chance association. Having thought of one phrase, the poet goes on to the next, without regard to what each is doing to the thought and feeling of the poem or how one relates to the last.

Themes can be clichés, too. For example, all the courtly imagery in the opening stanzas: trumpets, livery, jewels, perhaps even the carpet. Myrtle has probably never seen a court except in costume movies, but she's not drawing on her experience for these clichés. She's drawing on books, on conventional ideas of what sounds poetic. And this court scene sits like a bad egg in the melting butter, the world honeycombed by subways and oozing glue, beneath a sky full of maiden fingers and militantly flying banners.

Such incongruities occur in a poem, cheek by jowl, because the Myrtles of this world (at least half of whom are men, by the way) seem utterly to lack a sense of humor. Myrtle's poems are very funny, but not to Myrtle. They are like the singing of Flora Foster Jenkins, a wealthy lady of some years past who considered herself a singer but who apparently couldn't detect, even from recordings of her own voice, that she was always excruciatingly off-key. Yet she hired and performed in concert halls with great success as an unconscious comedienne, never perceiving the irony in the critics' mock-rave reviews, never catching on that when the crowd broke into applause in the midst of her songs, it was to muffle their uncontrollable laughter.

People given to thinking and writing (and speaking) in clichés apparently don't hear the discord when one image jars against another—the slumbering sun spreading like melting butter, then washing his face in dew and drying it on the flag. It's people like Myrtle who tell us to keep our shoulder to the wheel and our eye on the ball with a stiff upper lip. She doesn't hear the clash of crude realism (the flag squeaking up the pole) with trite fancy (the maiden fingers) or the clash of the majestic notion of a divine symphony being deflated by the coarse notion of bragging. The lawn is like a carpet. The sun spreads like melting butter. These are separate clichés in Myrtle's head, and the humor of their combination, forcing us to imagine a mess on the run, never occurs to her.

What You Bloody Well Mean

Clichés are evidence not only of incoherent thought but of a compulsive need to decorate. People who use them are like those who clutter their lawn with plaster rabbits and other kitsch. At the other extreme are those who give no thought to decoration at all, or, as I mentioned about Jiménez, deliberately strive for a "naked" style of simple statement. I'm sure every poet at one time or another yearns to do what Steve Kowit says in one of his poems, "I pretty well say what I bloody well mean."

But unfortunately, that rarely works in poetry or, at least, in good poetry. This poem says what it means:

LIFE

Sometimes I have good days,
When everything seems to go right,
And I think I'm lucky
As I go to sleep at night.

But then there are days
when I can't make a buck
And have to go to bed
Cursing my bad luck.

But in my heart I know,
Come happiness or strife,
I must take both good and bad,
For it's not luck, but LIFE!

At least it sounds sincere.

I call that "belly flopping," remembering a joke about a farmer who entered a fancy diving contest and won no points from the judges for his belly flop. On the way home his wife consoled him, "At least you got in the water fustest."

It's pointless to criticize such a poem. One might point out that the meter is a bit creaky in places, the rhyme is hackneyed, the language uninspired, the thought conventional. But all this is irrelevant. Many fine poems have creaky meter, hackneyed rhymes, uninspired language, and conventional thought, but no amount of revision could save this one. The problem is that the poet pretty well said what he bloody well meant—and landed flat on his belly in the water.

Sincerity is always a refuge of poor poets. Though it would seem natural to think that the most honest and direct statement of a feeling or idea would be the most effective, it doesn't work that way in art. Good poetry can be clear and simple, and even sincere, but always, when one judges language as art, one must ask *how* it is said. Form is equal in importance to content, and form includes not just meter and rhyme, but word choice, imagery, tone—all the suggestive qualities of language that qualify meaning.

Perhaps a poem by A. E. Housman, which superficially resembles "Life," will illustrate the point:

> Could man be drunk for ever
>   With liquor, love, or fights,
> Lief should I rouse at morning
>   And lief lie down of nights.
>
> But men at whiles are sober
>   And think by fits and starts,
> And if they think, they fasten
>   Their hands upon their hearts.

That poem is about as forthright as "Life," but many readers are confused by it because they can't quite believe the poet is coming out in favor of "liquor, love, or fights." But "lief" means "willingly" or "gladly." There's no getting round it: The poet says that if men could always be drunk, he would gladly get up and gladly go to bed, but men are occasionally ("at whiles") sober and spasmodically ("by fits and starts"—like an old car on a cold morning) use their brains, and when they do, they control their feelings ("fasten / Their hands upon their hearts").

If you have already decided that you don't like Housman's poem because you disagree with it, at least you can't complain that it's too indirect or obscure or long-winded. It's not clichéd or clumsy or conventional. It's just *wrong* in your opinion. Thinking about a poem that way is much like thinking that pure, unadorned statement of something you happen to agree with is bound to be good poetry. I hope to convince you here that your agreement or disagreement is an irrelevant response.

Though I would make no claim that "Could man be drunk for ever" should be classed among the greatest poems, Housman is a much better poet than whoever wrote "Life." (Hint: His initials are J. J.) I don't *agree* with Housman's poem, either: I have little faith in unchecked emotion, and I am able to rest easy only because I have confidence that people tend to be reasonable (and not stalk the midnight, like the madman in "Perhaps an Owl," Chapter V). But I admire Houseman's wryness, irony, surprise, understatement, even his boldness.

Compare that poem with this one on a similar theme by Ezra Pound:

AN IMMORALITY

Sing we for love and idleness,
Naught else is worth the having.
Though I have been in many a land,
There is naught else in living.

And I would rather have my sweet,
Though rose-leaves die of grieving,

Than do high deeds in Hungary
To pass all men's believing.

The title announces its deliberately immoral intentions, so perhaps if you are a moral person you skipped it. Both poems are related to the classical theme called *carpe diem:* Seize the day. In Ecclesiastes it is expressed this way: "A man hath no better thing under the sun, than to eat, and to drink, and to be merry." Often a note of mortality is struck, "tomorrow we die," as Pound does delicately, poignantly, with the line "Though rose-leaves die of grieving." A carpe diem poem is simply a reminder that life is short and we should make full use of it. Most poets have tried their hand at that theme from time to time. Here is a domestic version of mine:

CARPE DIEM

Our daughter has been using my razor. I found
it soapy on the bathroom sink.
Please finish your coffee and come back to bed.
It's later than we think.

And here's one that's less domestic:

BALLAD OF THE JOURNEYMAN LOVER

A day is long enough to find
  a night to follow after,
a lady of the loving kind,
  a morning of low laughter.

He walks with angled elbows and
   his feet point widely wide, oh.
On either side he swings a hand
   and swings a heart inside, oh.

He waylays maidens in the lanes
   and wives when they are lonely,
and little girls with growing pains
   outgrow them with him only.

He bears a bundle and a stick,
   a change of socks and sandals.
He travels light; he travels quick—
   and shows the world no handles.

"Just tell me when, my dear," he sings,
   "and I am yours for lending,
for whens descend on silent wings;
   there are no ifs to ending.

"The clouds move faster than the sun,
   and in a windy hour
the petals fly, the colors run,
   the sweetest milk will sour,

"No one will see me come again,
   and no one do I sigh for,
and no one knows where I have been
   or what I said goodbye for.

"I sprinkle salt upon the tails
   of birds I want to capture.
My melancholy never fails
   to bring the ladies rapture.

"Now in our grassy graveyard where
   we draw our breath and blow it,
our cheeks are warm, by dark are fair—
   but no one dead can know it.

"So lean upon the mound, my dear,
   and part your lips so quaintly,
and listen to the earth, my dear,
   which throbs not even faintly.

"And put your hand upon my chest

and kiss me now, and wonder
if loving on the earth were best—
or hugging nothing under.

"If you blush now, I cannot see—
and if you blush tomorrow,
I will be gone, and you are free
to say you blush for sorrow.

"A day is long enough to find
a night to follow after,
a lady of the loving kind,
a morning of low laughter."

We don't look to such poems for wisdom or advice on how to live our lives, but as memorable statements of one of humanity's perennial longings.

And it is their memorability that lifts them above the flatness of "Life." There is a tightness, a necessity, in the way those poems by Housman and Pound are written that imprints them in the memory. The poems seem to be chiseled in marble, so firm is their phrasing, so exquisite their balance and stately grace. I doubt that Pound had any more specific interest in Hungary than I do, but because of his poem, to do high deeds in that country will forever stand as a symbol for vain but heroic achievement.

Again I turned to Myrtle to help me distinguish between effective simplicity and utter flatness. I asked if she would modernize Housman's poem for me. She came up with this:

If man were all emotional
And never used his head,
Gladly would I rise at morn
And gladly go to bed.

But sometimes men are rational
And careful in their dealings,
And at such times, I'm sad to say,
Get a grip upon their feelings.

"It was a dirty job, but I did it," she commented, handing me her manuscript with a look of distaste. I decided not to suggest she work on "An Immorality." But I was glad, at least, to see her get away from clichés.

Appearance and Reality

Both clichés and commonplaces arise from faults of perception. If you allow yourself to be dazzled by or satisfied with the surface of reality rather than try to grasp it in all its complexity, you are likely to record only a jumble of contradictory impressions or a view that is too simple and empty to convey experience convincingly. Memorable language seems to reach beyond that surface to grasp some essence at the core. The phrases that resonate are those that seem to contain perceptions into the depths.

And though the poem itself, like "An Immorality," may be apparently clear and simple, its central experience is almost invariably paradoxical. You *know* Housman values thinking, no matter what he says in "Could man be drunk forever," because the poem itself is so tightly logical. It is aimed at the brain, not the gut. But he wants us to think about the limitations of reasoning. Similarly, the classical qualities and beauty of "An Immorality" belie the poem's advocacy of "love and idleness." One truly committed to those values probably wouldn't bother to write a poem about them at all. Even the little verse I quoted from Ecclesiastes is paradoxical: The preacher knows very well the vanity of eating, drinking, and merriment. But he wants you to think, to question, to test your values, to liberate you from smugness.

The more we learn about reality, the more paradoxical it seems—to the point that modern physics sounds more and more like Zen. Is light a wave or a particle? It all depends on what it's doing. Only the simpleminded, in poetry or science, view the world with tunnel vision. As a teenager I briefly fell for that simplistic vision.

My education, in both religion and poetry, largely consisted of learning to doubt, to question, to look beyond. I think that the ability to hear the echoes, to know that nothing is ever quite what it seems to be, is what you need to avoid both clichés and commonplaces, to find imperishable language to record your experience. You have to know that poems and words themselves never bloody well say what they bloody well mean and that every assertion (including this one) is bound to summon its shimmering opposite like a ghost from the beyond.

Once Archibald MacLeish and I were talking about how the images of the French poet Rimbaud planted themselves in the memory of readers, and the phrase MacLeish used to describe the effect planted itself in my mind, then in this poem:

ENVOI: THE TRAWLER

"Rimbaud . . . drives the fish hooks in . . ."
Archibald MacLeish

Unwind behind me, a little book,
each poem like a baited hook—

morsel of image, barb of thought—
that lips be lured and throats be caught.

Oh, I have strung my line this way
many a year and many a day

across a lake I cannot cross
again and never mind the loss . . .

but think how in your private deep
when boats are beached and trawlers sleep

your nose may lead your appetite
to swallow wire that bites your bite

and makes you thrash in dark alone
until flesh flakes from silver bone.

CHAPTER XIII:
THE
POWER
OF
SUGGESTION

Art always demands a sense of depth, something beyond mere flat representation. Compare it to our stereoptic vision and stereophonic hearing. When signals come in to each of our eyes or ears from slightly different angles, we are able to see and hear in depth. In the graphic arts perspective is achieved by illusion, a very precise, scientific way (discovered in the Renaissance) of representing depth and distance on a flat surface. Holographic art creates the illusion of three dimensions with laser beams. Modern painters have tried to enable us to see *into* reality, into its very atomic and subatomic structures and even into its immaterial nature, into feeling, thought, and abstract relationships.

And poetry creates a sense of third and fourth and many more dimensions by taking advantage of the suggestive characteristics of language. On its simplest level language can be used almost purely as a system of signs, as in mathematics. There are no ambiguities or emotional overtones in the statement $3 + 7 = 10$ or $ab\,bc = 6a$. Sometimes words are used almost purely to name. This sentence is composed of words. It has almost no more depth than $3 + 7 = 10$. I see a pine tree outside my window. That sentence may be a lie, but there is no doubt about what it asserts. The words function more or less as signs.

But words are also symbolic. They don't *merely* stand for a defined entity, as x might stand for 4 in an equation. When we say "pine tree," we are, true enough, denoting a specific biological phenomenon. But its greenness, its life, its commonness, its ability to retain its color through the winter—all these qualities of the pine tree are evoked to some extent by the words that name it.

If I say, "Still water runs deep," you know I'm probably not talking about water at all. That familiar homily is a kind of poem because one immediately senses a tension between its surface and its deeper (or "hidden") meaning. You know it may apply to a person whose placid exterior conceals profound thought or emotion, to a social situation where nothing seems to be happening but deep changes are occurring, or even to the weather when a calm precedes a storm. Symbols are open-ended, relevant to an endless chain of events, circumstances, feelings, ideas, or things. They are like mathematical variables, which can perform very specific functions but to which no fixed value is assigned.

Decoding Poems

As I explained in the last chapter, good poems almost never bloody well say what they bloody well mean. Unless there is a difference between what is said and what is meant, the poem lies flat and dead on the page. But too many people have been terrorized by the term *symbolism*. When they hear that the language of poetry is symbolic, they get the impression that "interpreting" a poem is like reading a code, one of guessing what the poet really meant in spite of what he said. Other, adept at the game, are not terrorized at all. Many write poetry in which they deliberately substitute a code for what they are talking about.

Both reactions distort the nature of poetry. In the first place you should know that *symbolism* isn't a technical term, like *metaphor* or *personification*, one of a list of "devices" one has to master. Symbolism occurs whether one intends it or not. We respond to symbols as Pavlov's dogs responded to dinner bells (which are, indeed, symbols), and we use them familiarly in all our communication. To some extent it helps to understand they are there and what they are doing, but too much conscious manipulation of symbols will turn poetry from an emotional into an intellectual experience, and good poetry is rarely primarily intellectual. Save the pleasures of puzzles for puzzles and those of poetry for poetry.

One of our most familiar symbols is the flag. A piece of cloth, colored and cut in a certain way, or a photograph, painting, or drawing of such a piece of cloth, or language that names or suggests it, has an emotional impact that most can identify, though the emotions may vary considerably from person to person and time to time. We all know what the American flag "means," though we may not have the same response to that meaning. Uncle Mortimer in the poem in Chapter XI put a flag to a quite original symbolic use. Blowing his nose on one is a symbolic act. That poem, in fact, is *about* symbols. What is "something sacred" which the speaker doesn't keep in his bureau drawer? If it were only a symbol of something sacred, it might have terrified Mortimer, as crucifixes are used to drive away devils.

A Crash of Symbols

One of the most common symbols in poetry is the rose—or, indeed, any blossom. One can hardly refer to a flower in a poem without suggesting transient beauty, but that doesn't mean that the symbol can't be used with originality. For example, William Blake uses the conventional meaning with astonishing power in this little poem:

THE SICK ROSE

O Rose, thou art sick!
The invisible worm,
That flies in the night,
In the howling storm,

Has found out thy bed
Of crimson joy;
And his dark secret love
Does thy life destroy.

But it is true that some symbols have grown so familiar they seem trite or pass unnoticed, and at times poets try to create new ones. That's hard to do, however. Much of the force of symbolism comes from the accumulation of emotional association over time. For example, Big Ben has come to be a symbol for London. A shot of its tower or the sound of the bell is often used to establish the locale in the movies. Suppose some filmmaker tried to replace it with a shot of a gigantic neon Exxon sign over Piccadilly Circus. That would hardly convey the same message, as an Exxon sign has already accumulated a weight of different symbolic meanings, such as commercialism, large corporations, oil, American industry, fast travel and quick stops. But if such a sign were erected there, it might, over centuries, come to be recognized as a fixture of the landscape, as the Eiffel Tower symbolizes Paris or the Statue of Liberty the New York Harbor.

You can't just assign arbitrary meanings to symbols any more than you can to words, unless you share Humpty Dumpty's philosophy:

"But 'glory' doesn't mean 'a nice knock-down argument,' " Alice objected.

"When I use a word," Humpty Dumpty said, in a rather scornful tone, *"it means just what I choose it to mean—neither more nor less."*

"The question is," said Alice, "whether you can make words mean so many different things."

"The question is," said Humpty Dumpty, "which is to be master—that's all."

Humpty Dumpty wouldn't make a very good poet, I'm afraid. We have to accept the fact that most effective symbols are so deeply engrained in our language and culture that we hardly recognize when they occur, yet we may still feel their effect.

For example, in 1900 Thomas Hardy wrote "The Darkling Thrush," offering that bird as a symbol of a faint, dim hope for the new century. The poem is filled with symbolism, but one would hardly notice the symbols unless someone called attention to them. Here is the first stanza:

I leaned upon a coppice gate
  When Frost was specter-gray,
And Winter's dregs made desolate
  The weakening eye of day.
The tangled bine-stems scored the sky
  Like strings from broken lyres,
And all mankind that haunted night
  Had sought their household fires.

Most obviously, the capitalized words, "Frost" and "Winter," symbolize much more than they literally say. Death seems to hang over the scene. Life is running out of the old century and has not begun in the new. It is also evening, another reinforcement of those symbols: cold winter evening = approaching end, dying light, the withdrawal of energy.

But the gate symbolizes a time of change, moving from one place or time to another. Lyres symbolize a civilization past, a beauty that has gone. Fires symbolize security, privacy, retreat. Even the poet's leaning has symbolic force, implying that his own energy has run out; he is tired, weak, dependent, passive, still, and thoughtful.

In this poem each of the images, from tangling and scoring to haunting and desolation, builds toward a unified emotional effect of exhaustion, hopelessness, bleakness, an approaching doom. I doubt that anyone could read it without grasping that meaning. Yet the poem says nothing about exhaustion, hopelessness, bleakness. It's all conveyed by symbols.

On the other hand, Hardy also wants to symbolize a glimmer of optimism with the thrush. Birds and birdsong, like flowers, are common symbols in poetry for brief, delicate, natural beauty. Often they are associated with dawn and springtime (which, of course, have opposite symbolic meanings from evening and winter). In this poem the single thrush is deliberately juxtaposed with the surrounding winter desolation. Like everything else in the landscape, it is wasted and nearing its end:

> An aged thrush, frail, gaunt and small,
>   in Blast-beruffled plume,
> Had chosen thus to fling his soul
>   Upon the growing gloom.

Even the phrase "fling his soul" has a symbolic association with death. But lest anyone fail to get the point, Hardy spells it out quite explicitly in the last stanza;

> So little cause for carolings
>   Of such ecstatic sound
> Was written on terrestrial things
>   Afar or nigh around,
> That I could think there trembled through
>   His happy good-night air
> Some blessed hope, whereof he knew
>   And I was unaware.

That one abstraction, "hope," is carefully placed so that it can't be missed or overlooked, making the symbolism of the bird's song explicit.

A couple of decades later we find symbolism being used in quite a different way. Here is a poem from Wallace Stevens's first collection:

DISILLUSIONMENT OF TEN O'CLOCK

The houses are haunted
By white night-gowns.
None are green,
Or purple with green rings,
Or green with yellow rings,
Or yellow with blue rings.
None of them are strange,
With socks of lace

And beaded ceintures.
People are not going
To dream of baboons and periwinkles.
Only, here and there, an old sailor,
Drunk and asleep in his boots,
Catches tigers
In red weather.

This poem probably strikes you at first as obscure, but it is as explicit, in its way, as "The Darkling Thrush." After the word "haunted" you know the white nightgowns symbolize ghosts, implying that the poet regards these people as wasted, dead, pale, dull, bleak (like the landscape Hardy depicted to symbolize the turn of the century). Half the poem is devoted to telling us what the nightgowns are *not*, but in case the splash of colors and mention of lace socks and beaded belts are unclear in intent, Stevens tells us—in an abstraction like Hardy's "hope"—that all these details add up to the fact that the gowns are not "strange." From that we can understand why he tells us what these people are *not* going to dream about: baboons and periwinkles.

None of these symbols—gowns with rings of various colors worn with socks of lace or beaded sashes, dreams of baboons and periwinkles—are traditional, yet the poet makes it perfectly clear that they symbolize strangeness. Take out that word and the poem becomes near nonsense. "Only," then, tells us that the remaining lines deal with an exception, a contrast. Unlike the people in white nightgowns, the occasional drunken sailor has traveled, seen strange sights, sleeps in his boots. I think he symbolizes unconventionality. His dreams are different: He catches tigers in red weather. And we don't need coaching, by this point, to recognize that such dreams are creative and, therefore, "strange."

Both poems are comments on the disillusionment the poets feel as they consider their world. The life has gone out of society. The old sailor, like the darkling thrush, is a symbol for a tiny, possible ray of hope in a scene of bleakness, deadness, and desolation. Stevens is much more specific than Hardy about what depresses him: conventionality, lack of imagination, conformity.

Hardy seems to feel some sympathy with the people who escaped to their household fires, but he senses some unnamed impending doom, which he doesn't name. We can deduce from the rest of his work and his biography that Hardy thought science and reason had destroyed society's spirituality, and that explains the gloominess of "The Darkling Thrush," but nothing in the poem leads us to that interpretation. Of the two poems, I would say Hardy's is the more obscure—yet by far the better poem. It is elegantly crafted, whereas Stevens's seems slapdash.

But the use of somewhat outrageous and unexpected symbols in "Disillusionment of Ten O'clock" is a deliberate device. Stevens was criticizing conventionality and lack of imagination, so he dramatized his protest with unconventional symbolism. Those who still symbolically wear white nightgowns and catch no tigers in red weather will, of course, never catch on to what he is saying.

Stevens uses dreams as symbolic of imagination, a popular idea in the twenties when the work of Sigmund Freud was first reaching public consciousness. And the symbolism of dreams set off a fad for putting bizarre symbols into poetry and finding them in poetry of the past. Some critics and professors delighted in scandalizing readers by pointing out that "coppice gate," for instance, might symbolize the female sex organ, and so on. Such planting (or finding) of Freudian symbols in a poem like clues to a puzzle may be an exercise many enjoy (for reasons Freud himself may have explained), but that's mere artificiality, not art, and the fad of Freudian symbolism seems to have passed.

Symbols of Social Turbulence

It is interesting that while some symbols, like the rose, seem to be immemorial, others are quite closely tied to their times. The colors in Stevens's poem remind me of a poem of mine which appeared in *Harper's* in the late sixties—a response to the social disorder and racial violence of those years. That led me to looking at other poems of mine written during the same period, and I see that the symbols that flowed "naturally" into the poems tended to reflect the concerns and issues of that specific historical period. In this one I used a kind of waking dream that the colors of the world had been altered to symbolize the common feeling that the time was (as Hamlet found his own time) "out of joint."

CHROMATIC

Owing to drugs or astronomic explosions
all colors were confused.
               I knew when I
woke on sahara sheets and gazed, alas,
at violet wifeflesh sleeping like a distant range.

Beyond her, orange slats across the sky—
pale green in the June morning. Black the grass
and utter white the boughs with their black leaves.
In the yard, my mauve feet cool in the black dew.

News
      on the pink screen
               explained nothing. Strange
that whole long day rotating in changing light,
and stranger still the rioting scarlet negroes
exploding like summer all the scarlet night.

Individual colors, such as green and blue, have traditional symbolic values, but in this chromatic chaos all such meaning is lost, though one of them, "scarlet" at the end, retains a suggestion of bloodiness. In another poem of the same period I used lightning as a symbol for the violence in the cities which, I felt, was bound to reach even those who imagined they had havens of escape:

THOSE SHEETS OF FIRE

These hot nights are broken
by soundless puffs of light

and, after gasps of time,
that disconnected rumbling.

(Each morning the news shows
walls have buckled, windows

are starry shards. We hear
air torn by sirens, the thud

of dark flesh, the sharp
information of shots, see

the hard lips under helmets.)
Hate squats on the heart

of the far city. Here we
kiss and kiss, after

each soft flash clinging,
counting, certain that sound

comes blackly on, at least
a thousand feet per second.

    Still another poem of that period (also in *Harper's*) depicts the paranoia of an Archie Bunker type mentality (though I believe the poem came before the days of Archie Bunker). In the speaker's incoherent tirade he sees symbols, symbols everywhere:

HARD

listen it's not only the Viet Cong but these
long-haired kids on BMW's naked at night
hauling off my substance like a train of ants
through jungles flakes of flesh in their mandibles
to roll it and smoke it somewhere out of sight

and these upstart bucks spreading violence
like popping pustules all over my USA
staring me down like my own daughter pregnant
with insolence cool you know like France
after all we've done for her acting that way

when all Washington know how to do is raise
taxes appoint a half-assed committee picks
some pipsqueak general to run Asia plays
007 with its Dogberry CIA you can't tell me
somebody isn't behind these foreign flicks

what we need is action castrate the Arabs
and wire 10 million volts into all these
electric guitars fry their beards send these mobs
to cotton patches in outer Idaho
and give SNCC back to the Chinese

its all right there in **LIFE** spread out in full
color conspirators from Havana meeting
in sheets burning draftcards to light their joints
you think the streets are safe? You think you'll
collect the rent each month and escape a beating?

me I'm taking more pills and enjoying them less
my wife looking gaunt dangerous antsy
my yard has gone to pot my kids dropped out
and you think just one thermonuclear device
in the right place would be you say chancy?

In that poem the meaning arises not so much from the individual symbols, such as motorcycles, long hair, pot, and "foreign flicks," as from their kaleidoscopic combination. And there is, of course, a tension between what these symbols mean to the speaker in the poem and what they mean to the reader. To the speaker one thermonuclear device in the right place would hardly be even chancy, but (I hope) the atomic bomb has quite a different symbolic force for you and me.

High-Tension Lines

Tension between real and apparent meaning is only one of the many kinds of tension that create a stereoptic sense of depth or resonance, bringing the words up off the page into a rounded, shapely form with many kinds of significance.

For example, there is usually tension between the title and body of a poem. If the title is "Life," and, sure enough, the poem with that title quoted in the last chapter ends with the momentous discovery "that's life!" the conclusion is an anticlimax. The title of a poem (unlike, say, an index card in a library) doesn't necessarily identify the contents of the poem. Rather, it is an element in a multidimensional artistic creation. Is Matthew Arnold's "Dover Beach" about Dover Beach? Only incidentally. Is this poem of mine about crabs?

CRABS

If you were to leave a burlap bag,
bunching and clicking, full of live crabs
on the beach, tied at the top, stuffed
with shifting shells inside its sag,
each sticky stalk-eye blind and tender,

claws pinching claws—or nothing—clacking,
hard, hollow bodies scraping as
legs worked them through the bodies, backing,
you would know how full of things I lie,
dry, out of reach of the folding sea,

inert and shapeless, were it not
for rattling crabs inside of me
that hear, perhaps, the long waves crushing,
the flute of wind through grass and sand,
remember the water, the cool salt hushing,

struggle to slit the burlap and
scatter in sideways, backwards courses,
like beetles, devils, flat as clocks—
these snapping wants, these shelled remorses—
to drag themselves beneath the rocks.

In line 9 you hear about vague "things" that are finally identified in the next to last line, "these snapping wants, these shelled remorses," so you know, at least, what crabs are a metaphor *for*. But I wouldn't say the poem is really "about" wants and remorses, either, though, certainly, one of its objectives is to describe how those feelings unsettle a person.

In fact, as a writer I never know what to say when someone asks me about a poem, story, or play, "What is it about?" If I'm working on nonfiction, like this book, it seems perfectly reasonable to answer that question—in one word, "poetry," or in a sentence or many sentences, depending on how detailed an answer my interlocutor wants. But, for example, since 1965 I have been working intermittently on a novel. It tells the story of a young white American painter living with his black model in the Dominican Republic during the period of the invasion by the U.S. Marines in the year I began it. When someone asks me what it's about, I can't honestly answer that the novel is *about* that artist, his model, the Dominican Republic, the invasion, or all of these. It's about art, about love, about revolution, about alienation from another culture, about our country's involvement in Caribbean affairs, and many other things—including the specific events it narrates. Above all, if I succeed in writing it well, it will take on a life of its own. It won't be about anything: It will just be itself.

Similarly, I can't tell you what "Crabs" is *about*. I hope that as a multidimensional work of art it stands alone, like a person or an object. What is a dog about? What are *you* about? The question really makes no sense. While, of course, it is possible, and often useful, to paraphrase a poem, its "meaning" is bound to be distorted when we express it in words other than those of the poem. As Archibald MacLeish said, "a poem should not mean / but be." That slogan can be quite misleading— even about the poem in which those lines occur, "Ars Poetica," which is very explicit in meaning as well as being. Good poems usually do have coherent, paraphrasable content. But we should always remember that the "meaning" so extracted is not equivalent to the poem itself.

It All Depends

Robert Frost said, "Poetry is what gets left out in translation." That was a way of emphasizing that the specific words, the way they are divided into lines and arranged on the page, constitute the real poem, and there is no equivalent for them any more than there is for a living being. A very simple example will illustrate the complexity of this problem.

Good poets are bound to test the limits of their art, and this poem by William Carlos Williams is famous as such an exercise. It is included in practically every anthology of modern poetry:

THE RED WHEELBARROW

so much depends
upon

a red wheel
barrow

glazed with rain
water

beside the white
chickens

That poem juts its chin in your face, daring you to say it's not a poem at all. It's a study in the minimal. Is it about a red wheelbarrow? Cover the first stanza and read the last three as a poem. What important ingredient is missing? Why does so much depend upon the lines "so much depends / upon"?

I am reminded of Willy Loman's wife in *Death of a Salesman* crying out, "Attention must be paid to this man!" She doesn't say exactly why Willy is so important or what kind of attention should be paid or what would happen if it were, but her speech is a kind of prayer to the Universe asking for recognition that the Death of This Salesman somehow Matters, even though the man may be insignificant in the eyes of the world. Similarly, Williams, in that first stanza, points and says *this matters!*

To show you how unsatisfying any particular interpretation of the poem might be, I'll make up a bit of literary criticism. Prof. Wood B. Shrink says:

Few can have failed to note that the word "wheelbarrow," which appears correctly as one word in the title, is broken into two words in the body of the poem, drawing attention to "barrow," a castrated pig. Also note that "wheel" is slang for a person of influence, as "chickens" can be taken to be young women (or even young men as homosexual sex objects). Thus what might at first appear to be a useful device for transporting heavy loads is seen as a symbol of impotence, the wheel pathetically useless in the rain among the possible young sexual partners.

Prof. Gloom N. Doom responds:

I agree that the tragic separation of "barrow" from "wheel" reverberates with significance, but the mournful sound of the word evokes an image of the barrow as burial mound, surely an Anglo-Saxon tomb in which a past civilization has disappeared under some vulgar "red wheel," perhaps of plastic, or a drive-in fast-food parlor, glazed or sugared over, dreary in the rain, surrounded by uniformed carhops that run around like a bunch of chickens.

But Prof. Art Fartsake objects:

You gentlemen are reading this much too literally. Breaking "barrow" from "wheel" is only the most blatant of a series of dramatic enjambments. Each of the four stanzas breaks into a unified phrase to isolate a two-syllable word on a line by itself. As we look more closely we see the first and last stanzas have four-syllable first lines, and the central stanzas have three-syllable first lines. Each of the first lines has two beats, and each of the second lines has one—"upon," an iamb, suggests a rising pattern, but that is immediately negated by the succession of trochees: "barrow," "water," "chickens." Each stanza has a strong and distinct asonantal pattern: the nasal sounds in the first, the rs in the second, the long a's in the third, the long is in the fourth . . .

But Prof. Sosh L. Kaws interrupted:

How long are you men going to remain in your ivory towers? We know that Dr. Williams was distressed by the poverty and suffering he saw on his rural calls in New Jersey. That red wheelbarrow is obviously wooden. Where do you find chickens running loose around a barnyard except on a small family farm? Already in the early part of our century he could see that these quaint little farms were threatened by the onset of agribusiness, and the way of life on which our civilization was built is now being glazed over by the tides of social change.

As readers we groan. We are bound to resent any specific interpretation that diminishes the resonance we feel from that vague "so much depends / upon." This is not to imply that a poem can mean anything and everything and that all interpretations are equally accurate (or foolish). Certainly Prof. Doom's conjuring up McDonald's in an Anglo-Saxon graveyard or Prof. Shrink's pitiful pig takes us out beyond silliness. But several of the specifics those imaginary critics point to are indeed elements of the tension that makes the little poem stand up with a multidimensional selfhood that can justifiably be looked at from many different perspectives like a thing in space.

One measure of the success of a poem is its ability to baffle any efforts to paraphrase it or even to tell exactly how it works. That isn't an invitation to write incomprehensibly, however. The best poems usually seem simple, at least on one level. It is only when you go back to them again and again that you discover how each element pulls against the other—meaning against statment, form against content, sound against sound, and image against image—creating the overall field of tension that, like a complex of tent poles and ropes, makes a flat creation stand erect.

PART IV:
THE
POET
AND
THE
PUBLIC

We have talked about some of the needs poetry fulfills for poets, some of the ways it relates to readers, and some of the dynamics working within poems, but, for better or worse, all of these considerations are deeply affected by a fourth factor, which we have so far considered only in passing: the social climate in which poetry occurs. If you plan to launch yourself into the world as a poet, you need to be aware of the currents affecting public taste and public reception of your art.

For the most part these currents are very transitory, more like fashions than enduring principles of great literature. Nonetheless, they are powerful forces that at times have a tyrannical effect on publishing and careers. Understanding them may help insulate you from disappointment and bitterness. Over a decade ago I almost totally stopped trying to place my poems in current publications, so disillusioned had I become with what I perceived to be the conflict between the values of our contemporary literary climate and those I associated with poetry of lasting quality. It seemed to me that my poetry was for myself and possibly for the ages, but it didn't fit into the current scene.

I have learned, I think, some acceptance and tolerance of that situation through understanding the relativity of taste in many different historical periods. It's fairly safe to say that good work is almost always out of fashion or, at least, that in every age much good poetry fails to find contemporary acceptance and only later comes to be recognized and valued by critics and the public.

Your work may be more fashionable than mine—and, if so, I wish you luck with it. But at any rate, you should understand how it relates to the external factors affecting publication and literary careers in our times. It is even more important that you clarify your goals for yourself. What kind of "success" do you seek in poetry? Do you want to make money? Have a wide readership? Be recognized by the literary critics? Or do you simply want to write the kind of poetry you find most satisfying and rewarding to read? In Chapter III I discussed the various audiences of poetry and the implications of writing for one or the other. In this section and the Appendix, I deal with that question in what I hope are practical terms for poets of our times. If you step out of the closet and expose yourself to public scrutiny, here's how to go about it and what you'll be getting into.

CHAPTER XIV:
POETRY
OF
SEX
AND
LOVE

We need a new beginning in regard to the poetry of love, and this is a good time for exploration. Many of the taboos that have prevented an honest and full expression of sexual concerns have been relaxed. But though love has probably motivated more poetry throughout history than any other emotion, not much good love poetry is being written today. It may be that the very concept of romantic love has come to seem invalid to modern poets—a curious phenomenon in an era in which formula romance novels are a rapidly expanding multimillion-dollar industry.

We may be caught in a literary bind. Love is a somewhat mystical concept, implying a spirituality that transcends sexual desire and satisfaction. At a level slightly above the physical we recognize what have come to be called "relationships." These are often, subtly or overtly, power struggles, and much of the most powerful poetry about sexual relationships in the last two decades has come from the women's movement. The poetry of such poets as Sylvia Plath, Anne Sexton, Marge Piercy, Nikki Giovanni, and Adrienne Rich tends to be an outspoken affirmation of women's rights and a critical examination of conventional sexual roles. It might be regarded as a poetry of sexual politics. But—for better or worse—that's almost the obverse of love poetry.

The Lady in the Tower

To understand our present state, let's consider briefly the tradition we have outgrown. We can no longer accept the assumptions that underlay the love poetry of earlier years, much of which is derived from the curious and now antiquated tradition of courtly love. Not many realize how unusual and relatively recent in human culture is the very idea of romantic love which we derive from this tradition. It has been said that before about 1100 a man might have about the same kind of affection for a woman as he had for his favorite horse. But as the castles of medieval Europe became centers of culture and learning (where there were many men and few women) the troubadors, itinerant poet-singers, began spreading a new conception of sexual relationship that was, according to *The Encyclopaedia Britannica:*

> . . . *dramatic in the extreme. The lover is always in a position of servitude; he must obey his lady's wishes, however capricious or unjust they may be. But it is his privilege, not his misfortune, to exist subject to her, for love, whether rewarded or not, is regarded as the source of all true virtue and nobility. Within marriage, such love is held to be impossible; the lover habitually addresses the wife of another, and secrecy is therefore one of the important conditions of any favour granted to him. The ritual which surrounded the whole situation was observed reverently and devotedly; as later developments make even clearer, the courtly lover often thought of himself in a semireligious context, serving the all-powerful god of love and worshipping his lady-saint.*

According to this tradition, the lover's heart is pierced by the eye-beams of the lady as by an arrow from Cupid's bow. He falls into deadly pallor, fear, and trembling, and the whole experience of love is one of noble suffering. The lady's cruelty and disdain can kill him. But if she grants a favor, perhaps a kerchief fluttering down from her moonlit tower, he can run around performing feats of derring-do, dedicating the dragons he slays to her honor.

Because of the "semireligious" nature of this kind of love, certain images and devices were borrowed from devotional poetry. Poets began using the language appropriate to worship of God in worship of their mistresses. Petrarch and Dante, two of the principal sources for many of the conventions of love poetry, alternately wrote of secular and divine love in much the same terms, for they were addressing idealized "mistresses" who figured in their imagination much like the Virgin Mary, an embodiment of aspects of divinity. From that practice were derived devices such as the traditional hyperbole of the sort typified by Robert Burns:

> And I will love thee still, my dear,
>   Till a' the seas gang dry.

and parodied by W.H. Auden (in "As I Walked Out One Evening"):

> I'll love you, dear, I'll love you
>   Till China and Africa meet,
> And the river jumps over the mountain
>   And the salmon sing in the street.
>
> I'll love you till the ocean
>   Is folded and hung up to dry
> And the seven stars go squawking
>   Like geese about the sky

The religious associations also explain why so many mistresses were described in terms of blinding light (transmitted by their eye-beams), as though they were divinities we dare not look upon, a rather disconcerting notion when applied to the next door. Indeed, in later centuries many poets (such as Shakespeare and Donne) satirized these conventions with anticourtly love poems, such as the well-known sonnet by Shakespeare beginning, "My mistress' eyes are nothing like the sun."

Eventually the tradition of courtly love was exhausted, and even satires of it grew tiresome. Though lovers continued to feel there was some kind of spiritual bond between them that surpassed their sexual relationship in importance and that sanctified it, they lacked a mythology to project that feeling. Moreoever, courtly love had nothing to do with a continuous domestic relationship. Shakespeare's *Romeo and Juliet* is a gentle parody and searching examination as well as a celebration of the assumptions of courtly love. But we can't imagine Romeo and Juliet settling down behind a picket fence to raise little Montagues. Courtly love was nighttime love. It began with a trational serenade and ended with a traditional aubade, when the lover takes his leave of his mistress at dawn. What happened otherwise between men and women wasn't thought of as love.

To My Lovable Klutz

The traditional love poem was of praise from a man to a woman. Curiously (and I would welcome evidence that I am wrong about this), very little seems to have made it into the annals of literature by women to men (the most notable exception being Elizabeth Barrett Browning's "Sonnets from the Portuguese," especially the one beginning, "How do I love thee? Let me count the ways"). When Archibald MacLeish wanted to write a poem of praise to a woman, he named it "Not Marble Nor the Gilded Monuments," taking his title from the first line of

Shakespeare's Sonnet 55, which he no doubt regarded as the archetype of this genre of poetry.* Typically such poems exalt the lady's beauty in vague terms and say very little else about her. The poem puts her on a pedestal to be worshiped, not to be touched. I doubt that modern recipients of poems which did that would consider themselves highly honored.

But, then, what *do* we say? I stated the dilemma comically in "The Superiority of Music" (Chapter VII). We can't exactly give a person whom we love our *reasons* for loving, for one of the peculiarities of love, is that it's irrational by nature. We tend to love *in spite of* rather than *because*. Which of these two statements would you be more likely to believe?

I love you because your features are well proportioned and animated. You are well adjusted, have popularly appreciated measurements, a high IQ, are skilled in domestic arts and know a profitable trade. You come up to my brow and complement me gracefully on the dance floor; you dress fashionably but inexpensively. As a potential mother of my children . . .

Or:

I don't know why I love you. You are scrawny, slovenly, and rather ignorant. I can't trust you or depend on you. You are self-indulgent and bittertongued. But I can't live without you . . .

The first sounds as though the "lover" were buying livestock. If we get the idea that we are valued for utilitarian reasons, we are likely to resent it. We want to be loved, as Frost said in "Hyla Brook," for what we are, for our innate value.

But we can't write poems saying, "I love you for your innate value." Should we really be honest? Here is a delightful—and to me, very credible—poem along those lines by John Frederick Nims:

LOVE POEM

My clumsiest dear, whose hands shipwreck vases,
At whose quick touch all glasses chip and ring,
Whose palms are bulls in china, burs in linen,
And have no cunning with any soft thing

Ironically, Shakespeare's sonnet happened to be addressed to a young man; moreover, the poem praises itself more than it does the person to whom it is addressed. It asserts that "this powerful rhyme" will outlast "marble and the gilded monuments" and that the young man will "live in this, and dwell in lover's eyes."

Except all ill-at-ease fidgeting people:
The refugee uncertain at the door
You make at home; deftly you steady
The drunk clambering on his undulant floor.

Unpredictable dear, the taxi drivers' terror,
Shrinking from far headlights pale as a dime
Yet leaping before red apoplectic streetcars—
Misfit in any space. And never on time.

A wrench in clocks and the solar system. Only
With words and people and love you move at ease.
In traffic of wit expertly manoeuvre
And keep us, all devotion, at your knees.

Forgetting your coffee spreading on our flannel,
Your lipstick grinning on our coat,
So gayly in love's unbreakable heaven
Our souls on glory of spilt bourbon float.

Be with me, darling, early and late. Smash glasses—
I will study wry music for your sake.
For should your hands drop white and empty
All the toys of the world would break.

Contemporary love is likely to be deeply involved, as in Nims's poem,
with a world that includes people, traffic, and housekeeping.

Even kids. A lover feels frustration when romance seems to get
bogged down in the opinions of others (such as parents) and the details
of domesticity. I once expressed that theme in a poem:

THE BARGAIN

Be beautiful as you are, and for
wit winking electric and your patience that
contains our family like a shore.

your tilted bones, your circular day
tending a household which, like a pile of fish,
needs perpetual putting away,

or, getting pound for ounce,
threading your spirit endlessly to patch
our metaphysical accounts,

yet leaping at dawn from the bed's warm pool,
landing on sand and flopping on to get
  dozens of daughters off to school,

  remain receptive as an eye,
enduring and softly holding as a glove
  which I completely occupy

  reliably as a nightlight glow,
and every other day I'll take out garbage
  and say again each decade or so

  in a poem, awkward, inexact,
how I am wealthier than all professors
  for having made this lucky pact.

Courtly love would not be likely to acknowledge such qualities as wit and patience, not to mention the delight one has watching his wife flop out of bed like a beached fish to get kids off to school. But the point of the poem is to show the absurdity of listing qualifications. I hope the reader (like the recipient) knows that the love the poem expresses is above, beyond, and in spite of those domestic details.

Geriatric Love

I have said often in this book that poets tend to try the limits. I am especially intrigued by long-lasting relationships that remain sensual—and I've seen very little poetry celebrating such love. But I have found love in the real world is very much involved with the qualities that enable people to hang together for the long haul. Thinking of that a few years ago, I calculated the number of my days and nights with Marty and was astonished by the figure:

AFTER 12,000 DAYS AND NIGHTS

Once on Lake Michigan
where waves come muttering in from foggy dawn
swirling and lapsing,

fanning thin on the sand,
sometimes reaching, sometimes not quite reaching
our bare, cold feet,

you said that you were glad
we did not live on the shore for you would lose me.
I said that fire

attracted me like water—
such various motion in so strict a form.
I lose myself.

Thank God I never found God.
I would disappear like snow on a black sea.
We did not then know

we held as sonnets do,
cupping together like an acorn—always
the same, almost.

But then I began to wonder about a *really* long relationship: Adam and
Eve's. I once heard a certain Reverend Moon extrapolate a wife for
Cain. No children of Adam and Eve other than Cain and Abel are mentioned in the Bible, yet Cain takes a wife. The Reverend Moon figured
out how that was possible by calculating the fertility rate of prehistoric
people. He concluded that there must have been thousands of women
of breeding age for Cain to choose from by the time he was about thirty.
(Obviously incest taboos must have come in later!) Since adolescence
I've been enchanted by that notion of a Neanderthal or Cro-Magnon
pair populating the earth in their own image. I wondered whether I
could capture in a poem both their sensuality and their genuine love.

THE YEARS OF EVE

*"And all the days that Adam lived were
nine hundred and thirty years: and he died."*

That apple wasn't good for his digestion.
I think he swallowed down a living worm
that gnawed him so—nine centuries it gnawed—
bottomless questions, worries, sudden doubts
flapping up unexpected in the night
like bats from his tunnel of brain, poor man. He woke
me with his tossing. *What was to be done?*
I asked. *What can we do now in the cold black?*
I'd put my robe on, sit and poke the fire
till orange played on the walls, the shadows slinking
back to their corners to lie in wait. Old Adam
would sigh—his lips parting the white silk
of his beard. His eyes seemed sparks that might ignite
his white loose curls. He stared and stared as though

                              That first stare—eons past—
he saw himself reflected in my eyes,
a tiny Adam staring at a tiny
Eve who stared back, and in the eyes of those
images—other eyes with other pictures,
and so on to infinity, he guessed,
like echoes in the canyon, softer, softer,
never ending—if one had ears, he said,
minute enough to hear them.

                         Those young eyes
still glowed in the old face. The cave was hot.
He threw the bearskin from his body—white
and long and firm. We age around the edges.
Face wrinkles, hair goes white, our knuckles swell.
Above the wrists and ankles skin stays smooth.
His muscles had all gone to flab except
his belly and loins. These never seemed to age.

I loved that man, the way he brachiated
around the Garden swinging tree to tree,
and loved the nights when he could not be sated
but still embraced the Garden, holding me.

Three hundred thousand nights he tumid stood
even when hair of the nest was white and thin.
What's to be done? he echoes with ancient smile.
I put my robe aside and lay with chin
resting on Adam's hipbone, teasing the elf.
You sway like a drunk, you mushroom, I said. Are you
the worm he swallowed? Or, perhaps, the serpent?
Don't hiccup. Say excuse me. Are you ticklish?
I scratched him with a fingernail then blew
a gentle breath which did not cool him. Adam
was grinning now, and groaning, as I watched
the shadow of the puppet sway on the wall.
And so we eased each other into sleep.

I sometimes think that Garden must have been
spun of imagination, youth remembered.
I glimpse us underneath a waterfall,
laughing and tumbling porpoises we were—
hair in our eyes, breathless in weight of water.
He shouted, This is now!

What?
　　　　　　　Now! *he shouted.*
He had in mind the way we bore the crush
of time that poured so roaring endless down
while we sat on that rock and hugged together.
I wonder whether that glimpse was a dream.

Well I remember sorrow: of birth's pain,
bread by the sweat of brow, the bruise of heel,
cleaving together in sorrow as virulence seeped
from our loins through the loins of reckless Cain.
Were these our kin—children of children of children
spreading across the earth like a rampant stain?
Daily on the savanna Adam would
encounter one of the daughters of sons of sons
and drop his game to dally, casting seed
indifferently as grass on which they'd lain.
And which of his babes were his he never knew,
for I was often on my hands and knees
bearing the thrust of strangers, sons of sons
who fertilized the region like the rain.

In luminous mist I dream I see a pair
of naked children playing under a vine,
picking the plump grapes, laughing, unaware
of pungent fermentation that makes wine.
Were those two in my keeping, would I dare
allow them knowledge that I took as mine?
A mother god would smother them with care
I'd wall the Garden tight and keep them there—
I say, and smile. The mist is in my eyes.
Confine them? I? One who could never bear
confinement? Mother of debauchery,
I would give them my counsel to escape,
teach them the freedom to be found in lies,
to squeeze intoxication from the grape.

And yet the old man, like the young, intent
on shaking meaning from the tree of stars,
for all his restless life kept tracking down
cause from effect, cause from effect, as though
truth left a trace, perhaps fur snagged on thorns.
His spear was at the ready. He would know,
someday, what life was all about, its whys

and wherefores, who was guilty, how we could
atone and find deliverance from sorrow.
Nights were the worst. He could not put his mind
to bed. It paced the cavern even as
he slept. He sought some revelation he
might pass along to Seth, significance
to consecrate the birthright. I take joy
in randomness, but he would tidy up
each last detail.
                          And lay here on this pallet
probing the silence with his dying breath.
I pushed his hair back with a tender touch.
He seized my hand with final boney clutch.
Surely, he must have thought, *there has to be
some answer at the end.* He looked at Seth
with panic in his eyes. And that was all.
The truth he sought was plain enough to me:
The curse was knowledge, the redemption, death.
At last one comes to rest. Life is a Fall.

She seems to me to have at last outgrown her infantile insecurities and
arrived at a love such as the world needs to sustain it.

Agonies of Sex

I have used a lot of my own poetry—in this chapter and earlier
ones—to illustrate poetry that attempts an outright celebration of love
because, frankly, I have not found much by other modern poets that
does so. But I am delighted when I find exceptions, such as this poem
by Heather McHugh which I came across in *The American Poetry Review*
(the same journal that printed, in another issue, the poem by James
Dickey that I criticized in Chapter XI):

THE TROUBLE WITH 'IN'

In English we're in trouble.
If you think of love as a place
we fall inside, sooner or later the beloved will ask
How deep? If time is measured in extent, sooner or later

someone asks How long? We keep
some comforters inside the box,
a heart inside a chest, but still
it's there the dark accumulates the most.

The end of life is thought to be
a boat to a tropic, good or bad.
A suitor wants to size up
what he's getting into, so he gets

her measurements, and wonders
how much is enough. The best man
cannot help him out—he's given
to a cummerbund himself. In English

boys and girls learn to regard themselves
in the worst half-light—too long,
too little, not enough alike,
and who could stand

to be made up for good? And who can face
being adored at all? I swear there is no frame
that I would keep you in. I didn't love a look
and find you fit it—every day

your sight was a surprise. You made
my taste, made sense, made eyes.
But when you set me up in high esteem
I was a star that's bound, in time,

to fall. The point's the sorrow
of the song. I loved you to no end
and when you said So far
I knew the idiom. It meant So long.

McHugh uses the ironies of English idiom to explore the very limitations I have been discussing here. No one wants to be put on a pedestal, and few know what it means to love without a "frame" that defines and delimits, to love "to no end." When he (I assume the person addressed is a he) began measuring their love in time—with a phrase that ironically refers to distance ("So far")—she perceived the beginning of the end. Though the poem records a failure of love, it nonetheless affirms the possibility of a love that our language and our ways of thinking about ourselves and one another seem determined to deny. It's a minimal whisper of a genuine love poem. Sadly, that may be as much as most modern poets are able to affirm on the subject.

When there is less love than "relationship," the theme is likely to be a tense awareness of boundaries, as between the man and woman depicted in this poem of Sandy's:

THE LAST FIRE

I lie awake for hours listening
to the wind rush through the pane-
less sash. In our summer bed you
roll against me hot with your fresh
dreams.
          I have my own dreams.
I slip away, eager to feel my bare
feet on the cold floor. Now, in my
own heat, I pace off the distance
between fire flies.
                Aroused by sun
burned dreams and creaky floor boards,
you sit up and strike a match. "Why
are you standing naked in the middle
of the room?"
            I shiver with cold
and fear. Oh, new love, last fire,
why must you shout so? All I hear
is, "I am the fire,
                burn here, burn here."
I stand dripping wax, waiting for cool
words to form on a hot tongue. Silence
irritates. You grind your cigarette
to its bone,
          thinking you've put out
the last fire of the night. Ashes fall
in sheets. I flicker in the dark,
an unsure flame. I tell you softly,
"Over here, over here."

Curiously, in an age of presumed liberation, contemporary sexual poems often seem tinged with guilt. For instance, "Leaving the Motel,"
by W. D. Snodgrass, contains these lines:

. . . Keep things straight: don't take
The matches, the wrong keyrings—
We've nowhere we could keep a keepsake—
Ashtrays, combs, things

That sooner or later others
Would accidentally find.

Check: take nothing of one another's
And leave behind

Your license number only,
Which they won't care to trace;
We've paid. Still, should such things get lonely,
Leave in their vase

An aspirin to preserve
Our lilacs . . .

Those lilacs seem to evoke not only the traditional note of tragic brevity
but also some internalized moral judgment on the transitory affair.
That stanza and the following one conclude the poem:

Our lilacs, the wayside flowers
We've gathered and must leave to serve
A few more hours;

That's all. We can't tell when
We'll come back, can't press claims;
We would no doubt have other rooms then,
Or other names.

There is precision in the phrasing, sophisticated management of the
rhythm and rhymes, yet the language is easy, conversational, and ac-
cessible. We can hear the voice of the poet, his bittersweet tone of wry
acceptance. Values and feelings are not merely expressed but dramatized, especially by the gesture of putting aspirin in the lilac water.
And moral awareness gives the poem a resonance beyond mere report-
ing of the experience. All that adds up to what I mean by a work of art.

But there's no joy in that anonymity the lovers are forced to adopt,
and if there was joy in the tryst at all, it isn't mentioned or suggested.
It's enlightning to compare that poem with a heartier and more confi-
dent poem on a similar theme—by Ben Jonson in the seventeenth century:

Cannot we delude the eyes
Of a few poor household spies,
Or his easier ears beguile
So removéd by our wile?
'Tis no sin love's fruit to steal,
But the sweet theft to reveal.

To be taken, to be seen,
These have crimes accounted been.

(You might enjoy comparing these poems on illicit love to my Philander poems in Chapter VIII.)

Jonson's poem reminds us that, of course, there is nothing new under the sun. Many of the Greek and Roman classics were sometimes torridly, often candidly sexual in their concerns. Ovid's *The Art of Love* is really not about love at all; it's a kind of seduction manual. Shakespeare's sonnets are perhaps the greatest poems in our language about both sex and love. They passionately and painfully explore sexual relationships among the strange triad: the poet, a young man, and a dark lady (with the shadowy figure of a rival poet sometimes hovering in the background). John Donne was one of England's best religious poets and, as Dean of St. Paul's Cathedral, the greatest preacher of his time. But he was also, in his younger days, author of many delightful and sometimes bawdy lyrics on themes of sex and secular love.

What is relatively new in our century is greater autobiographical realism of poets who, with apparent honesty and courage, wrestle with the problems and pleasures of sexuality.* There's some comfort for all of us in learning that, regarding these matters, we're not necessarily alone, though we may be still repressed, as I said here:

A ROUGH AVERAGE

The normal person has a thought with some
sexual content every twenty-five
seconds on the average.
                    I drop the book
in my lap—which stirs awakened like a spring pond.
Research psychologists people my dream
as moles crisscross and hump the even lawn.
In unisex white coats they are strapping wires
to downy arms or watching telltale needles
twitch on the rolling sheet.

---

*I'm sure exceptions can be found in which autobiographical candor on sexual themes occurs in older literature. For instance, Wolfgang Goethe's "Das Tagebuch" is an amusing confessional in which the poet, on a speaking tour, takes the maid in a country inn to bed. But his thoughts of his wife at home make him unable to perform. So while the girl sleeps he sits in bed beside her and writes his wife about the experience: "Honey, I'm yours, in Turkestan or Rome. . . . Impotence proved me superman." See the translation by John Frederick Nims in his Sappho to Valéry: Poems in Translation.

Tell us your thoughts.
That spasm of ink reads nine on the Richter scale.
What fault is slipping in your depths? What buckling
of which impinging continental plates?
Your resistant skin is damp with dewy beads.
Tell us,
        they whisper, probing like jealous mates.

I check the second hand and welling up
comes Beverly in a bikini, miles
from shore, leaning to leeward, snatching a patch
of seaweed with a boathook.
        Look at the life!
She points to seething creatures dwelling among
the pale, air-pocketed tangle of stems and leaves:
shrimp, crabs, bugs—God knows what—a populous island.
But my eyes have sunk in tanned cleavage to
the secret edge of white. She and her husband
will never know my thoughts, which will not focus
on marine biology. I hear her words.
I will never know her thoughts.
        Now the shovel
slices the tunnel of the city of worms.
Eyes glued to lens we witness venery.
The laboratory is all black and white,
but color squirms on the slide, squirms in our minds.
I am normal, I desperately say, but do not say
what the silent second hand seeks out and finds.

The Press of Flesh

For all their talk about sex, the poems I have been discussing have generally avoided or refrained from presenting it sensually. Poets may deliberately avoid graphic description of sexual behavior because they don't want to distract readers with sensual titillation. Such poetry quickly veers toward pornography, which is how many would class much of the poetry of John Wilmot, Earl of Rochester (1648-80). I will quote only a few lines of his "The Imperfect Enjoyment" for illustration:

Naked she lay, claspt in my longing Arms,
I fill'd with Love, and she all over charms,
Both equally inspir'd with eager fire,

Melting through kindness, flaming in desire;
With *Arms, Legs, Lips,* close clinging to embrace,
She clips me to her *Breast,* and sucks me to her face.
The nimble *Tongue* (*Love's* lesser *Lightning*) plaid
Within my *Mouth,* and to my thoughts convey'd
Swift Orders, that I shou'd prepare to throw,
The *All-dissolving Thunderbolt* below.

But if the poet's object in these opening lines seems to be to arouse the reader, it quickly becomes apparent that his real intent is to disappoint. The poem is about premature ejaculation: "Trembling, confus'd, despairing, limber, dry, / A wishing, weak, unmoving lump I ly." It ends in violent cursing of the part that let him down, and the overall suggestion of the poem is one of disgust and disillusionment with sensual experience. Such disgust is astonishingly widespread in the sexual poetry of the world. For example, Shakespeare's sonnets (and, indeed, passages in his plays) become savage when they delve into concrete sensual experience. This may be an inverse way of affirming the spirituality of ideal love.

At other times poets express delight in sensual and sexual experiences, but they seem rarely able to find ways to describe them positively and convincingly without obscenity. These lines by Robert Wallace (from "Mimi" in *Girlfriends and Wives*) manage to convey the experience vividly, excitingly, without being titillating:

THE BLOND AND LOVELY

love we
  made, over and over,
  slow,

full, love-oil
  on breast
  and cheek, fingers

curled to the skulls
  under hair, blood
  and breath rope-tight,

toppling
  at last
    like two cut flowers
    to the single blade.

Wallace's final image reminds me of one of my own poems on the same theme:

THE TIPPING

Slow building is best, the card-
on-trembling-card kind of slow
piling of sensation, hard
aching, reaching and just touch,
so that the lines of one skin know
those of the other, any thought
likely to pull all down, and much
turning of the mind, batting soft
as a moth with one wing warm, not
quite daring to cross the flame, intent
on sense and senselessness, the trough
feeding drop-by-drop into the pail,
imperceptibly filling, bent
on the process, not the filling, clean
and convex surface swelling until
at some instant almost unforseen
you tip and sigh to feel the spill.

One of the difficulties a writer faces in writing about sexual experience is that its pleasures are defined and enhanced by privacy. When the language of poetry becomes too intimate, readers are likely to snicker or to be offended. Similarly, indecent words, even in our relatively liberated age, may intrude in a poem like a hog in the house, evoking a negative or inappropriate response to a positive experience. Delicately suggestive language is likely to be more effective, such as that used by John Keats in this stanza of "The Eve of St. Agnes." The hero, Porphyro, is hidden in Madeline's boudoir, watching her undress by moonlight:

Anon his heart revives: her vespers done,
Of all its wreathéd pearls her hair she frees;
Unclasps her warméd jewels one by one;
Loosens her fragrant bodice; by degrees
Her rich attire creeps rustling to her knees:
Half-hidden, like a mermaid in sea-weed,
Pensive awhile she dreams awake, and sees,
In fancy, fair St. Agnes in her bed,
But dares not look behind, or all the charm is fled.

The words "warméd" and "fragrant" are especially voluptuous. Keats doesn't say, but makes us think of what warmed them and whence comes that fragrance. The slow removal of those jewels "one by one" creates subtle suspense and involvement. We behold this striptease in dim light from a safe but tempting distance. Like the hero of the poem, we look on, worship, and desire while allowing Madeline to remain inviolate.

But if you read Keats's narrative in its entirety, you find that instead of the wholesome kind of love that accepts another person and the terms of life fully, the love of Porphyro for Madeline is traditional courtly adoration. And today you will not find much poetry that expresses even that.

Rediscovering Love

The scarcity of strongly affirmative poetry of love seems to me symptomatic of a profound failure in our culture. As I explained in the Introduction, it was, above all, T.S. Eliot's "The Love Song of J. Alfred Prufrock" that brought me in my late adolescence to my calling of a poet. But that is a strangely loveless and songless poem. As a young man trying to learn how to live in the world, especially how to live with my own sexuality, I took it as a cry from somewhere near the heart of our civilization. Eliot depicted a society of superficial and empty relationships in which sincere emotional expression seemed unthinkable. Indeed, it was the society of "sexual politics" currently described by our feminist poets.

Another poem that deeply influenced me in adolescence defined the problem more explicitly. That was W. H. Auden's "September 1, 1939," a poem brooding on the destiny of mankind on the eve of World War II. He says, in part:

> For the error bred in the bone
> Of each woman and each man
> Craves what it cannot have,
> Not universal love
> But to be loved alone.

Another stanza (which Auden expunged in later revisions) dramatically proclaims the necessity of overcoming that possessiveness:

> All I have is a voice
> To undo the folded lie,
> The romantic lie in the brain

Of the sensual man-in-the-street
And the lie of Authority
Whose buildings grope the sky:
There is no such thing as the State
And no one exists alone;
Hunger allows no choice
To the citizen or the police;
We must love one another or die.

(You may remember an allusion to that final line at the end of Shapiro's prose poem "Lower the standards," in Chapter XI.) I take the "romantic lie" to be a reference to that "error" of our desire "to be loved alone." But the "universal love" he calls for is not to be confused with any myth of "Collective Man," whose "buildings grope the sky." We can't depend on governments to save us from self-slaughter. As I understand him (and personally believe), peace on earth can only arise from individuals developing a capacity for nonpossessive love of one another, a recognition and joyful acceptance of their fleshly interdependence.

Love poetry is not going to bring us peace on earth, of course, but the values and ideals we express in our literature have immemorially prefigured the aspirations of civilization, and it would help us all if poets were doing a better job of creating a lively vision of a workable world in which people were bound to one another in love and delight. Dr. Lewis Thomas, in *Late Night Thoughts on Listening to Mahler's Ninth Symphony,* says,

> *I maintain, despite the moment's evidence against the claim, that we are born and grow up with a fondness for each other, and we have genes for that. We can be talked out of it, for the genetic message is like a distant music and some of us are hard-of-hearing. Societies are noisy affairs, drowning out the sound of ourselves and our connection. Hard-of-hearing, we go to war. Stone-deaf, we make thermonuclear missiles. Nonetheless, the music is there, waiting for more listeners.*

I think poets have a responsibility to amplify that music. Good poems on the theme of love should, I think, open vistas of human possibility. I believe that a credible and exciting expression of emotion helps others extend their emotional range. And a poem that deeply, intensely, and passionately affirms the value of another person and the reality of spiritual union may suggest alternatives in a society of otherwise empty relationships and bitter interpersonal struggles for power.

And, while we're about it, can't we have love poetry—albeit of domestic middle age—that sings a little? Here's an effort to start the song:

HARVESTING TOGETHER

I dream you in the tawny time
  when days are bright and sere
and nights have teeth like diamonds,
  black laughter flecked with diamonds,
those satin nights and starchy days
  in tawny time of year.

I dream your rusty colors and
  your wool and leather feel,
your taste of lemon, tart and clean
  like air of autumn, tart and clean,
in kraut and mustard days of chill
  stamped with a golden seal.

Our love now weathers like a rock
  riding the gusty season:
when sumac bends and darkens red,
  weighted with berries dry and red,
and moments drift like milkweek by,
  our rock lies still as reason.

We shed the rain, are glad in snow;
  we store the steady sun.
Our lichen, rough as corduroy,
  our creases mossed with corduroy,
gripping the earth with all our might,
  and smiling ton by ton.

I dream you in our harvest time
  of ruddy bushels swelling,
in rugged hours and resting hours,
  in firelight-quiet resting hours
with boots and sweaters piled aside
  in times of tender telling.

I bring brown nuts and bittersweet
  served on a wooden plate
these days of garnet wine and tang
  of fruit fermenting sweet with tang,
of humming days and evening chill—
  your warmth to celebrate.

CHAPTER XV:
TRADITIONAL, MODERN, AND POST-MODERN

In the last chapter I talked about sexual politics. Does it surprise you that there is a poetic politics as well? Just as sexual politics has little to do with—and may actually be subversive of—love, poetic politics has little to do with the genuine experiences of poetry and cause a lot of bad poetry to be written in order to prove a point. But it is this struggle for power and influence on the surface that many readers and poets first encounter. You have to fight your way through the politics, like Christian in *The Pilgrim's Progress* slugging his way through the Slough of Despond, before you can arrive at the Celestial City of literature.

Which Side Are You On?

Surely someone wearing a firm smile of belligerence has already asked you whether you favored Traditional or Modern poetry. *Are you for us or agin us?* the question implies, and it is likely that for the person asking it the "right" answer is Traditional, which means you support the Red, White, and Blue, Mother's Love, the sanctity of marriage, and God knows what else—but He keeps the Traditionalists informed as the need for updating arises.

When I think of Traditional poetry, my mind drifts back to a high school classroom in Houston, Texas, in the spring of 1942. Motes slowly rotate in the slices of sun that have evaded the green blinds. Mrs. Bloom has a fluting voice to express her tone of reverent appreciation for the offering upcoming in our anthology. Secretively I am working at a pimple under my left jaw. I am uneasy because I know we are about to have a Significant Experience. We are to read "Thanatopsis," by William Cullen Bryant.

Now, you can't find a more Traditional poem than that. Mrs. Bloom tells us that thousands upon thousands of loyal Americans (my adolescent mind imagines those loyal Americans "upon" one another like a towering sandwich) have learned the poem by heart. She is not requiring that of us: All we have to memorize this semester is "Tomorrow and Tomorrow" from *Macbeth*. But, she tells us, when the *Titanic* sank, the passengers were having an evening's entertainment of amateur performances, and several American businessmen offered to recite "Thanatopsis." One of them was probably doing just that as the ship went down. To this day when I read the poem I imagine the last heroic *gurgle gurgle* of punctuation from some anonymous American businessman on the tilted stage.

Mrs. Bloom tells us that Bryant wrote the poem in 1811 when he was sixteen. She looks around the classroom severely. We are nearly that old ourselves, and not one of us was about to write any such poem. And we shouldn't get the idea that "Thanatopsis" was Bryant's first poem, either. The little tyke had had a book of his poetry published when he was ten, and at fifteen he had written a political satire, *The Embargo*. That poem attacked the efforts of President Jefferson to keep the United States from getting embroiled in the Napoleonic wars and called for the President's resignation from office. It was a best-seller, quickly going into a second edition.

In Mrs. Bloom's class we were really squirming now. We had all let President Roosevelt dally for two years before he got us involved in the European war. And then it was the Japanese attack on Pearl Harbor, not any political satire that we had written, that inspired his belligerence. Not one of us had raised a peep—let alone write a best-seller or ask for the President to resign.

Alas, my respect for the Traditional was already hopelessly underdeveloped. Instead of awe, I felt resentment. What kind of creep was this kid who wrote a poem with an unpronounceable and incomprehensible title? Did he have any notion of the misery he would inflict on other teenagers 130 years later?

The Rude Swain

With a funereal expression on her face Mrs. Bloom stands before us holding the book like a hymnal. (We note that she hasn't learned it by heart.) She warbles. I didn't understand a word of the poem she read. She had explained that the title, "Thanatopsis," meant a meditation on death, which, of course, was the sort of thing any fellow growing up in the wilds of western Massachusetts at the beginning of the last century would know. To me the poem sounded like death warmed over, giving me a vision of an eternity in which we were forever trapped in a class-room with Mrs. Bloom trilling like a stuck record. Reading the poem to-day, I can make out its meaning—which is mighty slender for its 81 fat lines—but the only impact it had then was of amorphous and unre-lieved gloom. Part of it goes like this:

> . . .—Yet a few days, and thee
> The all-beholding sun shall see no more
> In all his course; nor yet in the cold ground,
> Where thy pale form was laid, with many tears,
> Nor in the embrace of ocean, shall exist
> Thy image. Earth, that nourished thee, shall claim
> Thy growth, to be resolved to earth again,
> And, lost each human trace, surrendering up
> Thine individual being, shalt thou go
> To mix for ever with the elements,
> To be as brother to the insensible rock
> And to the sluggish clod, which the rude swain
> Turns with his share, and treads upon. The oak
> Shall send his roots abroad, and pierce thy mould.

I asked Myrtle Whimple if she understood those lines, and she gave me this modernized version to clear it up:

> It won't be long before the searching sun
> Will fail to find you when his work is done,
> Nor will your pale corpse any more be found
> Where weeping folks have laid you in the ground
> Nor will you float out in the ocean blue:
> The Earth that fed you can ingest you, too.
> No more will you be any single creature,
> But all dissolved—feature by human feature,
> As anything that's eaten soon will be
> Reduced in time to basic chemistry.
> Your kinfolk then will be the rocks and clods
> The farmer plows up, then upon them trods.
> The oak sends out a million tiny roots
> Which, when they hit you, will not give two hoots.

"You'll notice I put it into rhyme," she said. "I figgered it'd be more Traditional that way. But the poem still gives me the shivers. Why did those old-fashioned poets have to be so morbid and negative and obscure and why did they keep using words that send me to the dictionary?"

I doubt that Mrs. Bloom had any idea what the poem means. As a good Christian woman, by her lights, she would have been shocked at its deism (or even atheism) if she understood it. There is no mention of soul or immortality. I noticed that she didn't offer to discuss what the poem was about (other than, in general, "death"). She intoned it, looked at the ceiling a moment in silence, then snapped the book closed. So there. We'd *had* "Thanatopsis."

She taught me a lot about those who pledge allegiance to the Traditional. You tune out. You put yourself on automatic pilot and let the drone run through your head like tape through a machine. Every once in a while a bleep such as "rude swain" or "thee" or "thy" or "all-beholding sun" reassures you that you're still reading or listening to poetry. She taught us that what poetry says doesn't really matter. Poetry demands a certain grandiloquence, resonant clichés, uplift, formality, freedom from vulgar words or any suggestion of common speech or thought, and no great clarity of intention.

These lessons had little to do with Bryant. Actually, for his time, he was remarkably lucid. His handling of blank verse (unrhymed iambic pentameter—not to be confused with free verse) is skillful. His grammar is a little shaky, which is why the poem is so hard to understand. But Mrs. Bloom didn't realize that Bryant was not a Traditionalist at all, but a Modernist. The editor of the magazine to which the poet's father sent the poem couldn't believe it was written by an American. Obviously, it was by someone up on the latest work from the "Graveyard School," including Thomas Gray, William Cowper, and Edward Young (though it showed little influence of Blake and the emerging Romantic poets).

Mrs. Bloom wasn't really equipped to teach us much about Bryant. On the other hand, as systematically and strictly as she could, she taught us to have nothing further to do with poetry. It is amazing, given that there are still many Mrs. Blooms in the schools, that a few students continue to be interested in the art. Some model themselves on the teacher and go on praising the traditional and scorning the modern. Others, like myself, spend a lot of energy getting back at the image they retain of Mrs. Bloom. So goes the politics of poetry.

Fashion and Timelessness

There is no simple distinction possible between traditional and modern poetry if you use those terms without their political capital letters. All poetry is traditional, and it's all modern at the time it is written. In the seventeenth century the word "modern" had primarily a pejorative meaning—used for things that were merely modish, fads. "Thanatopsis," for all its strengths, is a mediocre poem specifically because it is too modern in that sense, too derivative of the fashionable poetry the precocious young man was reading. Surely some Mrs. Bloom out there in Cummington, Massachusetts, tried to steer him away from the modish Graveyard School. She probably wanted him to read, instead, good, traditional bowdlerized Alexander Pope and Samuel Johnson. But maybe he was sick, or played hooky, or did as I did—dozed and didn't listen to the teacher. Rebellion takes many forms.

It's really too bad that a boy growing up then, with Bryant's sensitivity and talent, didn't find an authentic vein to express his poetic gifts. You can get some sense of what his daily life might have been like from Eric Sloane's *Diary of an Early American Boy*. I'm sure he saw his family, friends, and neighbors in the fields every day—and there was ne'er a rude swain among them. One does not hear in "Thanatopsis" the voice of a young man contemplating death at all. Surely he must have known death at first hand, must have poured out adolescent grief at the departure of a favorite cow or uncle, at his growing awareness that his own developing body was doomed to death and decay. But there is nothing of that in the poem, none of the sparkle and awe and horror that, for example, make Emily Dickinson's meditations on death so incandescent. Like many writers in the new America, especially on the frontier, he was self-conscious about his distance from the European centers of culture. He must have trembled with modesty as he set his pen to write something that might be compared with Seneca and Lucretius, not to mention Cowper and Young and Gray. And so he set out to impress his elders rather than record his immediate experiences with life.

But the poetic politics of the day led him astray. Good poetry of any age escapes that narrow branding of the times in which it was written. If I were to confront those who claim to like Traditional poetry with passages of Chaucer, Shakespeare, Milton, Wordsworth, Browning, Dickinson, or Whitman, they would find them as difficult and forbidding as they claim to find the poetry of Eliot or Yeats or more modern poets—if they thought about them at all. More likely, they would switch to the automatic pilot.

And they wouldn't be open to new experiences, either. Mrs. Bloom would not, of course, be familiar with any poetry written since the turn of the century, but if she were interested in meditations on death, she might have found quite a number without thees, thys, and rude

swains. For instance, Allen Tate's "Ode to the Confederate Dead,"
1928, is about the same length as "Thanatopsis" and puts a somewhat
more positive emphasis on mortality:

> Autumn is desolation in the plot
> Of a thousand acres where these memories grow
> From the inexhaustible bodies that are not
> Dead, but feed the grass row after rich row.

And a few years after she taught us, she might have found that we who
failed to urge Roosevelt into the war were encountering mortality firsthand in strange lands, as recorded by Randall Jarrell in this brief meditation:

THE DEATH OF THE BALL TURRET GUNNER

From my mother's sleep I fell into the State,
And I hunched in its belly till my wet fur froze.
Six miles from earth, loosed from its dream of life,
I woke to black flak and the nightmare fighters.
When I died they washed me out of the turret with a hose.

Jarrell's friend Robert Lowell, himself a pacifist, mourned his cousin
who was killed at sea in that war in "The Quaker Graveyard in Nan-
tucket," a long poem containing these lines:

> Sea-gulls blink their heavy lids
> Seaward. The winds' wings beat upon the stones,
> Cousin, and scream for you and the claws rush
> At the sea's throat and wring it in the slush
> Of this old Quaker graveyard where the bones
> Cry out in the long night for the hurt beast
> Bobbing by Ahab's whaleboats in the East.

These, too, are Classics—stately, rhymed, eloquent, expressing hu-
mankind's eternal, elemental shudder before the fact of death. We
might find passages on the same theme from Aeschylus to Job to Dante
and Frost, the formal threnodies in which our kind has contemplated,
perpetually uniquely and freshly, the meaning of mortality.

But all that would have been lost on Mrs. Bloom. These are Modern
poems—no matter when they were written. They are poems that wake
readers up, sharpen their senses, demand their attention, pluck the
chords of their deepest feelings. Mrs. Bloom wanted a lullaby.

An Exercise in Nostalgia

To view the matter more sympathetically, I think the yearning that traditionalists feel has little to do with poetry. They may not care very much for poetry at all. Those I have asked become very vague when I ask them whose poetry they really liked. Longfellow is often mentioned—more often mentioned than read, though much of his poetry is very good. Traditionalists and I might share a fondness for, say, James Whitcomb Riley or Eugene Field. One of my favorite Christmas poems is Field's "Jest 'fore Christmas," of which this is the first stanza:

> Father calls me William, Sister calls me Will,
> Mother calls me Willie, but the fellers call me Bill!
> Mighty glad I ain't a girl—ruther be a boy,
> Without them sashes, curls, an things that's worn by Fauntleroy!
> Love to chawnk green apples an' go swimmin' in the lake—
> Hate to take the castor-ile they give for belly-ache!
> 'Most all the time, the whole year round, there ain't no flies on me,
> But jest 'fore Christmas I'm as good as I kin be!

Of course, Mrs. Bloom didn't bring that poem to my attention. Poetry was part of our family life, and my teenage aunts read Field and many other poets to me before I started school. Incidentally, it's hard to find a copy of that poem in modern anthologies, and you'd have a hard time getting such a poem published today, not only because it's in dialect and uses words like "ain't" but because it good-humoredly satirizes the hypocrisy of children who are mischievous all year, then clean up their act to ensure goodies under the tree at Christmas. For some reason editors today don't consider funny and realistic poetry to be a good influence on children.

It may be that what the Traditionalists are seeking is an America that had already disappeared when they were children. It's the Kansas Dorothy left for Oz, the Indiana of Riley's Raggedy Man and Little Orphan Annie, of Booth Tarkington's Penrod, the Wisconsin where Peck's boy was bad, the world of Little Women and Rebecca of Sunnybrook farm, the Missouri of Tom Sawyer and Huckleberry Finn.

If I am right, many who claim to be Traditionalists actually share Huck's outlaw urges and secretly long, like him, to "light out for the territory" and escape the suffocating effect of tradition.

If that is true, I sympathize with them because I share that nostalgia. Some of those "traditional" values—in Huck's case, putting friendship above property value, freedom above conformity—sustain an America we can love together. Another "traditional" value often missing in modern poetry is that of sheer pleasure and fun. For instance, if there is any single poem that a vast number of Americans know at least partially by heart, it is not gloomy "Thanatopsis," but a poem published a few years later than Bryant's, "A Visit from St. Nicholas," which Clement Clarke Moore (1779-1863), a professor of biblical learning, wrote for his own children. Without Moore's permission a friend sent it to a newspaper, the *Troy Sentinel* (Troy, New York), where it was published anonymously on December 23, 1823. Nothing else that Moore published, including a Hebrew lexicon and a volume of poems, is remembered, but that poem continues to bring joy to millions. Let's look closely at it to see whether it represents what Traditionalists are really advocating in poetry.

Moore almost invented the modern idea of Santa Claus, though the idea of a kind of magician-elf (replacing the traditional St. Nicholas and Father Christmas) had been current in New York since Knickerbocker days. (In Dutch the name of St. Nicholas had been reduced to Sinter-claes, from which we get Santa Claus.) Any child can tell you that Santa "really" has eight reindeer (and Rudolph is only a story). Many still know there "real" names, invented (I assume) by Moore. I don't know where the red suit of modern Santa comes from. Here, remember, is how he is represented in the poem:

> He was dressed all in fur from his head to his foot,
> And his clothes were all tarnished with ashes and soot;
> A bundle of toys he had flung on his back,
> And he looked like a peddler just opening his pack.
> His eyes how they twinkled! His dimples how merry!
> His cheeks were like roses, his nose like a cherry;
> His droll little mouth was drawn up like a bow,
> And the beard on his chin was as white as the snow.
> The stump of a pipe he held tight in his teeth,
> And the smoke it encircled his head like a wreath.
> He had a broad face and a little round belly
> That shook, when he laughed, like a bowl full of jelly.
> He was chubby and plump—a right jolly old elf,
> And I laughed when I saw him, in spite of myself.

In modern illustrations and enactments the pipe and soot tend to be omitted, but most of the other details persist in our imagining. And American Christmases have also been influenced by the staunchly secular and hedonistic tone of the poem. For better or worse, it helped make Christmas fun, even rather funny, and, according to poet Howard Nemerov (as we will see later), materialistic.

What makes such a poem so influential and durable in our culture? One element is certainly its rocking meter (anapestic tetrameter). Notice that most lines break into halves, like the ancient poetry of *Beowulf*. A sharp detail is usually buried in each unit. I count eight similes in those fourteen lines above, and that pattern of providing a colorful comparison for each detail is consistent through the poem.

St. Nicholas is in the house for only twenty-two lines, of which the fourteen quoted above are devoted to description. There is surprisingly little action, little dwelling on the gifts themselves:

> He spoke not a word, but went straight to his work,
> And filled all the stockings; then turned with a jerk,
> And laying his finger aside of his nose,
> And giving a nod, up the chimney he rose.

Sixteen lines tell of the arrival of the miniature sleigh and reindeer on the roof, four of their departure. But perhaps the most memorable section of the poem (and this may be only because it is first) is its relatively long (fourteen lines) introduction. The sleeping children (how many or of what sexes we do not know) get only a couplet, but we imagine them vividly, nestled snug, dreaming of sugarplums. The parents get another couplet, comically rendered in kerchief and cap. The hush of the house (with "not even a mouse" stirring), the clatter outside and drama of flinging open the window, the beauty of the scene of snow in moonlight, occupy most of the introductory section.

Most of the phrases and sentences are simple and direct, but the couplet about the moon (which "Gave a lustre of midday to objects below") is more complex, and perhaps the most haunting and beautiful passage is an elaborate, long comparison:

> As dry leaves that before a wild hurricane fly,
> When they meet with an obstacle, mount to the sky,
> So up to the house-top the coursers they flew,
> With the sleigh full of toys—and St. Nicholas too.

That may be too complex for small children, but I enjoy the slow build, the change of pace it brings to the poem. When the reindeer fly away, the image is clearer and simpler—"like the down of a thistle."

Nothing about the poem seems condescending or cutesy-pie, and though it is highly imaginative, it doesn't strain the imagination. Indeed, the elf is made very real and domestic, an object of fond laughter. We never get tired of such a poem; we go back to it, as we do to old songs, *because* it is so familiar. We go back to it because we go back to it. But how does a poem lock itself into a culture's repertory?

While I was writing this a seven-year-old girl gave me a clue. She interrupted me to ask whether I would come downstairs and read "The House That Jack Built" to her and her three-year-old companion. They giggled while I read, and when I finished, the older girl sighed. "I love that story," she said. Some hours later I asked her why. "The way it rhymes and goes faster and faster," she explained, and she laughed again, just to think of it. Certainly much of the content is obscure—a priest all shaven and shorn, a cow with a rumpled horn, a rat that eats, of all things, malt. Form, speed, repetition, lots of specifics—and, of course, no message or moral. No one is more resistant and sensitive to moral lectures than children.

And in this respect Moore's poem captures something very basic and traditional about Christmas. In ancient Rome the celebration of the winter solstice was the Saturnalia, a time of merrymaking and present-giving. The association of the birth of Jesus with this holiday was late (fourth century) and artificial, and it seems not to have changed much the essentially pagan nature of the celebration. While I am much moved by the story of Bethlehem, it only confuses me to think of that austere stable scene of the Judean desert mixed with snow and twinkling lights and the sound of sleigh bells, school out and eggnog flowing, relatives (those paunchy Magi) clogging the highways, their cars laden with spray-on myrrh and plastic frankincense. Dylan Thomas got it right in "A Child's Christmas in Wales"—snoring uncles and tiddly aunts, useful and useless presents, but mostly escape from the house into the snow, where one could throw snowballs at cats. No matter how imaginary its elves and flying reindeer, good literature has to be grounded in recognizable reality—and for this acid test children make good litmus paper.

One could never imagine children (or Traditionalists) being attracted to this modern poem (1960s) by Howard Nemerov:

SANTA CLAUS

Somewhere on his travels the strange Child
Picked up with this overstuffed confidence man,
Affection's inverted thief, who climbs at night
Down chimneys, into dreams, with this world's goods.
Bringing all the benevolence of money,
He teaches the innocent to want, thus keeps

Our fat world rolling. His prescribed costume,
White flannel beard, red belly of cotton waste,
Conceals the thinness of essential hunger,
An appetite that feeds on satisfaction;
Or, pregnant with possessions, he brings forth
Vanity and the void. His name itself
Is corrupted, and even Saint Nicholas, in his turn
Gives off a faint and reminiscent stench,
The merest soupcon, of brimstone and the pit.

Now, at the season when the Child is born
To suffer for the world, suffer the world,
His bloated Other, jovial satellite
And sycophant, makes his appearance also
In a glitter of goodies, in a rock candy glare.
Played at the better stores by bums, for money,
This annual savior of the economy
Speaks in the parables of the dollar sign:
Suffer the little children to come to Him.

At Easter, he's anonymous again,
Just one of the crowd lunching on Calvary.

Yet Nemerov is asserting the "traditional" value of spirituality and rail-
ing against the materialism of Christmas. My own response is ambivalent. I admire Nemerov's poem for its brilliance and wit, and I have
some intellectual sympathy with his attack on the commercialization of
the holiday. But I guess I must be, in part, a Traditionalist at the core. I
like "A Visit from St. Nicholas" more than I do "Santa Claus," and I'm
afraid that our family Christmases are more characterized by visions of
sugarplums than reminders that "the Child is born / To suffer for the
world." Needless to say, children, if they understood Nemerov's poem
at all, would be put off by its moralism.

Modern as the Model T

If Traditionalists want to read and write poetry like "Jest 'fore
Christmas" and "A Visit from St. Nicholas," more power to them—
and I'll gladly read and gladly follow their lead. If one objects that I
have talked primarily about poetry for children, the lusty ballads of
Robert Service might serve as examples for adult poetry. Of his poems I
would especially recommend "Bessie's Boil," "The Ballad of Salvation
Bill," "Touch-the-button Nell," "The Cremation of Sam McGee," or
such brief lyrics as this one, which I quote from memory:

Please, Mother, don't kill Father with the bread knife.
Remember, 'twas a gift when you were wed.
But if you *must* kill Father with the bread knife,
Please, Mother, use another for the bread.

If Traditionalists can't find magazines to publish such poetry, they should start new ones. Their potential audience is enormous. And we might again have a genuine grass-roots folk poetry which would help restore to our culture some of the values and ways of relating to others for which many of us yearn.

But unfortunately, the impact of most Traditionalists is much less positive. Many seem to be cranks whose only intent is to excoriate the Modern wherever they see it, by which they mean any poetry they perceive as different or unusual or disquieting. Such people frequently join poetry societies and writers' clubs to find a forum for their gripes. They don't buy books, but they vote with a vengeance. They don't write poems, but let one appear in the club newsletter that uses a quad-ruple-letter locution (to avoid the phrase "four-letter word"), and they cancel memberships, write letters to the editor, spread gossip, retract gifts, and mobilize the block. They do not go silent into their good night. But my chief complaint is that they intimidate other poets and corrupt the young. Many are, indeed, teachers like Mrs. Bloom. I am saddened and appalled by the young people who come to me asking, *Is this proper? Does this follow the rules? Is this allowed?* Not only will they be unable to write but they will be unable to hear poetry as long as they are burdened by such inhibitions.

But to some extent the anger of the Traditionalists is understand-able. They resent the fact that we pointy-headed intellectuals have tak-en poetry away from the people. And they have reason for such resent-ment. The Modernist movement very quickly took on an elitist tone. That movement, and the resulting controversy between Traditionalists and Modernists, started in the teens of this century, the era of the Mod-el T, and continues unabated seventy years later. The premises of the debate are about the same, but the poetry written by both political camps is a lot worse than that written in the teens and twenties. There is great irony in all this, for the intent of the Modernists was to widen the audience of poetry. They were quite understandably fed up with the heavy Victorian dullness of the dominant poets. They felt the old forms were exhausted, and to reach poeple they had to wake them up with something new. In fact, "Make it new!" became a motto of Ezra Pound, one of the most active protagonists of Modernism.

Thus, in its earliest stages Modernism was a consciously populist movement. Poets of socialist sympathies, such as Vachel Lindsay and Carl Sandburg, crisscrossed the nation declaiming vigorous poetry in the speech of the common man. They were rebelling against the genteel tradition which had by practice and theory defined poetic diction as a rare and stilted language never heard on the street or in ordinary conversation. The vision of the poets was to unite society with poetry of vitality and freedom, daring in form and democratic in content.

But from the beginning the new movement was schizophrenic. These new poets were being published in many new little magazines, but especially *Poetry: a Magazine of Verse,* started by Harriet Monroe in Chicago in 1912. One of the poets who quickly attached himself to that magazine was Ezra Pound, already an expatriate, living in London, Paris, and Venice and soaking up the influence of European poetry, ancient and modern. He became "foreign correspondent" for *Poetry* and began sending back to Chicago the work of new poets he was discovering, including W. B. Yeats, T. S. Eliot, and Robert Frost.

But many American poets, including Pound, have suffered from the same kind of cultural inferiority complex that caused "Thanatopsis" to seem so bookish and removed from life. Pound was born in the provinces—Idaho—and raised near Philadelphia. Like other poets of the time, he had an early populist and socialist bent. But he seems to have felt a need to compensate for his background with superficial but recondite erudition. He hoped to enable backward Americans to stay up to date on European culture.

The schizophrenia of the resulting combination of populism and elitism can be seen by contrasting two mottoes. *Poetry* carried on its masthead a quotation from Whitman, "To have great poets there must be great audiences too." The motto of *transition,* a little magazine started by Pound in Paris after World War I (which published parts of James Joyce's *Finnegans Wake,* was "The common reader be damned." There was no way to thumb a nose at the public and at the same time draw it in as a readership. In cold economic terms it is interesting to note that before World War I publishers actually sold enough poetry that poets could make a living from book sales. That has not been possible since for any of our major poets.

But if the Modernists didn't succeed in creating a mass audience for poetry, they did manage to get poetry into the news. The debates of poets and critics raged in the little magazines and were reported by the national press. Those debates often seemed preoccupied with form, and the antipathy between the political camps has most often been seen as one between Traditionalists who believed in rhyme and meter and Modernists who believed in free verse.

But that was really only a superficial aspect of more profound differences. The older poetry expressed conventional bourgeois sentiments about nature, religion, and patriotism, the traditional values of home and hearth. The Modernists wanted poetry to deal with all aspects of life, and to emphasize that they very often turned to themes that were shocking, morbid, ribald, and critical. And, following the lead of Pound and Eliot, they peppered their poetry with esoteric allusions and enough quotations to keep armies of professors busy for years supplying footnotes.

Form and Function

When I think of Modernism of the era of the Model T, I can see a trend that affected poetry as it did our other cultural products. If you compare Tin Lizzies to the carriages they replaced, the cars appear to be very technical, noisy, ugly, fast, dangerous, and functional, a list of adjectives that could be applied to much of the poetry hailed as Modern between 1908 and about 1927, the period in which over 15 million Model T's rolled off the assembly line. The last of those adjectives, "functional," needs some explanation, as it is perhaps the most central to the concept of Modernism.

Functionalism became a seminal idea in all the arts, especially architecture, in the twenties. Louis Sullivan had issued the dictum "Form follows function," which meant that things—especially buildings—should look as though they were made for the purposes they served, a reaction to the "gingerbread" of Victorian architecture and decor. The Model T perfectly exemplified functionalism. It looked like a machine on wheels, which is what it was. One box contained the motor, and another contained the passengers. Buildings constructed under the influence of the Bauhaus school of design looked like massive boxes of glass, concrete, and steel; whether they actually were or not, they appeared to be severely economical ways to contain space.

The counterpart in poetry was free verse. The shape of the poem was determined by its content, not some imposed and artificial form. The poems didn't look like skyscrapers, of course; and, in general, they were the opposite of boxy. They actually looked squirmy on the page. But that was because the poems were saying a lot of squirmy things. Their message was revolutionary, and their form (including not only meter but diction, imagery, even grammatical structure) was designed to overthrow the old, to shock, to attract attention—much like the gaudy advertising that began to emerge in the same period.

But while advertising attempted to draw buyers in, Modernist poetry ultimately had the opposite effect. Revolutionary poetry, which flouts conventional bourgeois taste and values, speaks only to those already converted—the intellectual elite. I doubt that many have ever changed their values because they read poetry in which their values were savagely attacked. When we feel threatened, our values are reinforced, not weakened, in reflex. When readers felt that poets were, in effect, spitting in their faces, they responded as might be expected—initially with outrage, then with indifference. Poetry, they came to believe, was something they could do nicely without.

I think they are wrong about that; a culture needs a poetry that truly does what some of the early Modernists wanted to do—unite a people by expressing in their language their values and concerns. Now the social analysts are telling us we're in a postindustrial age, and terms like "poststructural" and "postmodern" are appearing in the annals of art and literary criticism. In architecture that means that the monolithic Bauhaus style is beginning to be replaced by eclectic borrowings from earlier periods and a variety of new forms in which function is not the primary aesthetic criterion. New architects believe that a house or building ought to be designed so that people actually want to live and work in it. Maybe it is time for a post-Modernist poetry created in such a way that people actually want to read it.

I can only speculate on what such post-Modernist poetry might be like. If I knew how to write it, that's what I would be doing, and so far readers have not beaten any great paths to my verses. But I am sure that its first injunction has to be *Rise above the fray!* Poetic politics have almost killed off poetry altogether. We have no popular poets writing today anywhere nearly as skilled as James Whitcomb Riley or Eugene Field or even Edgar Guest, poets who really know how to use vivid imagery, lively diction, complex rhythms, and ringing phrases to amuse, tell stories, and render the rich variety of the lives and attitudes of ordinary people in forms that they can recognize, enjoy, and remember. Nor have we any Modernist poets nearly as good as Pound and Eliot were in their early days. The best of our "serious" or "literary" poets, some of them very skilled writers, seem utterly to have lost the common touch that enabled poets such as Frost, MacLeish, Sandburg, even E. E. Cummings to reach mass audiences. Where are the Browning Societies of yesteryear?

Like post-Modernist architecture, post-Modernist poetry will have to explore the byways of the past to see what themes and forms could have modern applications. For instance, I thought once, on a lark, one might write a love poem in traditional form using computerese:

BOOTING UP

You touch my reset button, making
my screen go wavy, and then blank.
My disc-drives groan. My system checks
and loads. Then I have you to thank

for software lighting up my hardware
and rippling signals through my CRT.
My ROM begins to tingle when your RAM
absorbs the data from each input key,

filling our memories with kilobytes
of information processed, indexed, stored
in streams of on and off which bring to life
inert connections on our circuit board.

Oh, never shall my drive refuse to log
so long as chips have juice—and you to boot.
Come slip into this port: my CPU,
without your floppy disc, cannot compute.

That may not be the language of the street, but it's also not that of the
elite literary journals. In my *Homage to Shakespeare* series I took themes
from Shakespeare's sonnets and rendered them in contemporary images:

#26

Odds are against us. Even if lovers find
their opposite number in the possible range,
and juices fuse inside the wiry mind
where signals pulse across the world's exchange
they soon are disconnected. Though one goes
on shouting the empty line, flipping the book,
dialing the code again and again, he knows
that busy buzz means love is off the hook.
Yet I would slip my token in the slot
of this machine and finger out my choice
and think it lucky if at most I got
three minutes in the darkness of your voice,
  unraveling the automated gods,
    connecting mind with mind against the odds.

And the paradoxes of photography seemed to me appropriate to describe those of sensual experience:

NEGATIVE

I have lost the print, but in this negative
you can see her shape, if not much more. That black
is beach. Her hair, here white, was black. That white
is water, laced with black. Its roar and that
of the wind (not pictured here, except as her hair
flies out from her grey shoulders—they were brown)
drowned all our conversation. We lost track
that sun-bleached day (the sun here makes her frown)
of hours, words, kisses, sandwiches and beer,
all used in colorful affirmative.

We left our imprint on the sand. The sea
or wind in another season cleaned this away,
and now all black and white in each our minds
remains some blurry dent on how we lay,
some negative of warmth of other lips,
some scrape of sandy thighs, some taste of salt.
I forget now how it was, but how it ends
is negative, the afterglow of a glimpse,
turned inside out, unfleshed, with strength for fault,
remembered in the nerves transparently.

And I've tried at times to affirm rather than attack bourgeois domestic values.

EASING IN DURING THE LATE SHOW

It's all right
            wanting it this way that way, even not
wanting it's all right (though I'd rather you not want me
not to want it).
            I've checked around, and it's all right
black white old young fat thin, even (as we are) being
thickly forty, muscles giving way
                        boing! twang! like
rotting straps. (I studied our bodies in the long mirror
in the bathroom. They're all right.)

Some get their kicks being
faithful unfaithful desired desiring undesired.
Some feel guilty all the time,
or inadequate,
which is a drag for them and others, but if that
is what they can't help feeling,
I guess it's all right.
Some object
to being used as objects.
I kind
of like being used,
but if they want to hang their egos
on it that's all right with me.
It's difficult
in the bathtub or generally under water.
On the grass in the rain
it's fine, but itchy after.
On the rug by the fire it's splendid
if the kids don't come downstairs.
(The woods are overrated.)
Surreptitious is fun (notes, winks, squeezes under
tables, afternoons, no squeaking—
sneaking home).
Flagrancy is also fun
(orgies, everybody flopping
around, switching, pot, AC-DC, the works—
sounds
great, but I've not had the opportunity to).
Romantic is all right (dress up, go out, theater,
maybe the Bahamas—
though I can't see it adds that much).
In fact, in spite of
revolution and the dis-
approval of the young and its being
middleclass unintellectual inartistic and socially unconscious
while the new world blooms around us like dogwood in the bracken,
it's all right, just us,
our bed in the suburbs,
bourbon
and flicker of the set.
Hard to believe that home
is best,

      but I've found no improvement on your nudging
back in my lap, just lolling along
                          (even dozing, even
stopping to potty the boy,
                no sweat,
                          there's always more
where that came from).
                  Come once twice don't come,
                                it's all right,
drawing it out like taffy,
                and if you fantasize
on Joseph Cotten's monotone,
            that's you,
                  and it's all right.
    Perhaps one of these directions, or some combinations of them,
points the way beyond Modernism.

CHAPTER XVI:
OCCUPATION: POET

I am at a poetry workshop held on the grounds of what was once a beautiful baronial estate, now managed by a foundation as an arts center. A couple of hundred people, mostly women, have paid something like ten dollars each to attend this all-day affair. They will be served box lunches and wine and listen to four of us talking about and reading our poetry. Then there will be an "open reading" at which some twenty poets from the area will each read a few poems. Tables are set up near the entrance of the former coach house, now an auditorium, to peddle our books. I was paid two hundred dollars to be here, plus coast-to-coast air transportation and "hospitality." I suppose the other three speakers were paid approximately the same. I will gross about sixty dollars on book sales that day, twenty of which is profit. That's about how it goes at these affairs. The big beneficiaries, of course, are the airlines and motels.

Obviously, ticket sales of a couple of thousand dollars won't cover the costs. The foundation probably made the auditorium available for little or no money. Even so, the publicity, office work, catering, transportation costs, honoraria, and other items probably exceeded the cash intake. Several volunteers worked very hard to put all this together, and some may have contributed funds. The family of one of them generously opened a home for a reception. I go to workshops like this a few times a year and am grateful for the junkets and the pay. Especially after that wine at lunch I am in a rosy mood. Hooray for poetry.

Robert Creeley, the best known of the four of us performing that day, started the *Black Mountain Review,* with Charles Olson, Robert Duncan, and others at Black Mountain College in North Carolina in the mid-fifties—the group that first promulgated "open form," discussed by X. J. Kennedy in a quotation in Chapter XI. He is a little older than I am, and he's still doing what I did in my "professional" days: holding an academic position and taking time off now and then to run around the country doing gigs like this on a tight schedule—between university sessions. Yesterday he gave another workshop or reading across the nation, and he will leave us early to make it to a third a few thousand miles away, jetting here to there with socks, underwear, and books of poetry in his satchel. One can pick up several hundred dollars on a weekend that way. Poets better known than Creeley and I get a thousand or more per performance, mainly at colleges and universities. I call these "gunslinger raids" when I do them, as I leave the farm only to pick up some cash. I enjoy the little bit of public exposure they give me, but after some years on our communal farm each trip beyond the mailbox seems like a visit to an alien planet.

Waiting my turn on the platform, I look around the airy, sun-dappled room wondering, *Who are these people? What do they want?* Almost all think they are poets or are trying to be poets. Some few might admit they came just for entertainment, for the pleasure of hearing poetry, hearing literary talk, taking in some of the rather shoddy glamour associated with the speakers. Most, though, think they have come for educational purposes—such as you might have in reading this book. They want to learn how to write better or at least more successfully. Maybe it is to learn something about what it's like to be a poet. Some are editors or volunteers associated with one of the literary magazines of the region. Sample issues are for sale on the display tables. They may pick up some subscriptions. Like the others present, they are rubbing shoulders, making contacts, doing the sort of thing businesspeople do at conventions, including making social arrangements for after hours.

There's a lot of hustle going on in the world of poetry these days— and where there is hustle, there is bustle. The first speaker, a man I would guess to be in his thirties, wears a T-shirt that reads *POETRY MAN* in big letters. He says he wears it to attract the attention of kids. As head of the Poets-in-the-Schools (PITS) program in his state, he has contact with hundreds of children, and he says he sees each as a potential customer for his books of poetry, which are indeed (he tells us) selling well (more than I can say for mine—and probably more than Creely can say for his). The "poetry man" is paid over twenty thousand a year for his work with PITS, and it's obvious that he wields substantial power in allocating money to other poets, who get a hundred or more per day for working in the schools.

He recommends that poets get in on the bonanza. PITS money comes from the National Endowment for the Arts and is allocated through state arts councils. (It works somewhat differently in each state.) Its administrators are usually political appointees, so you can find out about it through the political party currently running your state government. To qualify, you have to have some half-dozen poems published in magazines, but that should be easy, as many of the magazines and small presses are also supported by NEA, directly or indirectly through state arts councils, or by the Coordinating Council of Literary Magazines (CCLM), which gets part of its funding from NEA.

Never has it been so easy for an unknown poet to get into print (though getting read is more difficult). There are hundreds, indeed thousands of small presses and little magazines because government (and foundations) are in the arts as never before—though some think still not enough. Consequently, a lot of jockeying and politicking and backbiting is going on among the small presses, magazines, poets, artists, arts groups, and what have you, scrambling for this unprecedented flow of funds. And, in addition, most poets I know have thrown their hat into the ring for one of the numerous $10,000 (or higher) Creative Writing Fellowships handed out annually by NEA.

Yet dollar-for-dollar payment for poems in the few magazines that pay anything at all for poetry is hardly better now than it was at the turn of the century (when a dollar per line for magazine or newspaper publication was not uncommon), and book sales of poetry are actually worse. What has grown has been what might be called poetic activity—a proliferation of little (nonpaying) magazines, awards, prizes, workshops, conferences, and fellowships. I fear that what has principally diminished is the number of readers.

The Personality Game

We live in an age of personality cults in which gossip columns and news about private lives sustain many magazines. If you write prose, your publisher will be considering your talk-show potential along with your manuscript. Poets (not counting Myrtle Whimple) don't often make it to talk shows, but workshops and readings are a substitute—on a much lower scale. Dylan Thomas, in the fifties, brought poetry back to the platform in America, in the tradition of Vachel Lindsay and Carl Sandburg. Thomas read excellent poetry—his own and that of others—but I'm not sure that was the main appeal for his large crowds. He had a voice that could make a list of want ads sound like the Book of Job, and, besides, his talent for self-dramatization created a titillation that may have smothered appreciation of poetry. *Would he show up at all? Would he come on stage drunk? Would he make a fool of himself at the party afterward?* Who really absorbed "Fern hill" or "A Refusal to Mourn. . ." in that context?

In his wake came the Beats, who added color to their performance much as rock groups have done since—stripping off clothing, reading to musical accompaniment, clowning, and shouting obscenities. What a thrill. Going to a poetry reading was like going to see King Kong chained onstage. Some critics proclaimed that Bob Dylan was the greatest poet in America, and though the lyrics printed on his album covers were at best bromide and at worst gibberish, he sure put them over in performance, which was less singing than rasping recitation.

Poet Donald Allen (and others, such as Anne Sexton), who traveled the circuits a lot in the sixties, warned that poems might become no more than scripts for performance, and, in fact, that has happened. Much of the most notable (and vital) poetry being written today is conceived of as oral entertainment, written by the new jongleurs. A book of poems by, say, Edward Field, is in effect a collection of monologues for stand-up comedy. One can almost imagine parenthetical stage directions: *scratch head, shrug, grin, pause.* Allen Ginsberg used to appear shaggy and scruffy; now his beard is trimmed and he wears a business suit. But he still chinks finger chimes and drones mantras at his reading. Robert Bly wears Halloween masks. So far I haven't heard of a poet doing lariat tricks like Will Rogers, but that may happen.

Or we may have cable video channels interspersing enacted poems like the current videotapes of rock music. Maybe poets will bypass print altogether. But that wouldn't be as shocking a development as it may appear. Poetry ancient and modern has been primarily an oral art, an art of performance. The current prevalence of poetry readings is quite in keeping with the tradition of the bards and scopes and actors in their buskins. Maybe we are past the days of the constipated poetry, too tied to the printed page, of poems like intellectual exercises to be pondered, decoded, and solved like crossword puzzles. The pendulum seems to be swinging the other way.

Anonymous Artists

But I think there is an unhealthy dependence upon the personality of the poet in performances. An epic of Homer's or script of Shakespeare's or composition of Beethoven's is great precisely because it does *not* require the personal presence of the artist to work effectively. To some degree art is an expression of self, but it is more significantly a transcendence of self. Whitman's *Song of Myself* is a definitive example. In spite of the title's promise of an exercise in egocentricity, and in spite of the pervasive voice throughout of a distinct personality, the poem reveals almost nothing of the man who wrote it. His voice suffuses its many parts as that of Shakespeare animates the individual voices of his plays. Whitman wrote as though he wanted to press his very flesh to ours. But when his poetry is great, it is so in spite of—not because of—that impulse.

When we overemphasize the poet in the flesh, we forget that the trick of art is to create perpetual motion. It must fuel itself. If you have to run along behind, as some inventors do with their experimental aircraft, leveling a wing or lifting a tail or giving a shove, your poem fails. And, alas, not much of the poetry written during the last ten years flies on its own, not even so well as the brain-bound academic poetry of the midcentury. For example, Robert Lowell began as a promising poet, but he became a public personality, appearing in the newsmagazines, and his later poetry is unintelligible without a detailed knowledge of the events of his life. He swirled down the sink of self, epitomizing what was happening to the best and the brightest.

Meanwhile, all this funding stimulates and sustains mediocrity, and mediocre poetry (like bad currency) drives out good. Since much of the money comes from the government, there has to be a certain emphasis on its democratic spread. Too much quality would seem elitist. If you want a grant, be sure to promise to publish children, the elderly, the minorities, all the folks we haven't heard from. And while I am glad to see the poor and downtrodden and overlooked getting a chance and to see even mediocre poets get money, I am not sure this environment is good for the art.

Hanging Out Your Shingle

The PITS man advertised himself on his T-shirt. Creeley told an anecdote about identifying himself as "poet" when they asked for his occupation in a police lineup. The third speaker, a young housewife-poet, told us how she manufactured poems out of any common experience—spilling coffee on a dress, seeing a robin escape a cat, getting flustered on the freeway. She was right. Anyone can do it, though probably not so well as she can. The general message was that all those in the audience should be brave and hang out a shingle announcing themselves as poets. The PITS man carried that message to the schools: He got all that money for going around anointing each child as a poet. And I have to agree with their message. Sure, we're all poets. Get in the act. See my poem "You Have to Toot Your Own Horn" in Chapter II for advice on this subject. Anyone who writes what he or she calls a poem is a poet, and most people have done that at least once in their lives.

But the implication of what I was hearing was something more. At the same time they said anyone can do it, they also implied that the status of poet was something special, like being born again. The Muse will speak to you if you just listen. *Afflautence* will come over you (I just invented that portmanteau word, combining "afflautus," "flatulence," and "affluence." They weren't talking about a craft involving any particular knowledge or skill. They emphasized how easily, naturally, their poems came. They weren't teaching people how to write poems. They were saying, in a kind of humble-pie patter, *I don't know how I do it. Spirits must be working my fingers as I sit at the typewriter.*

I wondered what the two hundred were getting out of all this. I was reminded of sitting in church as an adolescent, my heart aching for the spirit to speak to me. It never spoke. (I finally lied and said it had so I could join. Each must be wondering, *Am I a Poet?* (The capital *P* distinguishes that special status from that of someone who simply writes poetry from time to time.) Would they lie to join the church? Would they agonize in the night, wondering whether they really *were* Poets, wondering whether the world would ever find them—or find out they were frauds. Could they qualify for a grant? Could they get into PITS and go out and anoint schoolchildren for one hundred dollars a day?

But, then, I play devil's advocate so often it's beginning to feel like typecasting. Who asked Jud to puncture the balloon? I certainly agree that every child and every person has unused imagination, that each should be encouraged to express it. And among the things taxpayers' money is spent for, poetry and the arts are surely among the least harmful. Could government and foundation money make every individual in the nation deeply aware of and joyous about his or her spiritual nature and innate worth, I, too, would rejoice.

But I don't think that's what's happening. I worry about real heads in real ovens—the record of poetic suicides being very high, and related, I think, to this sense of special status in that word "Poet." Some develop agonizing self-doubt when they try to live up to their reputation and often have to face a void within. I think even Dylan Thomas's death by alcoholism (the hospital described it as "an insult to the brain") was a kind of suicide resulting from the hopelessness of trying forever to outshine his last performance.

And, though it may be presumptuous of me, I worry, too, about those who make such pronouncements and then do *not* see a void when they look within. I wouldn't pick on my other fellow panelists (the PITS man and the woman) by name because they are not nationally known, but I do wonder what Robert Creeley sees when he looks within. Here is a fairly representative example of the poetry that has earned him a reputation that keeps him in the jet set:

SOMEWHERE

The galloping collections of boards
are the house which I afforded
one evening to walk into
just as the night came down.

Dark inside, the candle
lit of its own free will, the attic
groaned then, the stairs
led me up into the air.

From outside, it must have seemed
a wonder that it was
the inside *he* as *me* saw
in the dark there.

That's no script for a stand-up comic. I don't know *what* it is. To me it seems to have no meaning, imagery, vitality, energy, thought, rhythm, or sonority. There was a movement called *minimalism* in the sixties in which, according to *The Harper Dictionary of Modern Thought*, "all elements of expressiveness and illusion are minimized." It meant seeing how little paint you could put on a canvas and still sell it in an art gallery. Maybe this 1959 poem was a precursor of that movement, an effort to find words that to the slightest degree possible disturb the blankness of the page. Most of Creeley's poems I have read—some of them quite long—are equally vaporous. He's making a career of noncommunication.

I had never met him before that workshop, nor have I met him since, but I genuinely liked the man—as did the audience. He is sweet, unassuming, quiet in manner, reading and talking in an agreeable mumble which makes one blame one's incomprehension on hearing or acoustics in the auditorium. As literary curiosities go, he is certainly one of the most harmless. I can see why the cops who had him in their lineup and heard he was a poet let him go.

Except he might be charged with devaluing the currency. I worry about readership—the people who pick up these proliferating publications, who see prose dribbled down the page artlessly, ostentatiously, self-indulgently, or incoherently. Will they develop a taste for Keats and Shakespeare and Frost and Eliot? For my poetry? For yours? Even if they buy my books, will they read them? I am beginning to think that the cornucopia of poetry, poets, and publications everywhere is a plague. As early as 1978, poet Felix Stefanile was protesting (in *Tri-Quarterly Review*):

In each of the categories cited—the movement, the schools, the govern-ment programs . . . the mounting evidence of NEA influence is clear. By now literally millions of dollars have been given to the magazines. There exists a monolithic and automatic filtration system connecting the schools with CETA, PITS, and the Creative Writing Fellowships, still more and more millions of dollars. I have not so much been pointing out components on a grid as to one vast chaos of poetry palaver, misnamed renaissance, state arts councils, neighborhood betterment projects, new educational plans . . . and so forth.

It would be different if poetry were a wholesome and innocent art, like painting by the numbers, which people could practice on Sundays for their own amusement and development and the pleasure of family and friends. But, no, poetry demands an audience—specifically one that does *not* consist (at least exclusively) of families and friends.

And just as many sing in showers and few at Carnegie Hall, few write poetry well enough to hold the attention of an audience. They settle for two things that are very different from an audience—publica-tion and status. Unread poetry must by now occupy more printed pag-es than unread government statistics (publication paid for by the same taxpayers). And status is as cheap as a Smiley button. All you have to do is wear a T-shirt—or not even that. Just toot your horn.

POET as Verb

Troubled by these thoughts, I took a hike after the workshop into the surrounding wooded mountains, thinking of our own log cabin in the mountains a few jet hours away. The workshops I experienced there were among the most enriching occasions in my life. Real people dealt with real problems, and though their poetry may not have been immortal, it served to open the way for exchanges regarding profound human concerns, among them art and literature. That all seemed very distant from this workshop on the front line of the poetry game. I wished some poet could function for that crowd as the old stamp col-lector functioned for me, helping them sort out the factitious from the genuine. I tried, when it was my turn to speak, but the resentment in the auditorium was palpable. I wasn't old and revered enough. Maybe I myself wasn't genuine.

PLEXUS AND NEXUS

I can prove who I am. I draw my wallet like
a six-gun. Look what all these numbers show:
core, corpse, corpuscle in many systems. Stopped,
I see in the mirror an upturned radio.

That tall young nun studies the mirror daily
learning to show emotion on her face.
That black boy sits in the darkness staring at
the image in the mirror of his race.

But I with light and sticky step may travel
the web of the world, springing the tense strands,
sensing the signals at each intersection,
darting the way my heart (it seems) commands.

I am the fly in the network and the network.
I exist at many levels, if at all.
I am the thousand images receding
in every surface of the mirrored hall.
I diffuse at the speed of light.
                              Remember me!
the honest ghost, the wave, the pulse, the fleet shape
imprinted on and by all I have met.

Experience runs through me like a tape.

APPENDIX: PUBLISHING POETRY

A poem exists as soon as it has been composed in the mind. It is "published" as soon as it is written down or recited—made public. Anyone can publish poetry by copying it out in handwriting, typing it with carbons, or using a photocopy machine. But that doesn't satisfy most. The poem still doesn't seem quite real until it has been "accepted" by an editor and appears in a periodical or book. That's what we usually mean by the term "publication." It is as though the creative act were dependent for its completion not only upon the judgment of others but on the vicissitudes of the marketplace. And for most poets, *printing*, which is one thing, and *publication*, which is quite another, are shrouded in mystery.

This appendix is intended to dispel the mystery. You should become as comfortable with the processes of printing and publication as you might be with singing in the shower or showing guests through your garden. Even poetry that critics judge to be poor may serve important functions for its author, and it may bring pleasure and enrichment to others. But the mystique of publication inhibits the flow of creativity and tends to contain the art as the province of a privileged elite.

On Becoming Rich and Famous . . .

I'm all in favor of poets being recognized and paid as much as possible. But if recognition and payment are what you are after, poetry is one of the worst possible ways to go about getting these. Hundreds of my poems have been published during the past forty years, many in highly respected magazines, yet I assure you it has brought me little fame and fortune. For one long series of poems (the first six of the *Rumors of Change*) I received $500. *Ladies' Home Journal* once paid me $10 a line for a twenty-line poem. Several anthologies paid me $25 to $50 for reprint rights for individual poems. These were top rates for the times, and it's a good thing I wasn't trying to feed my family on the proceeds—or indeed from the proceeds of writing. I have written a dozen published books, literally hundreds of articles, stories, plays, essays, and reviews for magazines, columns in various magazines (including *Writer's Digest*, for whom I have been writing monthly for over a quarter century), and my writing has never brought in more than about $5,000 per year. I'm neither bragging nor complaining. I just want you to be realistic about your own prospects.

A dozen acceptances in a year from respected, paying markets (e.g., *Harper's, The Atlantic*) at less than $100 a poem would mean a year of dazzling success for the best-known poets in the country. An advance of $500 on a collection of poetry from a major publisher would be generous, and the book would be almost certain to earn no royalties beyond its advance (I'll explain later what that means). Poets don't support themselves writing poetry. Some few draw healthy fees from readings, as I mentioned in Chapter XVII. (I usually get about $250 per reading a few times a year.) Others are able to publish more profitable prose (e.g., James Dickey's novel and film *Deliverance*, the novels of Marge Piercy). Their reputation as poets might even help those sales, and prose might help the sale of their poetry, too. Erica Jong's first two books were poetry, and no more successful than most, but after her novel *Fear of Flying* was a best-seller and subsequent novels extended her audience even further, a collection of poems, *Ordinary Miracles*, 1983, came out in an edition of 5,000 hardcover and 25,000 paperback copies—an astonishingly large printing for "serious" poetry.

So how do poets get by? Some subsist as Robert Lowell did—almost entirely on inherited wealth. I recommend that route, though for some reason I have never been able to follow it. Wallace Stevens was an insurance executive. William Carlos Williams was a doctor. Some sponge a lot. Some live hand to mouth, doing odd jobs. Many are teachers or professors, as I was for twenty years. Some are supported by their mates. But for none that I know of is poetry a full-time profession. You don't become a poet as you become a doctor, lawyer, or business executive. You become a doctor, lawyer, or business executive and then write poetry if and when you can.

It would be almost impossible to write poetry "full-time" anyway. I was once at a writers' and artists' colony (the Huntington Hartford Foundation), primarily to work on verse plays. For a few weeks I was to be relieved of the pressures of job and family. They put each of us in a cottage and brought us our lunches in a basket so as not to interrupt our work. We were forbidden to disturb one another during the day, though we were allowed to socialize in the evenings. I can be very prolific under those conditions. I finished my official project—the verse play I had started before I came—then two more, then decided to use my remaining couple of weeks writing poems. Given that opportunity for concentration, I started turning out the *Instructions for Acting* series, some of which you saw in Chapter IX. I was finishing one, two, or three poems per day—and rapidly going bananas. In the past I might have worked on a single poem off and on for years, but not for hours and days at a time. I couldn't concentrate on reading or any other activity because I thought I should be writing, and a couple of hours of concentration on a poem would exhaust me. It was like feeling obliged to make love all day long. Luckily for me, if not for her, one of my daughters got sick and I had to leave the foundation early. Then I went back to my normal rhythm, squeezing time from other things a few times a month to work on a poem.

These conditions I am describing are probably healthy for poetry. If the rewards were comparable to those for, say, television scripts, so, probably, would be the products. I just compared writing poems to making love, and the analogy is instructive in many ways. Not many are willing to pay me for either activity, or not much, or not steadily, and that's probably just as well. It it were otherwise, what I would be making would not long be either poetry or love.

Fame is a lot easier to acquire through poetry than is an income. I was told that when Wallace Stevens won the Bollingen Prize, one of our most prestigious literary awards, his book, *Auroras of Autumn,* had sold sixty-six copies. But, then, the Bollingen Prize carried a handsome cash stipend—$50,000, I believe—so his problems of fame and fortune were solved at a single stroke. All he needed then was an audience.

But fame is tricky and corrupting. Whose opinion do you respect— and why? One might think that the critical appreciation a poet would most value is the approbation of a tiny but knowledgeable community of fellow poets. But in fact, the opinions poets have of one another's work (including those I have expressed in this book regarding poetry by my colleagues) are even more suspect than those of critics who are not poets. Poets have a row to hoe—a kind of poetry we passionately value—and we are inclined to dislike other kinds just as passionately.

So we all yearn to be recognized—but by whom? It's helpful when one's name is known by magazine and book editors, and they can keep their opinions to themselves so long as they publish our work. I am pleased when crowds turn out to hear me on the basis of my name, even though I realize few of those who come are familiar with my poetry. We all appreciate grants and awards and favorable reviews. But fame is a thin reward compared to the satisfaction in the poetry itself. Writing remains that lonely art Dylan Thomas described (see Chapter VII). In spite of his fabulous success during his lifetime, Thomas earned little by writing, which forced him into the orgiastic reading tours, capitalizing on his fame, which killed him. He will be better rewarded by the lovers through the ages who pay no praise nor wages. And you'll be a happier and better person if you can put both praise and wages out of your head—though that isn't easy.

Should I get an agent?

Forget it. There may be some "agents" who will send your poetry around for a fee (instead of the conventional 10 percent of the sale price), but such people are seeking to exploit you. Few respectable agents handle poetry at all, and then only for writers who are successfully selling prose and for whom poetry is a sideline. Most poetry—even by famous poets—is published in literary magazines which pay very little or nothing. (Many pay only in contributor's copies.) I know of only a handful of national magazines sold on newsstands that buy any freelance poetry at all. Payment from these magazines ranges upward from about $25 for a poem, which would mean upward of $2.50 for an agent. If an agent placed a book for you that brought a $500 advance, he'd make $50. That's not enough to make it worth the agent's time.

For a poet an agent would be like an accountant for a boy with a paper route. Rod McKuen (see Chapter XVI) no doubt has an agent or, more likely, a business manager and maybe a chauffeur. But I think your circumstances will let you know when that is appropriate. If you indulge your vanity and engage an agent (such as one that advertises in writers' magazines), you will be charged accordingly, for the only ones who will take your work have to profit from you directly, not from your poetry. No, you don't get an agent. You peddle your own work—and I'll tell you how to go about that in a later section.

Should I copyright my work?

Only if you want to restrict its circulation, and it's hard to imagine why a poet should want that. Your work is copyrighted by common law until it is published in a book, magazine, or newspaper, so you don't need to copyright it before mailing it out to editors. When it is printed and offered for sale or free distribution to the public, it becomes "public domain" unless it is marked "Copyright" or © with the year of publication and name of the person or entity holding the copyright. It need not be registered with the Copyright Office, but if you want to register it, write the Copyright Office, Library of Congress, Washington, D.C. 20559, for an application form, which you return with two copies of the work and a small fee. They will also send you an explanation of the law.

If your work is copyrighted, others may not publish it without your permission. When someone requests such permission, you may require a fee for the privilege. (And you may ask them to indicate that the work is copyrighted, in whose name in what year.) If it is public domain, no permission or fee is required, though in practice most editors ask permission, and, if they are paying for other material they are using, they will usually pay you a reasonable fee.

Usually you needn't concern yourself with this process. If a magazine accepts your work for publication, the editors should (and usually do) notify you when it will appear. If the magazine pays, you might be paid on acceptance or on publication. Ask if the magazine is copyrighted. Some little magazines don't copyright each issue, though most do, and your work is protected by that copyright. When requests for reprinting are received by the magazine, the editor usually forwards those to the author as a matter of courtesy. If you want the copyright in your name, you may ask the magazine to assign it to you, and most do so as a routine matter. Or if you want to use your poem in a book and have not arranged for transfer of copyright to your name, you should ask the magazine for permission to use it or, at that point, have the copyright assigned to your name.

Book publishers usually take out a copyright in the name of the author, but you sign a contract granting the publisher the *exclusive* right to publish that work. If you want to use your poem elsewhere after it has appeared in a book, you need the publisher's permission to do so—but it is almost certain to be granted as a courtesy.

So much for theory. In practice I ignore all that folderol. I have deliberately put much of my work into the public domain because I *want* people to spread it around, and there is so little money to be made on poetry at best, I don't see much reason to protect it.

Though I know it is heresy for any writer to say this, I don't see that copyright serves the poet's interest. Like patents, copyrights are intended to enable creators to profit from their work, and if what you write is likely to earn big profits, that may well concern you. Certainly it concerns commercial publishers: As I will explain later, copyrights are the mainstay of their business. And one reason you might want to protect your copyrights is to have something to sell to publishers. But since a poet is likely to derive little income from his work at best, and none at all unless there is some public demand for his work, and since copyright limits circulation, I don't see why a poet should want it. I just pulled out of the wastebasket one of the dozens of privately printed first collections of poetry I receive each year from poets who hope I will review or comment on their work (which I rarely have time to do). It bears this imposing notice:

Copyright © 1984 by _____

I just broke the law by copying that notice on my word processor! The poor lady may have paid some lucky attorney to help draw up that statement, but I hereby grant you permission to copy it for your own book if you want to use it. Just think what you will have achieved. You will have prevented some lonely fellow from reading your poems to his girlfriend over the phone in the middle of the night, since he can't possibly get your written permission at that hour. You will probably prevent teachers from making photocopies to use in their classes, since few plan ahead carefully enough or bother to get written permission in advance. Indeed, you will have prevented any spontaneous spreading of your words—except for one detail. No one really pays much attention to such notices. If your work is really good, it'll no doubt get spread around without your permission, in spite of all your legalistic snarling.

If it were my book, I would say, "I beg you to reproduce or transmit in any form or by any means, electronic or mechanical, . . . etc." Someone might hear of or benefit from my work. Some commercial publisher might track me down and ask to bring out my next collection. Someone might want to hire me to write something for money.

But I warn you, my attitude is idiosyncratic. I believe patents are violations of the principle of free and open communication of scientific discovery. And I believe that literature is only cramped and corrupted by notions of private ownership. I'm grateful that most of the literature we treasure was written and published before anyone ever came up with the idea of copyright.

Should I submit my poetry to magazines?

Probably, but I hope you'll think about some of these things before you do. Do you read poetry in magazines. Which magazines? Do you know people who read poetry in magazines? Do you want them to read your work?

In the seventies my own answers to these questions were so negative I more or less stopped bothering with magazines. Sure, I read the poems in the general magazines that happened into my hands—usually in some place like a doctor's office. And I usually couldn't figure out why the editors had chosen to print what I read. I certainly saw little that encouraged me to think they would like what *I* wrote. Literary magazines come to me by the bundle because the editors want me to mention them in my column in *Writer's Digest,* and I make it a point to read a few poems in each one. But, again, I rarely find much that I really enjoy or am engaged by. My friends don't read much poetry—and when they do, they usually prefer the older work in the anthologies to what is currently published.

I asked myself, *For whom am I writing these poems?* Back in the fifties and sixties, when John Ciardi was poetry editor of *Saturday Review,* my poems published in that magazine often brought me letters (which I deeply appreciated) of comment from readers. I still occasionally hear from someone who has been carrying a poem of mine for years—probably one clipped from *Saturday Review.* But I've rarely had that experience with poems published elsewhere, certainly not in the little literary magazines where most of them appeared. By the seventies, of course, I had had enough acceptances that I knew I could get poems published if I tried—and I imagine most of you will want to prove yourself in that fashion, though I'm not sure what you're proving. If you want a commercial publisher or even a good small press (see discussion later) to bring out a book of your poems, you'll probably have to rack up a list of credits in good magazine publications first. So you have to go through with it. But just don't expect too much gratification from the process. Someone once compared the thrill of having a poem appear in a magazine to that of dropping a leaf in a well and listening for the splash. Unfortunately, though, we have few other ways of making any splash at all.

So how do you go about it? When I was regularly sending out poems, I kept about a dozen envelopes in circulation at a time, each containing some three to five poems. I kept careful records of where I had sent them, starting with the general magazines such as those I have mentioned, then when they returned, sent them right out again to the next magazine down the list, first to the ones that paid, then to those with greatest prestige among the ones that didn't pay, then to less well known literary magazines—often to publications I had never seen, whose names I got from market lists.

If you submit to magazines you don't know firsthand (all editors advise against it), be sure the magazine at least publishes poetry. It is, of course, much wiser to study sample issues before submitting, but you can use *Writer's Market, Judson Jerome's Directory of Publishers of Poetry* (both published by Writer's Digest Books), and *The International Di-*

rectory of Little Magazines and Small Presses (published by Dustbooks, Paradise, CA 95969) for descriptions that will give you some idea of what kind of material these magazines use, whether and what they pay, and any instructions they have for submission (e.g., some consider manuscripts only during specific months of the year). These reference books should be in your library, and they're updated annually.

Of those directories, *Writer's Market* has more commercial listings, *International Directory* lists many more small literary magazines, and the new publication I will be editing as of 1985 should be more complete in regard to both, but it won't, of course, include magazines or publishers that do *not* take poetry. As a writer you should be familiar with all three.

Another good way to find out about markets is to spend time in library reading rooms, especially of university libraries, which often have collections of little magazines. If you happen to live in a large city, there may be a literary bookstore that stocks small-press publications. In the Washington, D.C., area there is a Writers' Center with an excellent collection of little magazines and small-press books, and other areas may have similar facilities. Moreover, in the libraries, bookstores, and writing centers you can meet other poets and share information about publications.

What format should I use for my manuscripts?

They should be typed (or word processed), and poems, especially, should be letter-perfect. Some editors are prejudiced against dot-matrix printers, but that attitude is changing as printers are improved. The print should be dark and *look* like typing.

If the poem will fit on one page double-spaced, double-space it; but if double-spacing makes it run over onto an extra page, it might be better to single-space it. The *appearance* of the poem, the integrity of lines and stanzas, and the overall spacing are usually the most important manuscript considerations. But some contests and some book publishers have specific requirements—for example, that all manuscripts be double-spaced. If in doubt, send an SASE (self-addressed stamped envelope) for guidelines.

Your name and address should be at the upper right of the first page of *each* manuscript—that is, each poem—and your last name and short title of the poem on all subsequent pages of each. Always enclose a SASE with sufficient postage to cover return of all the material you send. Some poets use 9"x12" envelopes so they can send their poems flat, but that's not necessary. An ordinary #10 envelope, folded, will do.

There is a difference of opinion among editors about whether a "cover letter" giving a brief indication of previous publication is advisable. Some editors like to have such information when they are considering an author's work, but in my years of magazine editing I found cover letters annoying—just more words and papers to deal with. I wasn't about to give a poet more, or more careful, consideration for having been published elsewhere. And a letter saying in effect that you are submitting the enclosed material for possible publication and so on seems redundant. Why else send the manuscript to the magazine? I noticed, too, that it was the most amateurish of writers who chattered in cover letters about such things as "first American serial rights only." It's like a job applicant who starts off his interview asking about the retirement plan. Simplify the process. Write poems that hold the attention of editors. Discussion of details can come later if there's anything to discuss. But, as I say, editors differ in their tastes. There is no *harm* in including a note about prior publications. Try it both ways.

If you are a member of a church, club, or special interest group (e.g., senior citizens, gun collectors, horse breeders), you may know of newsletters or other publications that aren't listed in the directories mentioned above. And these may reach the audience of most interest to you. Local newspapers serve the same purpose. But if your hope is to gain critical recognition as a poet, only the "quality" general magazines (*Harper's, The Atlantic, The New Yorker*) and the literary quarterlies and little magazines are relevant to that purpose. Look at the credit page in the front of books by poets you admire to see where *they* were published. That will help you find the literary ambience in which you are most likely to flower.

But a lot of postage and stationery and the time of a lot of poets and editors are wasted in the process. And a lot of poetry goes straight to obscurity that way—appearing in a little magazine with few readers and quickly forgotten. I have stacks of such magazines where my poetry appeared over the years, and they are small but sad reminders of the excitement I had writing those poems. They remind me also of the hundreds of poems by other poets in the same magazines, poems I never read. What was it all about? Communication? Nil. Fame? Little— and what little occurred was mostly a nuisance. Wealth? Nil. Art? Who's to judge? The professor who this year happens to be poetry editor of the *Plottsville College Quarterly?* I found the whole scurry of submission, rejection, and acceptance (note the degrading emotional overtones of those words) a distraction from poetic concerns.

But there is really no alternative. Yes, you should try the magazines—with judgment. Buy sample copies. Most of those little magazines are published on a shoestring, and much of their circulation has to be among folks like you who are getting acquainted with the literary world. And maybe you'll find soulmates and allies in improving the dreary scene, or maybe you won't find it as dreary as I do.

To which publishers should I submit my collection?

Many publishers won't look at poetry at all. Check the directories I have mentioned before trying any. Better yet, look in the modern poetry section (the 850s in the Dewey Decimal System) of your library and check your local bookstores. See who has published the poetry *you* like; they may be the publishers who're most likely to respond to your work.

The few volumes published each year by the big trade publishers are the ones most likely to be reviewed and to win awards. Such publishers bring out poetry primarily for prestige. Over the years it pays them to have a Robert Lowell or Sylvia Plath on their lists, but most of the poets who seem significant in any given year are bound for obscurity. So the editions are small, the publishers make minimal efforts to distribute most of them, and the bulk of even the small editions (often only a thousand or two) are remaindered (that is, sold at reduced prices to book wholesalers in order to clear the warehouse). If you have been publishing widely in the quarterlies, little magazines, and quality general magazines, if your name is bandied about on the cocktail circuit, if you have friends in the literary Establishment, or if you are famous or notorious for reasons other than poetry, it might be worth your while to submit to the big trade publishers. Personally, I never bothered. It's expensive and time-consuming, and the likelihood is that your manuscript will be returned after only cursory examination.

For these reasons even well-established poets are turning increasingly to the small publishers and university presses. Some of the latter, especially, have quite distinguished series, such as those published by Wesleyan University and the Carnegie Mellon University. Many believe that the future of publishing in this country for all specialized interests, including artistic writing, lies in the small-press movement, which is flourishing today. We are in the midst of a process of decentralization in which New York and the other major cities are losing their grip on the arts in general and literary publication in particular.

Moreover, much interest (and publication) of poetry today reflects regional interests. If you live in the Pacific Northwest, or the Southwest, or the Deep South, look first for the small publishers (and magazines) near home with which you can identify. It always helps to know the people involved personally, to know the work of other regional poets, and to participate in readings, workshops, and other literary activities in your area.

For all publishers, big and small, query (with SASE) before sending a whole manuscript. Your query might include a sample (e.g., up to about five pages) of your work. If you are dealing with a small press, inquire whether you will have to contribute to the cost of publication and what the terms will be. Many poets enjoy and benefit from participating in the whole process—from financing to printing to sales—and many small presses rely on this kind of participation. But be suspicious of flattery. I will discuss vanity publication later, but it is often difficult for a neophyte to distinguish between small presses of high quality, some of whom require subsidization from their authors, from vanity presses. A good publisher has no need to be lavish with praise—and a good poet would be suspicious of it, anyway.

When you know—as I hope you do by now—that it is difficult to sell even the best poetry, beware of promises. Ask the press how they handle advertising, distribution, and what kind of reviews of their books they have been getting, keeping your phoniness-detector turned on at all times. Beginning poets are notorious suckers for all kinds of scams. But always remember that there are literally hundreds of honest small presses of high caliber with a genuine interest in finding and promoting good poetry. They need your help just as they need your poetry (if it's good). Genuine interpersonal relationship and friendship are often your best guide—along with your taste for the sort of work the press publishes.

A little reflection should help you understand why these conditions are so difficult. Some small-press publishers do succeed in getting their books into bookstores (usually on consignment, which is a pain for the publishers) and getting their books reviewed in little magazines. Some also advertise in little magazines, where the rates are not prohibitive.

But who buys these books in bookstores? Who reads these reviews? Do you, for instance? I don't—and I've been working in this field a long time. Who orders books he or she has seen ads for? What would the state of poetry be like if it were dependent on people like you (or me) for sales? I'm amazed that poetry does as well as it does in our economic world.

If you consider yourself a poet and are interested in getting a book published, and presumably would like people to buy that book once it appears, you might ask yourself how many books of poetry you bought in the last twelve months. Where did you find out about them? What impelled you to buy them? Did you read a review and send your check to the publisher? Did you find the book in a bookstore? Your answers to questions such as these should be a guide to what you may expect when you enter the market with your poetry.

What is a publisher?

Don't confuse printing with publishing. Printing is simply the manufacture of multiple copies, and it will be discussed in a later section. You can print your work yourself, but economical and aesthetically pleasing printing can best be done by equipment too expensive for most individuals to own and too complex for most of us to use. You can publish your own work, too, simply by making it available to the public in any form. Self-publication and home printing are ancient and honorable means for poets to reach readers. Robert Frost's first book was a single poem in an edition limited to two copies, one of which he gave to his girlfriend. Walt Whitman not only set type for his *Leaves of Grass* but wrote (anonymously) many of its reviews. Through most of the history of literature the relation between poet and public has been much more direct than it conventionally is today—and that was probably a benefit to literature.

For information on self-publishing write COSMEP, Committee of Small Press Editors and Publishers, P.O. Box 703, San Francisco, CA 94101. If you join, you get a packet of pamphlets on various aspects of printing and publishing and a subscription to a small-press newsletter. There are also a number of useful books that COSMEP can lead you to. *How to Get Happily Published* (Harper & Row) is a good general guide you can find in your library.

A printer manufactures books. A bookseller buys these and markets them for a profit. But in between, in modern practice, there is likely to be a publisher. Some publishers, for economic reasons, have their own printing plants, but their function as publishers is incidental to that, and many farm out some or all of their printing.

A publisher is essentially a broker. You want your work printed and into the hands of booksellers, but you don't want to pay the printing bill and you don't want to, or can't easily, distribute to sellers. So you engage a broker. If the publisher sees it to his advantage, he may agree to pay the printing bill in exchange for exclusive control of your copyright. Just as manufacturers buy a lot more patents than they ever use, partly to keep competitors from using them, publishers contract for a lot more books than they expect to sell. And they usually include a requirement that you submit your next book to them, so they, in effect, have rights for two books in each contract.

To understand how that works, consider my father, an oil royalty broker. He bought and sold mineral rights of farms that had not been drilled and, in many cases, on which no one had any intention of drilling. Should oil happen to be struck anywhere in the area, it was a great advantage to have the mineral rights sewed up. He had nothing to do with the actual drilling or selling of oil. He just sat on the rights and hoped for a chance to collect, like a fisherman with a lot of lines in the water.

Similarly, publishers contract for and bring out nominal editions of many books that they never advertise or make any serious attempt to distribute to booksellers. They are sitting on the copyrights—just in case. Should there suddenly, for some reason, be a surge of interest in an author, the publisher is in a position to make a profit. That need happen with only a few books each year to make the business profitable and to pay for dozens of books that never made it out of the warehouse. When my first novel was published by a major house, I asked my editor why no advertising had appeared. "Oh," she said, "we don't advertise books to sell them. That would be bad business. We advertise books that are already selling."

But, I wanted to know, how do they get to be "already selling" in the first place? Before publication booksellers receive review newsletters from advance reviewing services. They order on the basis of those reviews. When the books are published and reviews begin appearing in newspapers, a reader can go immediately to the bookstore and pick up the book he wants if the bookseller has ordered it. My novel was bombed by a bad advance review, though its newspaper and magazine reviews were good. If any readers went to buy it, they wouldn't find it in the bookstores (and most readers don't bother to order books they don't find in the store, and, indeed, most booksellers today won't special-order). So there was no chance it would ever be "already selling," so no reason to advertise. It was kept in the warehouse like a state secret for a decent interval, then remaindered. Needless to say, it is rare for books of poetry to be involved in this process at all. They are sustained, if at all, by library sales of established poets or those reviewed favorably in library journals.

The usual book contract, in exchange for exclusive rights, provides the author with an advance (very small in the case of poetry). It promises that the book will be published by a certain date, but it usually doesn't specify how many copies will be printed. (A thousand is a fairly normal edition of a book of poetry published by a major trade publisher.) The author is usually promised ten free copies, may buy more at a 40 percent discount, and will receive 10 percent of the retail price of books sold after his advance has been paid off. Thus, if the advance is five hundred dollars and the book sells for five dollars, the poet would begin receiving royalties after the first thousand were sold. Since that many copies of a book are rarely sold, the poet, in effect, has sold his book for the advance plus his ten free copies. Maybe there'll be a few reviews. Maybe it will be bought by a few libraries. But in most cases, that's it for that book of poems. I bought a hundred copies of my first book to give away, which probably accounted for most of its distribution until I bought up the remaindered copies, stored them in my attic, and began selling them myself by mail order.

One might think that if a publisher went to the expense of paying to have a book printed he would try to sell it, but, in practice, the efforts of most publishers to market books are nominal at best. If all the tens of thousands of books published in the United States each year were advertised, the media would be flooded with nothing but book advertisements. Besides, few people buy books on the basis of ads. Or on the basis of reviews.

Why people buy books and which ones they will buy seem to be mysteries to which publishers haven't a clue. Some best-sellers (not poetry, you may be sure) are created by concentrated publicity campaigns, but that accounts for a very small proportion of the book business. Publishers seem not even to know where books are sold. An author doing a magazine article on ski resorts recently had a book (on another subject) published by a major publisher. He wrote me:

> I told my publisher I would be all over the place in New Mexico, Utah, Colorado, and Idaho and was willing to give autograph parties or whatever. His secretary wrote back to tell me my promotional efforts were appreciated, but there were no bookstores in New Mexico, Utah, Colorado, and Idaho. Maybe he thought literacy stopped at the Mississippi. There are two bookstores in every major ski resort in the U.S., but publishers don't know it. (Those bookstores get a lot of traffic, mostly from bored wives who don't want to ski all the time like their husbands do.)

If you think salespeople from major publishers hover around the stores where books move—in airports, train stations, hospital gift shops, even natural-food stores near college campuses—you are mistaken. Some do have salespeople in the field stopping at some of the larger bookstores, but the salespeople have hundreds of books on their lists and can't push them all. They may even pointedly neglect books they don't happen to like personally, so as to avoid cluttering their presentations of those they most hope to sell.

In short, the marketing of books (other than textbooks, for which publishers make very serious sales efforts) is a chaos into which publishers seem rarely to venture. Of all writers, poets have the least to expect from publshers. They carry a few poets on their lists to enhance their image—the illusion that they are interested in literature as well as profit. Increasingly today the big publishers are but subdivisions of corporate conglomerates with no more interest in literature than detergent manufacturers have in public health. There are many dedicated individual editors in publishing houses who do what they can to counteract the purely mercenary corporate interests, but they are bound to have a limited effect on the overall picture. We may read with misty eyes how Henry Holt & Co. helped Robert Frost establish himself as a poet in the United States (after, it's true, a small English firm had published his first collection), but it would be a mistake to dream that the same thing could happen today.

What is the vanity press?

Just what the name implies, though vanity publishers don't call themselves that. They use the term "subsidy publishers," which is misleading because there are many nonvanity arrangements by which authors partially or completely subsidize the publication of their work. For example, that is how many scholarly works, for a limited audience of specialists, have been and continue to be published. University presses are often "subsidy publishers." Since their primary function is not to make a profit, many of their books are subsidized—sometimes by the university itself, sometimes by organizations, sometimes by authors. Indeed, the commercial publishers of high repute are open to subsidy contracts—for instance, to publish the findings of a study funded by a foundation, when the foundation may also pay part or all of the printing costs.

What people call the vanity press is a high-cost printing business that parasitically imitates the conventional publishers. It takes many forms. For example, you will often see poetry "contests" advertised in magazines. If you enter, you will find your poem immediately "accepted" for an anthology, and a letter suggests that surely you'd like to order an advance copy for thirty-five or forty dollars. Maybe you'd like your picture in it, too, for another fifty dollars. If you don't order a copy (though they might not tell you this), your poem won't be printed at all. If you do order a copy, you'll get a poorly printed volume containing your poem and those by all the other suckers who bought a copy—when and if the scam works well enough actually to justify printing it. Wherever you see words to the effect "Poems Wanted" in an ad, beware. No one wants poems. They want your money, and they will ply your vanity to find a way to get it.

Most commonly, though, the vanity press consists of book publishers who contract to print your book for you if you pay the costs. There's nothing wrong with that arrangement—many good authors have done it. But the vanity publishers are usually much more expensive than ordinary printers. Check that out by getting an estimate from your local printer on the same manuscript. The vanity publisher promises to send out review copies and publicity, but these are a waste of your money. Reviewers spot vanity-press publications instantly and, fairly or not, ignore them. The "publicity" might be flattering news handouts to your local papers, which might or might not use them. Worst of all, though you have paid to have your books printed, in many cases you'll find you don't own them. The contract might give you perhaps forty "author's copies" and the right to buy more at a discount. Sometimes they don't even bind the books they print until someone, usually the author, buys them (having already paid to have them printed and bound).

But vanity presses have thousands of perfectly satisfied customers. Their correspondence oozes flattery. Sometimes one of the "editors" may even visit you in your hometown, especially to persuade you to sign a contract. They do everything they can to make publication "feel" like an auspicious occasion. Their literature is filled with noble-sounding justification which makes it seem as though they were the last bastions of freedom of the press. Indeed, their function is quite legitimate, and they have published many good things which would otherwise not have been published. Occasionally one of their books actually sells.

But I have talked with a lot of poets who have gone that route, and they are universally hurt, ashamed, and embarrassed. Some have gone on to success with other publishers. They admit they were naïve to have started with the vanity presses, but their plight is understandable. Those publishers are mighty slick and persuasive, and writers have very little means of finding out what is really going on or how the publishing business works. I know no good answers to the question of how to get a book of poetry published, but I'm fairly certain that the vanity press is the worst.

What is a printer?

A commercial printer has equipment for hire. Very little commercial printing is literary: It may be anything from advertisements to instruction booklets to business forms to newspapers. It's not the business of the printer to judge literary value, but simply to provide what the customer wants, though the printer may advise the customer on technical aspects of publication and may refuse to print material that is in violation of the law. It's a straightforward business: You get what you pay for, with no flattery and no tricky contracts regarding discounts, royalties, and the rest. All copies printed are yours.

To work directly with a printer seems to me by far the most sensible choice for most poets—and not a bad one for the rest. Just check your yellow pages and go down and talk it over with a local printer. Or you may prefer to work with a low-cost mail-order printer. I have in front of me an ad from a writers' magazine in which a printer is offering to do chapbooks of poetry in editions as small as ten copies—twenty-four pages for $20. You supply camera-ready copy (which I'll explain below). For literally thousands of poets such a tiny edition would be enough. They could give copies to their family and friends, and thay may be all they need. The same printer offers a hundred copies of a forty-eight-page chapbook for $145, or $1.45 each. Sell half of them for $3 each and you're home free.

When you're paying a printer to do your book, the responsiblity is squarely on you to design the book well and to make sure your manuscript is letter-perfect (though most printers try to catch obvious typos). One thing to consider is how large a page you need, and for this you calculate the number of characters per line and number of lines per page in the type size and page size you will use. For example, iambic pentameter will fit comfortably on a 4¼" page width, but iambic hexameter, or anapestic pentameter, or longer lines require a wider page. (Run-over lines are a nuisance—and they eat paper.) How many of your poems have lines longer than iambic pentameter? If there are several, it would probably be worthwhile for you to use a 5½" width or even larger page. But if your lines are shorter, or if most of your poems are short, and you want only one poem to a page (which many poets prefer), there is no reason for you to pay for all that white space on the larger page. A smaller book is cheaper to print and to mail, and you'll be taking it easier on our weary forests. With the printer's help and instructions you will need to design the book, for instance to decide whether to start poems on odd or even pages. (Two-page poems should usually start on even pages so as to be open to the reader's eye at once.) If there is an awkwardly broken stanza gobbling up a whole page with a few leftover lines, that's because you didn't do your job of designing carefully. Someone has to make those decisions—and in my view the poet is the best one to do so.

Once a book is printed, how can I distribute it?

By "distribute" you probably mean sell, and it may be naïve to think you can sell even a single copy. I know I buy very little modern poetry, and I'm a professional in the field. Nor have I bought most of the poetry I have learned from and loved in the past: I read it in school, in the library, or I got free copies for one reason or another. Most of the poetry sold in the United States is in textbooks, assigned for college reading. Many who buy poetry at all buy anthologies, not works by individual writers. Most of us are a lot more eager to have other people read our poetry than they are to read it, so maybe we should pay them to do so.

If you paint pictures or do embroidery or weave baskets, you probably don't expect to sell your products; perhaps you shouldn't expect to sell your poetry, either. I don't know what makes amateur writers take on such a professional air, but many behave much more commercially about their art than they do about anything else they love to do. The best way to distribute poetry is to give it to your family and friends. But let's consider some of the more profitable alternatives.

Should I send out review copies

There's no harm in it if you're rich enough, but you should know that most review copies of poetry, even from major publishers, are not read. And of the few read, few are actually reviewed, and few people order books on the basis of having read reviews. Good reviews do help build a reputation, but that may mean little in terms of sales. If you do send out copies, select those periodicals that you know will review poetry. If possible, address the book to the person primarily responsible for reviewing poetry in that magazine. A little research in past issues in the library will help. Also read the *Publish-It-Yourself Handbook* (Dustbooks) for tips. Look at two journals from Dustbooks: *Small Press Review* and *Margins,* both of which do review self-published and small-press editions of poetry. Quotations from reviews may be valuable in advertising and other promotional efforts.

But do you really want a critic's opinion of your work? (How about your embroidery, basket weaving, or gardening?) Dozens of authors send me their books each year asking for my opinion, and, as I toss them into the box where I keep them (or into the wastebasket if a glance tells me I won't want to look at that book again), I think, "You don't really want to know." I don't like to hurt people's feelings, but, as you may have gathered, I am not given to easy enthusiasm about new poetry. Perhaps you enjoy playing the piano—and maybe your friends enjoy hearing you. But it would help neither you nor the world of music for you to get a professional music critic's opinion of your performance. Why should you care? Spend a few hours reading modern poetry in anthologies and literary magazines. Would those editors and poets like your poetry? Does it matter? Do you really *want* them to review your work?

Should I try bookstores?

In the back of *A Directory of American Poets and Fiction Writers* (a book you should know in any case—available from Poets and Writers, Inc., 201 West 54 St., New York, NY 10019) there is a list of bookstores that "consistently stock poetry and literary magazines. Most will also single-order poetry and fiction books." It is a geographical sampling, and no doubt there are many more around the country. That is the kind of store you need to find if you are going to try to place your work in bookstores. Try in the vicinity of college campuses or in artistic and craft-oriented neighborhoods in cities. Most bookstores buy at a 40 percent discount on consignment only (that is, they pay only for what they sell, and you pick up the copies left over). Some distributors (see the *Publish-It-Yourself Handbook*) will handle small-press and self-published books, but they, of course, require an additional discount (and it's not easy to get one to handle your work). You can make a career for yourself, if you lack one, traveling around to bookstores, talking to managers, persuading them to take a few copies on consignment, checking back to see how (or if) they are displayed, collecting bills and unsold copies. But it won't pay your gas money.

Go into a bookstore and look around. Try to imagine what would happen to your book if it were there. It would have the best chance of selling if displayed up around the cash register. What books are presently displayed there? How many books of poetry? If you live in a town or neighborhood where you are known, a bookstore manager might be willing to feature your book for a while—perhaps even to have an autograph party for you in the store. But you can probably count the number of copies you sell that way on your fingers, and you may well wonder whether it is worth the bother.

Should I advertise?

By now you should be able to predict my answer. Where? What would you say in the ad? Who reads the magazines in which you can afford ads? How many order books on the basis of ads?

Maybe your experience will be better than mine, but I tried advertising a book of poetry in *Writer's Digest* once. My name is fairly well known, especially to readers of that magazine. The ad cost eighty dollars (one column, two inches) and brought in about two dozen orders for a two-dollar book, by no means enough to pay for the ad, let alone the books. This had nothing to do with the quality of the poetry: People who read the ad can't judge that. Advertising is just not the way to sell most books, especially books of poetry.

Should I send complimentary copies to well-known writers?

I've mentioned the dozens of such volumes I receive each year, and I would guess other poets and writers receive many also. I usually glance at a poem or two, write a note of thanks to the author, and dispose of the book. Sorry. I mean no offense. But what am I going to do with it? I haven't room to keep it on my shelves. Given my choice, there's a lot of other poetry (and prose) I would rather read. I review very little poetry in magazines. I don't even know anyone to whom I might give such volumes. And it's sad to destroy them, for they cost someone money, and I have an aversion to wasting paper. But I can think of no alternative. And it is true that I have occasionally been struck by one I received and commented on it in *Writer's Digest* or elsewhere, so I understand why poets send them.

If you can afford it, maybe you want to take a chance. You just might hit some poet who is enthusiastic about your work and will promote it. Also, you might be picked up on the street to star in a movie with Robert Redford or Barbra Streisand.

Well, then, what do I do with all these copies of this book I just paid to have printed?

I hope you didn't buy too many. A couple of hundred are quite a few for a poet to dispose of. I get best results (and they aren't outstanding) by mailing announcements to friends, enemies, to anyone with whom I may have corresponded or to whom I am fairly certain my name is known. But I get a lot of mail and am better known than most beginning poets. The announcements give a sample of the poetry, enough so that a person can guess whether he might be interested in reading more. I don't try to describe it, or praise it, or quote comments about it. I know of no graceful way to toot one's own horn. Some few buy—maybe because they like my poetry and maybe because they'd just like to help me out. I appreciate it when they do.

Why, then, bother at all?

As Myrtle says, poetry is its own reward. It'd better be, for there is very little other reward for it, as for virtue. Yet is is satisfying to have your poetry printed in a handsome booklet—something cheap enough that you don't mind giving it away (or a graphically beautiful book, with illustrations and fine typography and rice paper and leather binding with gold embossing, if you can afford all that!). If you give poetry readings, you should certainly have copies to sell to the audience and should be unembarrassed about making them available. That's one instance in which a sale may have real meaning: People have heard the poetry and like it enough to want to have a copy to take home. In time you may build up a general interest in your work, sufficient that even the Establishment publishers may want to bring out an edition. But don't live in such castles in the sky. Meanwhile, you can get a fine chapbook of poetry printed for less than a hundred dollars and enjoy having it and giving it to those who care. Moreover, I think of publication as a way to shore up against oblivion. I feel posterity will be thrilled to find my poems stored in a hundred attics.

Except for Exceptions . . .

One poet sent me a mimeographed booklet of his wretched rhymes with the claim that he had sold more than ten thousand copies of them. He ran a gas station, and he must have had the gift of blarney, for he was able to palm them off on customers for a couple of bucks each. Myrtle's on all the talk shows. McKuen's poetry in boxed editions can be found in the bookstores alongside the Bibles and Kahlil Gibran. You may well discover some way to market your wares I haven't thought of (prizes in boxes of detergent?). Or you may be situated, like the man in the gas station, in some way that gives you better than average access to a paying market. I have never heard of an instance in which a relatively unknown poet submitted an unsolicited manuscript to a large trade publisher, had it accepted, reviewed, and sold to a relatively large audience (say, of more than a thousand). Who knows, though. It may have happened. Or you may be the first!

Poets and Printers

Today almost all printing is done by a photographic process which makes it possible for ordinary typewriting or printouts from word processors (or even handwriting) to be printed in a book. With instructions from a printer, you can prepare your own "camera-ready" copy and not only save some money on composition but exercise very exact control over what the printed page will look like.

Typing, though, looks like typing. Most printed writing looks different from typing because of "proportional spacing." That is, an *i* takes up less space than an *m*, though they occupy the same space on most typed manuscripts. Moreover, if the printing is prose, the right margin will probably be "justified"—made to come out even by irregular spacing within the line, which is impossible except on specially constructed typewriters and cumbersome on many word processors. Justification is of no interest to most poets (for the poetry in their books, that is; they may have front matter, jacket blurbs, or other prose they want justified), but proportional spacing—available on most composing machines (those used to compose type for print)—makes a page look professional. Composers are much more expensive machines than word processors or typewriters. If you want your type to be proportional or justified, you'll probably pay the printer to compose it. But if you know the approximate number of characters he gets to the line and the number of lines per page, you can set up your book in manuscript on an ordinary typewriter in a very close approximation of what it will finally look like.

A number of poets and small-press publishers still use the old-fashioned "flat bed" presses, with metal (or "cold") type, set by hand, inked by rollers. Sometimes you can find old machines at very low prices, since they are rarely used commercially anymore, and it might be fun to print posters, broadsides, and postcards—excellent media for single poems. But book printing by such a process would be a heroic contest like that of John Henry racing the pneumatic hammer. If one of your tastes is for fine printing, however, these presses do far more beautiful work than inexpensive modern photographic processes.

When I wanted to publish my work or that of others, I used mail-order printers such as advertise in magazines for writers. Local printers usually charge more, but they offer the advantage of personal service; they have office staff, are available by visit or telephone, and can help a neophyte answer the innumerable questions and make the many choices that arise in the process. I decided that it was worthwhile to save money to learn enough about the process so that I didn't need the personal service, but if your venture into publishing or self-publishing is not extensive, you may benefit by taking the luxury route.

Some Questions for Printers

If you go in to talk to a printer or correspond with a mail-order printer, it will help you to know a little about the technical aspects and probable costs of printing. First, consider binding. Hard covers will add a few dollars per copy if you are having only a few hundred printed (and who needs more?). Quality paperbacks have flat spines: You can read the titles when they are filed on a shelf. That is called "perfect binding," and it costs extra. If your book is more than about sixty-four pages, it will probably have to be perfect-bound, but if it has fewer pages, you have a cheaper alternative. Pamphlets or chapbooks are usually "saddle stitched" or "saddle stapled"—simply folded and stapled (or sewn) at the crease. You can even buy a saddle stapler at an office-supply store (less than ten dollars the last I knew) and put the books together yourself.

If what you want is simply to put an inexpensive chapbook together, you might even work with a neighborhood quick printer. First let's consider page size. Fold an ordinary piece of typing paper in half, and you have four sheets, 5½"x8". Tuck ten such sheets together and you have the "dummy" for a forty-page booklet. The outside sheet, of course, represents your cover. It will probably be printed on only one side, and you may want to buy some paste-on "transfer" headline type for the title, your name, and, if you wish, some invented name for the "press" (I used "Trunk Press" because I had once advised poets to get ahead the way Emily Dickinson did—try your trunk.) The office-supply store probably also has decorative borders and other designs in transfer-type kits, and you can paste on graphics borrowed from magazines or other printed materials if you wish. Avoid colors.

You may want to consult your printer about the overall design of the cover. For instance, you can put your photograph and a bio note on the back. Select a photo. The printer can "screen" it (copy it through a marked glass for half-tone reproduction) and reduce or enlarge its size appropriately. You might want him to compose the bio note on his composing machine, with justified type, to look more professional. You will probably want to buy heavier, perhaps colored, paper for your cover—for example, 100-pound offset. It depends on how fancy you want to be: The cover can cost you as much as the rest of the pamphlet.

Now leaf through your dummy, numbering the pages. The first will probably be unnumbered, then comes your title page (again, with the title and your name and any other material you wish in transfer type), and you must put your copyright notice on the front or back of that page. Perhaps the next page on the right will be used for a table of contents. Look at other pamphlets you have around the house for ideas regarding prefatory material.

The first page of text is on the right, and your actual numbering will probably start with page 2. Once you have numbered through the book and taken your dummy apart, you will see why you need that dummy. The pattern of numbers on the two sides of the pages is complicated, and you will have to work it out carefully in order to know where your poems will be placed. Don't try to put the text of the poems in the dummy. Just write on each page what will go there—for example, how many lines of which poem. The dummy is for reference purposes only. Note that the whole pamphlet, including any unnumbered prefatory material, has to be number of pages divisible by 4. Otherwise, you'll end up paying for blank pages.

Once you have designed the book, you are ready to start making a "master" for each page. "Camera-ready" simply refers to a page ready to be photographed. You don't have to type your poems on half-pages (though you may if you wish). I suggest you use pica type, space and a half, on regular typing paper, and ask the printer to photo-reduce it to the 5½"x8" page size. The text will be perfectly legible, will look more like printing than typewriting, and you can get more poetry into less space that way.

Leave ample margins, remembering, especially, the "gutter," the side that goes into the fold (left on odd-numbered pages, right on even). The printer requires at least a quarter-inch of space on each edge, and you'll probably want more than that. Remember, too, the book will be trimmed—top and bottom and outer edge (right on odd, left on even pages). Use a good, dark—preferably carbon—ribbon. If you need to mark the page, a blue pencil will not show in the photograph—handy to know if you're cutting and pasting and need marks to help in alignment. Use "white-out" or paste white paper over anything you want to delete. Correction tape and erasures show through. Remember that the camera will "see" every smudge or imperfection. If you make a mistake halfway through a poem, you can retype the stanza or section on a clean sheet of paper and paste it over the old copy. The camera won't see the edges of paste-ons if you are careful not to have a roll of glue along them. (I use a glue stick, with as little glue as possible.) Calligraphy, line drawings, or other graphics can be pasted onto the page, too, and entail no extra printing cost, though they do, of course, take up space. Photos all have to be screened by the printer, which will cost you a few dollars for each. Just indicate (with blue pencil) where they go and what size they should be. (Remember, if you are following my suggestion to have your master photo-reduced, the photos and graphics will be in reduced size, too.)

When your master sheets are all typed and numbered, take them and the dummy to the printer. You will have to select a paper color and weight—usually white paper, twenty-pound bond or fifty-pound offset (these are about the same weight, but the offset is of higher quality). You also select ink color; black is cheapest and most dependable. The printer may have samples of stock to show you for the cover.

Remember, your masters are of *pages*; the printer has to convert them to *sheets*, each representing four pages. With the aid of your dummy he can assemble the pages—shooting and reducing two pages at a time for each side of each sheet. When you pay for the printing, you pay by the number of sheets, printed both sides. Your printer probably has posted prices for 8½"x11" sheets printed both sides—the basic cost of your pamphlet

After printing both sides of the sheets, the printer has to run the pages through a folding machine, collate them (there are machines for this, too—gathering the pages and putting them in order), and trim them (so the center pages won't pooch out beyond the edge of the outside pages). You can do your own folding and collating if you want to save money, but trimming is very important and requires special equipment. The cover has to be trimmed separately, a little larger than the page size (an office paper cutter won't do the job). Then the book is ready to staple together—by either you or the printer. And, *voilà*, you're a publisher!

You don't need anyone's permission. Just do it. Take your life in your hands. Incidentally, if you self-publish, nothing prevents your using the same poems again in a commercial book should some opportunity for more auspicious publication present itself in the future.

INDEX

Other Books of Interest

General Writing Books
    Beginning Writer's Answer Book, edited by Kirk Polking $14.95
    Getting the Words Right: How to Revise, Edit, and Rewrite, by Theodore A. Rees Cheney $13.95
    How to Become a Bestselling Author, by Stan Corwin, $14.95
    How to Get Started in Writing, by Peggy Teeters $10.95
    If I Can Write, You Can Write, by Charlie Shedd $12.95
    Knowing Where to Look: The Ultimate Guide to Research, by Lois Horowitz $16.95
    Make Every Word Count, by Gary Provost (paper) $7.95
    Writer's Encyclopedia, edited by Kirk Polking $19.95
    Writer's Market, $19.95
    Writer's Resource Guide, edited by Bernadine Clark $16.95
    Writing for the Joy of It, by Leonard Knott $11.95
    Writing From the Inside Out, by Charlotte Edwards (paper) $9.95

Magazine/News Writing
    Complete Guide to Writing Nonfiction, edited by The American Society of Journalists & Authors $24.95
    Magazine Writing: The Inside Angle, by Art Spikol $12.95

Fiction Writing
    Fiction Is Folks: How to Create Unforgettable Characters, by Robert Newton Peck $11.95
    Fiction Writer's Market, edited by Jean Fredette $17.95
    Handbook of Short Story Writing, edited by Dickson and Smythe (paper) $7.95
    How to Write Best-Selling Fiction, by Dean Koontz $13.95
    Storycrafting, by Paul Darcy Boles $14.95
    Writing Romance Fiction—For Love and Money, by Helene Schellenberg Barnhart $14.95
    Writing the Novel: From Plot to Print, by Lawrence Block $10.95

Special Interest Writing Books
    Children's Picture Book: How to Write It, How to Sell It, by Ellen E.M. Roberts $17.95
    Complete Book of Scriptwriting, by J. Michael Straczynski $14.95
    The Craft of Lyric Writing, by Sheila Davis $16.95
    A Guide to Greeting Card Writing, edited by Larry Sandman (paper) $7.95
    How to Write a Cookbook and Get It Published, by Sara Pitzer, $15.95
    How to Write a Play, by Raymond Hull $13.95
    How to Write & Sell (Your Sense of) Humor, by Gene Perret $12.95
    How to Write "How-To" Books and Articles, by Raymond Hull (paper) $8.95
    How to Write the Story of Your Life, by Frank P. Thomas $12.95
    On Being a Poet, by Judson Jerome $14.95
    Poet's Handbook, by Judson Jerome $11.95
    TV Scriptwriter's Handbook, by Alfred Brenner $12.95
    Travel Writer's Handbook, by Louise Zobel (paper) $8.95
    Writing for Children & Teenagers, by Lee Wyndham $11.95

The Writing Business
    Complete Handbook for Freelance Writers, by Kay Cassill $14.95
    Freelance Jobs for Writers, edited by Kirk Polking (paper) $7.95

To order directly from the publisher, include $1.50 postage and handling for 1 book and 50¢ for each additional book. Allow 30 days for delivery.

Writer's Digest Books, Dept. B, 9933 Alliance Rd., Cincinnati OH 45242
Prices subject to change without notice.